Something is Out There

Much of the material in this book is based the personal accounts of individuals and does not necessarily reflect the views of the authors. All stories have been taken in good faith and all photographic evidence supplied in good faith. Neither is meant to provide conclusive evidence of the paranormal. No images have been significantly altered by the authors or the design team.

Something is Out There

Unlocking Australia's Paranormal Secrets

JULIE MILLER & GRANT OSBORN

ARENA
ALLEN&UNWIN

For Jo and Karen, and our parents Isabelle, Danny and Dolores, for their unfailing support and encouragement during our bizarre adventures.

First published in 2010

Copyright © Grant Osborn, Julie Miller

All rights reserved. No part of this book may be reproduced or transmitted in any form or by any means, electronic or mechanical, including photocopying, recording or by any information storage and retrieval system, without prior permission in writing from the publisher. The Australian *Copyright Act 1968* (the Act) allows a maximum of one chapter or 10 per cent of this book, whichever is the greater, to be photocopied by any educational institution for its educational purposes provided that the educational institution (or body that administers it) has given a remuneration notice to Copyright Agency Limited (CAL) under the Act.

Arena Books, an imprint of
Allen & Unwin
83 Alexander Street
Crows Nest NSW 2065
Australia
Phone: (61 2) 8425 0100
Fax: (61 2) 9906 2218
Email: info@allenandunwin.com
Web: www.allenandunwin.com

Cataloguing-in-Publication details are available
from the National Library of Australia
www.librariesaustralia.nla.gov.au

ISBN 978 1 74237 132 0

Internal design by Bookhouse, Sydney
Set in 12/16 pt Spectrum MT Std by Bookhouse, Sydney
Printed and bound in Australia by Griffin Press

10 9 8 7 6 5 4 3 2 1

Mixed Sources
Product group from well-managed
forests, and other controlled sources
www.fsc.org Cert no. SGS-COC-005088
© 1996 Forest Stewardship Council
FSC

The paper in this book is FSC certified. FSC promotes environmentally responsible, socially beneficial and economically viable management of the world's forests.

Contents

Acknowledgements vii
Introduction x

Part 1 Supernatural

Chapter 1   Haunted houses   3
Chapter 2   Terror towns   22
Chapter 3   Creepy convict colonies   40
Chapter 4   Paranormal prisons   58
Chapter 5   Wards of woe   71
Chapter 6   Theatres of fear   82
Chapter 7   Ghostly grottos   93
Chapter 8   Hotels from hell   101
Chapter 9   Possessed pubs   109
Chapter 10 The banshee in black   119
Chapter 11 Spooky cellars   126
Chapter 12 Australia's most infamous ghost   131

Part 2 Ufology

Chapter 13 Wycliffe Well – Australia's UFO capital   141
Chapter 14 The UFO hunter   153
Chapter 15 The great UFO flap of 1909   162
Chapter 16 Tully saucer nest   172
Chapter 17 The Westall UFO conspiracy   178
Chapter 18 The Valentich disappearance   193
Chapter 19 The Min Min Lights   204
Chapter 20 UFO hotspots   212

Part 3 Cryptozoology

Chapter 21	Yowie – Australia's biggest cryptid mystery	231
Chapter 22	The river monster	243
Chapter 23	Mega shark	255
Chapter 24	Giant ripper lizard	266
Chapter 25	Beware the bunyip	281
Chapter 26	The Binjour Bear	291
Chapter 27	Panthers on the prowl	299
Chapter 28	Phantom kangaroos	313
Chapter 29	The Queensland tiger	316
Chapter 30	The Tasmanian tiger	326

Epilogue	330
Glossary	335
Bibliography	341
Notes	345
Conversion table	363

Acknowledgements

A project as personal and subjective as an exploration of the paranormal world could not be achieved without the cooperation, assistance and support of many people. Over the course of our research, we interviewed many eyewitnesses about their experiences in this fascinating world, and it's only due to their openness and honesty that we could embark on this journey.

Special thanks to those who welcomed us into their homes for lengthy chats – Lew Farkas and all the staff at Wycliffe Well; Mark Schmutter, Robyn Schmutter, Gerry Wood and Bob Kennon in the Top End; Ann Taylor and Jasmine from the Blue Mountains; Vernon Treweeke, whose interpretations of UFOs left us spellbound; and Reg and Olive Ryan – it's always a pleasure to visit Monte Cristo. Also to Jenny and Tony Wilson from the Wartoook Teahouse in the Grampians; and to Rex and Heather Gilroy for your time and hospitality. And a special big thank you to Alan Ferguson – 'Keep your eyes on the skies', mate.

Also to Aaron Osborn, Sam Hutchison, Julie Zanker, Phil Martin, Keith Douglass, Andre Clayden, Mike Williams, Paul

Cropper, Matthew James, Shirley Humphries and Alan Bucholz. To Brett Green for so generously sharing his history of the Binjour Plateau and surrounding areas, and Sam Hill who, although we never quite managed to track down, left a fascinating trail of stories. A big thank you too to cryptozoologist Steve Rushton and to Chris Coffey, a lady committed to solving the panther puzzle if ever there was one. Also Alan Lanham, Richard Jennison, Maev Hitch, Marcia Osterberg-Olsen, the gracious Greg Dillon and the rest of the Campbelltown Theatre Group gang, Jane Roman from Campbelltown Visitor Information, David Neely, Attila Kardy, Trudi Toyne, Pat Collins, Stephen Smith and the staff of the Gearin Hotel, and Guy Filmer. Also to Joy Clark, Suzanne Savage, Dee Sardikay and Tania Butcher for sharing their personal experiences – may the truth prevail.

Special mention must go to George Simpson from the Australian UFO Research Network, a man very generous with his time and a great diplomat for the field of ufology. And of course Bill Chalker, one of the all-time greats of UFO research who extended eminent kindness in allowing us to access his comprehensive works on historic UFO events.

For those who showed us around haunted sites in the dead of night – Antesia Leigh and Nikki Parsons-Gardiner from Q Station, Danni Formosa from Picton Ghost Tours, Tim the Yowie Man and Tinny from Canberra Ghost Tours, Cori Camilleri and Dan Cove from Jenolan Caves, Caitlin Vertigan from Port Arthur, Brendan from Hobart Penitentiary Chapel, the team from Ghostseekers, and Andrea from Seppelt Wines, Great Western.

We also had assistance from several newspaper editors and staff writers who helped us track down leads – special thanks

Acknowledgements

to Matt Cunningham and Rebekah Cavanagh at the *Northern Territory News*, Jane Boler, who provided some fascinating articles from the *Hawkesbury Gazette*, Jill Slack of the *Gayndah Gazette*, and also Mark Russell from *The Age* and Sarah Vogler from the *Courier Mail*.

Thanks to Virgin Blue and Tasmania Tourism for their valued assistance in getting us to the Apple Isle, Queensland Tourism for their assistance in visiting Boulia, and the National Trust of Victoria.

We must also thank the visionaries whose wisdom we leaned on when the paranormal world grew dark and murky: Arthur C. Clarke, who saw the future before it was written, then went ahead and wrote it; and Dan Aykroyd, a beaming light of inspiration for anyone on a mission to seek the truth about UFOs.

We must also give a nod to the members of paranormal, cryptozoology and ufology societies around Australia, whose dedicated research, generally for no financial gain, can only be commended.

Of course, none of this would have been possible without our super-agent, Pippa Masson of Curtis Brown; and special thanks to Louise Thurtell, Ann Lennox and the editing team at Allen & Unwin for their support and patience.

Last and certainly not least, thanks once again to our families who support our bizarre passion for this subject matter and tolerate our absence when we're off chasing ghosts, UFOs or strange creatures. Promise we won't bring any back with us.

Introduction

'In this world nothing can be said to be certain, except death and taxes,' said doddery 84-year-old Ben Franklin back in 1789. A timely quote, considering the following year that great man would be staring the Grim Reaper square in the eye. But while the end of life is surely inevitable, perhaps Franklin was a little off the mark – for what lies beyond remains one of the world's great mysteries, a shadowy realm enshrouded in uncertainty.

It is through these indefinable and mysterious edges of our consciousness that we journey in these pages, exploring the strange and often challenging world collectively known as the 'paranormal'. For the purposes of this book, we have categorised this subject into three broad areas: UFOLOGY, the study of flying saucers and extraterrestrials; CRYPTOZOOLOGY, the search for strange and bizarre creatures which are alleged to lurk on our planet; and of course the SUPERNATURAL, which encompasses all things ghostly that go bump in the night.

The more immersed we became in the paranormal, the more we began to encounter the vast networks of people who pursue these dark and edgy fields with a passion often bordering on obsession. And in many ways, we found the members of these mysterious and in many cases secretive subcultures of ufologists, cryptozoologists and ghosthunters to be as fascinating as their elusive quarry.

Of course, the paranormal is generally viewed through the prism of pseudoscience; with methodologies not necessarily adhering to the accepted scientific way, it lurks in murky corners on the borderline of accepted knowledge. In venturing into these corners and crossing these borders, we were surprised to find pseudoscience not without its virtues.

Whereas established science, rigid and rigorous by definition, might bow to accept a new discovery only when laden with suitable proof, pseudoscience is more than happy to plough straight ahead and make spectacular flights of logic from conjecture to hypothesis to theory on the wings of nothing but sheer imagination alone.

Perhaps this maverick edge is one of the reasons the subject matter of flying saucers, monstrous animals and spine-chilling phantoms continues to entice and enthral us; despite the scepticism of the scientific establishment, which would argue it does little to add usefully to collected knowledge. But one of the gleeful things about pseudoscience is it both relies upon and inspires the imagination. And as Albert Einstein, one of the greatest scientific minds, was famously quoted, 'Imagination is more important than knowledge. For knowledge is limited to all we now know and understand.'

And there is much we don't understand. For example: what are those shiny saucer-shaped objects flitting around the sky, reported so often and seemingly photographed so regularly? For more than half a century ufologists have committed themselves to solving this conundrum. Are they just plain nuts?

Not unless you consider a third of us nuts. A recent Nielsen poll for the *Sydney Morning Herald* which revealed 68 per cent of Australians, or roughly two out of three of us, believe in God also revealed 34 per cent of us believe in UFOs![1] That's approximately one in three. This means half as many Australians who believe in God believe in UFOs. If you were a sceptic sitting at the bar in a pub, chances are one of the people sitting either side of you would be a believer.

Of course, with the advent of digital technology and the rise of the internet, UFOs are being caught on camera and posted for public consumption at a greater rate than ever. So why does cold hard evidence — a chunk of alien spacecraft, or a video or photograph so clear its contents are undeniable — continue to be so elusive? Over recent decades a panoply of experts, from ex-NASA technologists to ex-Apollo moonwalkers, has stepped forward to declare not only are flying saucers real, but their existence is being covered up.

Not being conspiracy theorists ourselves, we were indeed taken aback during our investigations to discover the sheer amount of both official denial and lack of government accountability when it comes to this subject. A good example is the Westall UFO case — dealt with at length in this book — which, despite having more than a hundred witnesses, many of whom insist the military swooped on the site soon after an alien encounter, is not listed on a single official document in any government department whatsoever.

Introduction

Our quest to search for flying saucers, and to get to the bottom of such mysteries, led us from the suburbs of Melbourne to the Blue Mountains of New South Wales to a tiny spot in the Red Centre called Wycliffe Well — self-proclaimed 'UFO capital of Australia'. The discoveries we made and the colourful characters we met along the way are contained in these pages.

From *The Day the Earth Stood Still* to *Close Encounters of the Third Kind* to *Avatar*, our fascination with the existence of alien beings is clearly deeply entrenched. But what about those mysterious creatures alleged to stalk the Earth and which are not of extraterrestrial origin? Reputed to prowl our bushes and lurk in our waters, such creatures are the fodder of cryptozoology.

Generally, these cryptids fall into three categories: unknown species, such as the giant hairy apeman called the yowie; beasts displaced in habitat, such as the phantom big cats that have caused so much controversy in the northwest of Sydney in recent times; and species lost in time, which although regarded extinct by science have an annoying habit of rearing their heads in front of shocked witnesses frequently enough that the possibility of their continued existence cannot help but be examined.

Since Australian species have been known to 'rise from the dead', the latter category is actually of particular interest. The mountain pygmy possum, previously known only from fossil records from the Pleistocene epoch, 2.5 million to 12,000 years ago, was found alive and well on the slopes of Victoria's Mount Hotham in 1966. Unfortunately, due to the incursion of man, Australia's only hibernating marsupial is now truly on the brink of extinction.

But what of the marsupial lion, a ferocious megafaunal carnivore which fossil records show to have perished 40,000 years ago? For more than a century witnesses on the Queensland hinterland have reported an agile and fearsome feline creature, known locally as the Queensland tiger and matching descriptions of the prehistoric big cat.

Then we have the case of the 'giant ripper lizard', a goanna known to have grown to the size of a crocodile but which perished in the same period. Unless, of course, we take into account sightings by terrified witnesses and an enormous and curious claw print collected by one of Australia's most high-profile cryptozoologists.

Our trek for the truth behind the existence of such creatures took us from Indonesia's prehistoric Komodo Island, home to the komodo dragon (recently discovered to have originated in Australia), to the windy peaks of Victoria's Grampian mountain range, where we stalked the region's rampantly reported puma. Despite many a terrifying moment ourselves, we fortunately managed to make it back uneaten and unscathed enough to write this book.

Then, of course, there is the shadowy world of the supernatural; a realm that punctuates all cultures, continents and ages, dating back to the dawn of civilisation when man first questioned, 'What's next?'

Ghosts are the ultimate unexplained phenomena – debated by science, debunked by sceptics, celebrated in fiction and movies, and an endless source of hair-raising dinner party anecdotes. Interest in this topic crosses gender, class and age; and with science unable to provide answers, belief becomes a matter of faith, backed by personal accounts or the occasional grainy flash of evidence on photo or video.

Many people assume that as authors with a longstanding fascination with this topic, we have a psychic connection to the spiritual world; but this in fact couldn't be further from the truth. While we can both pinpoint moments in our lives when our interest was piqued, whether through personal experience or purely on an entertainment level, we really only became involved when a commercial opportunity arose — making a television program about haunted places in New Zealand for that country's national broadcaster, TVNZ.

This project — a ten-part 'reality' series called *Ghost Hunt* — involved six intense months exploring the bizarre and sometimes infuriating world of spooks and spectres, throwing ourselves literally into the eternal deep end. Long nights in allegedly haunted places not only heightened our senses and connection to this world, but also introduced us to experts in the field, people with a passion far outweighing ours who were happy to share their time and knowledge.

During the course of our research, our minds and consciousness were broadened; experiences beyond rational, beyond logic, beyond reality bored into our brains, leading us to the conclusion that this is a very strange world indeed.

From the intriguing tale of the Lady in Black who haunts a road crossing a mountain range in New South Wales, to atrocities committed behind closed doors in Australia's most haunted house, to the eternal cries of despair from our convict predecessors, each story we uncovered during our research both confounded and delighted us. Based on historical fact, embellished by time and brought to life by passionate storytellers, these ephemeral tales preserve characters and incidents that would otherwise be forgotten. The seemingly insatiable public appetite for ghost tours is testament to just how intriguing and delicious these stories are, precious snippets of bygone times served in an enticing cocktail of history, folklore and anecdote.

At one point in our journey through the unexplained we discovered something always of interest to any writer — a new adjective, 'fortean'. The term and its associated noun forteana, derived from the surname of writer and researcher Charles Fort, are used to collectively categorise various anomalous phenomena.

At the turn of the 20th century the eccentric and iconoclastic Fort released several books dealing with such diverse oddities as teleportation (a term he is credited with coining), amphibious rain (frogs falling from the sky), poltergeist events, ball lightning (a still controversial electrical phenomenon), the existence of creatures held to be mythological, alien abduction and extraterrestrial hypothesis, all of which remain in print today.

Essentially, Fort was the father of strange phenomena. A cult grew around the writer, which also survives to this day in the form of the International Fortean Society and the monthly magazine *Fortean Times*. Thumbing his nose at conventional science, Fort was himself sceptical of scepticism, suggesting people with a psychological need to believe in marvels are no more prejudiced and gullible than people with a psychological need not to believe in marvels.[2]

In his first publication *Book of the Damned*, Fort imparts what we endorse as solid advice for anyone thinking about stepping out into the world of the paranormal – his ideal is that one should neither be a 'true believer' nor a 'sceptic' for 'the truth lies somewhere in between'.³ But beware how you step, for he is also attributed with saying, 'If there is a universal mind, must it be sane?'

Having submerged ourselves in this topic for the past ten or so years, that is a question that constantly arises: Do you believe in this nonsense? In the past, we gave the glib answer, 'We believe it's very entertaining.' But having had our consciousness raised, our eyes opened, our logical minds challenged in so many ways and so often, all we can say now is – anything's possible.

Part 1
Supernatural

Chapter 1
Haunted houses

Monte Cristo, Junee, New South Wales

Junee, New South Wales, 1961. A troubled young man exits the local movie theatre and steps out onto the streets of this small Riverina town. Above his head the marquee banner advertises *Psycho*, the Alfred Hitchcock thriller he has just seen, and which has terrified millions around the world. He stops to gaze up at a decaying two-storey Victorian era mansion perched on a prominent hill, overlooking the town. In his mind it coalesces with the Bates family residence; its lone caretaker with Norman Bates, the film's psychopathic protagonist.

Taking a rifle, the young man stalks up the hill and across the remnants of the crumbling estate's formerly grand gardens. Ambushing the innocent and unsuspecting caretaker in his tiny shed out the back, he fatally shoots him point blank. The killing horrifies the town's populace, and adds yet another layer of tragedy to a dwelling that will grow in infamy to become known as Australia's most haunted house: Monte Cristo.

We approach the sprawling property atop its gently sloping hill with a sense of déjà vu. We have been here before. Ten years earlier, in fact. In the time passed, Monte Cristo has lost little of its allure and none of its sense of foreboding menace. On our previous visit we were acting in our other roles as television producers. After a night of intensive filming with an extensive array of cameras probing every dark corner, our production crew captured two startling ghostly images: one a wispy silhouette of a craggy old lady in dark period garb, theorised to be the stern former matriarch of the residence; another showing ethereal 'ghost tongues' of fire licking at the cracked ceiling of the homestead's stables, exactly where a young stable hand was said to have burned to death in a tragic hay bale inferno.

Despite being provided with such dramatic evidence of otherworldly activities Australian television networks, deeming the subject matter 'too dark', failed to give the program the green light. Television executives in New Zealand showed more insight and creative vision — and after substantial reworking, the project was reborn as *Ghost Hunt*, a series that was not only successful across the pond, but also in the UK, the Middle East, Africa and throughout Europe. And as 'dark' became the new 'black', a slew of similarly themed television shows emerged around the world, many of which have travelled to Australia to investigate Monte Cristo.

'Let me tell you about the television crew from Poland!' exclaims Reg Ryan, the garrulous owner of Monte Cristo, after welcoming us back warmly to his haunted house. 'They were from the longest running supernatural show in the world. They asked to come and stay for three days and nights. But they were so terrified by the place none of them would spend the night. They would film until 5 p.m. and then run off to spend the night in the safety of a motel!'

Ryan and his wife Olive have lived in Monte Cristo since purchasing it as a decrepit ruin in 1963, two years after the infamous murder. 'We had no doors or windows when we first moved in,' he explains. 'We had no water. No electricity. We had three little girls. And Olive was five months pregnant. But I knew from the first day I saw it eight years earlier that I would one day live here.'

The couple toughed it out with their young family, despite soon coming to the realisation that, adding to other hardships, their 'renovator's delight' was spirit-infested. The first inkling came only days after moving in.

'We went down to town in the evening to buy some bread and milk,' Ryan recalls. 'It was on dark. As we drove up to the house, there was light streaming from every window and door. At that time we only had one kerosene lamp and it wasn't even lit. We both saw the lights and we stopped the car in the driveway. Olive wasn't keen on getting out. But I said, "That's where we're living – we have to go up." Then the lights disappeared.'

As Ryan continued the ongoing task of renovating his huge house, the spooky occurrences continued, spurring him to look into the history of the place. What he discovered was that even prior to the killing of the caretaker, the home was a veritable 'house of horrors'. According to Ryan, its paranormal problems relate primarily to the shenanigans of the family who built Monte Cristo – the creepily named Crawleys.

Something is Out There

Lord of the manor was Christopher Crawley, an imperious man and a natty dresser. As one of the earliest settlers of the region, he fell into fortune when the Sydney to Melbourne railway line cut through land he had acquired from a government grant. He duly built Junee's first hotel and general store, and business prospered. As a founding father of the burgeoning community, Crawley felt he needed a residence in keeping with his newfound status and had the imposing Monte Cristo built on a prime piece of hilltop real estate looking down over the town.

On the surface, Crawley was a respectable citizen and pillar of the community, happily married to his devoted wife. But according to Ryan, something sinister may have been lurking beneath his slick façade.

'I think Mr Crawley was very good on Sundays for an hour,' he jokes, before leaning forward conspiratorially to launch into a grim series of yarns about the Crawley patriarch. 'Some of the servant girls became pregnant while they were in service here. Mr Crawley was the most likely culprit.'

Legend has long had it that one of Monte Cristo's ghosts is that of a young servant girl who, upon finding herself pregnant to her employer, flung herself to her death from the mansion's first floor balcony. Along with Ryan, we crouch around the concrete stairs leading up to the front entrance, examining strange pale markings set in the cement.

'This is where she landed,' he tells us. 'The white stains came from the bleach they used to clean up all the blood. It soaked into the concrete.'

The tale only gets darker. Several years ago Ryan met a lady who had worked at the Crawley home during this period. As a 'day maid', she was fortunate enough to return home each day after work hours, thus avoiding the nocturnal philandering of the master of the house.

'This lady was on her death bed. She had no reason to lie,' says Ryan. 'And she swore she saw Mr Crawley actually push the girl off the balcony. It was all hushed up. She wasn't game to talk about it back then.'

So was Crawley the church-going philanthropist also Crawley the murderous sexual predator? It would go some way towards explaining why Monte Cristo is such a troubled piece of real estate.

'There's been a lot of sadness here,' says Ryan. 'And a lot of people pick up on the sadness.'

Since its refurbishment Monte Cristo has been open to the public as a heritage-listed museum, the front section festooned with Victorian-era furniture and artefacts, collected by Ryan during a prior career in antiques dealing. Over the years, hundreds of mediums and psychics from all over the world have visited this haunted mansion, many having severe reactions.

In 1977 the ABC television program *Big Country* profiled Monte Cristo, their film crew accompanied by a medium. According to Ryan, she vowed never to return, describing it as 'the most evil place she'd ever been'. Amongst other dramatic moments, she ran in terror from the property's stables claiming she could 'smell death'.

This led to the revelation of another tragic demise on the homestead's grounds, when another former day maid, Amy Babcock, came forward after seeing the program. As Ryan relates her story, he pulls out a black and white wedding photograph taken in 1907 showing the entire Crawley clan gathered in front of their impressive domicile. Two maids stand on the balcony, both of whom were sacked for the intrusion; Mrs Babcock gained employment at the house when she replaced one of them.

'When Mrs Babcock came over to visit she was 86 years old, but her memory was as clear as a bell,' says Ryan. 'She told me a young lad was burnt to death in the stables — exactly where the medium had sensed something. His name was Ralph Morris. He didn't get up for work one morning, saying he was too sick. So Crawley set fire to the straw mattress to chase him. But the boy actually was too sick and couldn't move. She said Crawley probably didn't mean to kill him. But it was manslaughter. The police came up to investigate but the Crawleys were a law unto themselves. They had it all wrapped up.'

The medium who accompanied *Four Corners* also sensed a tragedy inside the home's central stairwell. This too was confirmed by Mrs Babcock, who told Ryan the story of a nanny dropping one of the Crawley children down the stairs to its death — claiming to have been pushed by an invisible force. But the medium's strongest reaction occurred when she entered the shed in the backyard where the *Psycho*-inspired killing occurred. 'She went in there and got possessed,' says Ryan. 'She went off her head a bit.'

Ryan went on to discover this tiny shed was the site of even more misfortune: 'Only a few years back I discovered there was a housekeeper called Mrs Steele. She was Mrs Crawley's sister, and she had an illegitimate child to Crawley, called Harold. He was developmentally disabled, and he was chained up in the shed. After both Mr and Mrs Crawley had passed away, Mrs

Steele stayed on with the boy. When she didn't show up in town for supplies after a few days, authorities investigated. They found both mother and child on the brink of death. She was taken to the local hospital but died on the way. He was taken to Kenmore Mental Institute in Goulburn. Within a few days he also died. Apparently he fretted to death because he knew no other life than being chained in the back shed.'

This story was corroborated by the elderly owner of a Junee hardware store. 'When he was 12 years old,' continues Ryan, 'one of Crawley's sons, a local solicitor, asked him to go up with a horse and dray and pick up an old piano case, because they make good horse feed boxes. He and his mate pulled up in the backyard, and no-one told them about Harold Steele. He said, "This thing covered in hair came racing out of the shed and took up the slack in his chain — and we were off." He said Harold's hair hadn't been cut for 30 years and his fingernails were so long they'd curled up into his hands. It wasn't very nice.'

By this point our heads are spinning trying to keep up with the flow of ghastly events and ghostly folklore. We ask Ryan exactly how many spirits he shares his home with.

'Ten!' he states emphatically, going on to list them. 'Mr Crawley . . . Mrs Crawley . . . The caretaker who was shot . . . The servant girl who was pushed off the balcony . . . The stable boy who burnt to death . . . The boy who was chained up in the shed . . . There's a lady with a white hood who's been seen at the top of the stairs and a lady walking around the balcony — we don't know who either of those two are . . . There's the little girl who was dropped down the stairs . . . And the boy who was murdered . . .'

Wait a minute! A child was murdered here?

'Many mediums say a little Crawley boy was killed in his bedroom,' Ryan explains matter-of-factly. 'They think he was about seven years old. They say there was blood all over the walls. I can't prove that. But many mediums have sensed it. It is the only death certificate I have not been able to find. I have found all the others.'

As well as keeping assiduous research notes on Monte Cristo, Ryan has collected three thick scrapbooks full of ghostly photos and testimonials of hair-raising experiences from visitors to his home. We flick through them, agog at the cumulative evidence. One photo we find particularly chilling, taken on a camera phone by a woman who felt a strange presence while on a self-guided tour of the house. At first glance it looks like nothing more than a dark, grainy blotch. But when brightened, the translucent apparition of a little girl can clearly be seen staring directly at the camera. Could it be the spectre of the girl who was dropped down the stairs?

Ryan has never seen any of the ghosts himself. Instead he feels their presence, claiming to 'get on' particularly with the spirit of Mrs Crawley. After her husband died of blood poisoning caused by a carbuncle on his neck (in turn caused by the fashionably high, starched collars he favoured), she went on to live in Monte Cristo until her own death 23 years later. In that time she is reputed to have only ever left the house twice, spending the bulk of her time praying in a chapel she had constructed in a tiny storage room on the side of the expansive balcony.

Before we begin our nocturnal investigation Ryan refamiliarises us with the layout of the place. In the dining room, under the unsettling gaze of a pair of portraits of the Crawleys which he painted himself, he informs us he can feel the 'presence' of the house's former matriarch. Oddly, as we circumnavigate the enormous cedar dining table in the centre of the room, we can feel a distinctly cold patch — even though it is a warm night and there are no detectable drafts.

Wishing us a happy ghost hunt, Ryan leaves us to our own devices. We head upstairs to the rear section of the house, which functions as B&B-style accommodation for overnight guests, to collect our camera equipment. As we sit in the vestibule on an antique chaise longue, preparing our gear for the night's activities, we hear an erratic but insistent tapping noise. It seems to emanate from right beside us, but we can discern no obvious source. Confounded by the mystery, we determine to solve it before heading outside. Finally we discover the cause: a leak above a door frame, evidently caused by Monte Cristo's eccentric plumbing, is dripping water directly into the corridor. Satisfied the fluid is indeed natural and not ectoplasmic in nature, we remind ourselves to inform Ryan the next morning.

Armed with video and photographic cameras, we head out into the grounds of Monte Cristo, the crunching of our footsteps on the gravel echoing eerily. It is a dark night, and the beams of our torches slice through the blackness to reveal the tragic shed where both the *Psycho* killer struck and the developmentally disabled young man endured life chained up like an animal. Ryan previously informed us that when he first bought the property he found a disturbing sign scratched into the shed's door, reading 'Die Jack Ha Ha'. He has since had it removed, and is unsure to this day whether it was scrawled by the killer, or merely the morbid joke of a local prankster.

The spirits seem calm inside the shed, but our attention is drawn by a spooky screeching noise from the far side of the yard. We realise it is originating from an open door to a storage loft above the barn. It is swaying ever so slightly and irregularly in the breeze, even though there appears to be no breeze. We enter the barn to try and figure out what is causing this mystifying door movement.

The barn is cavernous, noiseless and dusty – stocked only with the skeletons of old horse buggies, the restoration of which is another of Ryan's passions. Against the rear wall we see a slender wooden ladder stair leading up to the loft. We climb its squeaking steps and find ourselves standing on the floor of the loft. In fact, if our bearings are correct, we are directly above the spot where young stable hand Ralph Morris met his tragic fiery death. The loft door, which we could see moving from below, is now still. We wait and observe but strangely it remains stationary. Perhaps the imperceptible breeze abated. Or perhaps Morris's restless spirit does not appreciate company. Either way, we descend the rickety stairs with the feeling of something looking down on us from the darkness above.

Back outside, as we ruminate on the stillness and quiet of the property, we try to shake off the sensation. Ryan has previously told us Monte Cristo is a virtually impossible place in which to keep pets, hypothesising animals dislike all the spiritual activity, to which they are alleged to be sensitive. According to Ryan, 'The first weekend we moved in we brought our pet cat. We put her down in the house. She went completely mad. Raced up the broken staircase and jumped off the second floor. We never saw her again. We brought our pet dog the next weekend, a little Australian terrier. We put him in the house and he ran around like mad, got out, and we never saw him again either. But there is a ghost cat.'

We, of course, are hunting more substantial paranormal prey. We traipse around the side of the building to Monte Christo's impressive front yard, decorated with ghostly white stone statues around a central fountain. A staircase leads up to the balcony, from which the lights of Junee sprawl beneath us. Apart from passing night trains the entire town appears dormant. Nevertheless, we sense company . . .

We tiptoe across the terrace, past the spot where the pregnant maid either committed suicide or was murdered. We turn a corner and in front of us is the converted chapel which was Mrs Crawley's fortress of solitude after her husband's demise. Its door is ajar, revealing an inky abyss within. As we cautiously approach we hear a rustle. Suddenly, the ghost cat leaps out!

It flies between us, landing lightly on an upper step of the stairwell — at which point we realise it is in fact a flesh-and-blood cat; a moggie, to be precise, and a friendly one at that. We pat it as our pulses calm, and make ourselves a new pal. But what on earth is a phantasm-fearing feline doing camping out in Mrs Crawley's private domain?

We discuss the encounter with Ryan over tea and toast the next morning. He explains the cat belongs to his son, who lives with his family on an adjacent property, and that it is the only neighbouring pet game enough to put in the occasional visit. Mention of Ryan's son leads us to ask what it's been like for he and his wife Olive bringing up a family of five in a haunted home.

'When the kids were younger it was just home and they just accepted things,' he explains. 'It was just "faces in the windows". It wasn't until they got a bit older they realised it wasn't normal. And of course by then they'd been living here all that time so it didn't worry them.' Except for their son Lawrence, owner of the cat, who gets spooked himself every time he goes upstairs.

This fact seems particularly odd when we learn Lawrence is one of the most fearless people on the planet – literally. Visitors to Monte Cristo are often surprised to discover Lawrence Ryan is in fact stunt performer Lawrence Legend – the 'Evel Knievel' of Australia. Ryan proudly shows us some of his son's memorabilia on display in the entrance to the estate. Among his many daredevil feats, Lawrence has jumped his motorcycle over 15 trucks, over 20 cars, and over 11 cars blindfolded! Our favourite photo of Lawrence in action shows him jumping over 38 motorcycles in a double-decker bus! But Lawrence's most bizarre stunt was staged in his very own backyard, when he jumped Monte Cristo itself. Billed as the 'Scariest Jump in the World', Lawrence made it over the roof of his ghost-ridden home and – obviously overcoming his fears of Crawley corner – landed safely back on Earth.

We ponder the irony of someone brought up in a house so steeped in death opting for such a death-defying career as we bid Ryan a fond farewell, departing Monte Cristo in far less spectacular fashion – with all four wheels firmly planted on the ground. In our rearview mirror it seems to take on almost anthropomorphic features – the two huge curved ground-floor Victorian windows like two eyes, the immensely wide and ornate front door a mouth – both beckoning and taunting at the same time.

The Abbey, Annandale, Sydney

In May 2009, a Sydney newspaper announced that a landmark historic house would be open to the public and its entire contents auctioned prior to the sale of the property later in the year.

Everything was to go – garden statues, grand pianos, gramophones, dusty books and a massive record collection – with one exception: the ghosts that call The Abbey home.

Looming over the inner-city suburb of Annandale, this magnificent 50-room Gothic mansion built in 1881 has always been shrouded in mystery, its ivy-covered sandstone turrets, gargoyles, chapel and stained glass a breeding ground for tales of the paranormal.

According to the report in the *Daily Telegraph*, any future buyer would not only inherit a multimillion dollar restoration bill but also its original occupants—including a 'lady in white' said to haunt the tower.

Stories of strange occurrences are part of the house's mythology, the newspaper said; ghosthunters have been lured here for decades, keen to investigate reports of windows and doors opening of their own accord, whooshes of cold air, and dark shadowy figures lurking in the corridors. 'Everyone has a ghost story to tell,' Francesca David, who was raised in the house with her brother Gervase and five other siblings, told the *Daily*

Telegraph. 'The seven children all know it is haunted by ghosts, especially the Lady in White. The basement and the main bedroom are notorious for ghosts.'[1]

The opportunity to peer inside this spooky old mansion and perhaps to get a glimpse of its otherworldly residents proved irresistible for many Sydneysiders; and on a sunny autumn Saturday afternoon, we join the throng exploring hidden nooks, squeezing through narrow corridors, and venturing down crumbling steps to gawk at the hidden chapel.

With more than 500 people packed into the grounds to attend the auction, there was barely room to swing one of the resident cats, who, just like Monte Cristo's, are said to be sensitive to paranormal presences. According to the *Daily Telegraph*:

> Gervase Davis and his wife — who live alone in the house at 272 Johnston St — use their trusted feline as a barometer of spectral activity. When Merlin the cat's hackles rise, Gervase knows to clear the room because something unseen has entered. 'If you live here you need a cat to warn you. Cats are sensitive to that kind of thing, that's how I know someone has come in,' Ms Davis said yesterday.[2]

Whether due to the auctioneer's drone or the presence of literally hundreds of curious visitors, the Lady in White kept a low profile during our visit; and time will only tell if she chooses to linger as The Abbey undergoes restoration.

In November 2009, The Abbey was sold for $4.86 million to an inner-west family who plan to move in and restore it to its former glory. It seems a live-in colony of ghosts is an investment not to be underestimated.

Studley Park, Camden, New South Wales

Another allegedly haunted house currently undergoing renovation is Studley Park, a grand Victorian mansion surrounded by the fairways of Camden Golf Course in southwestern Sydney. Once the clubhouse for the golf club, this imposing white structure was acquired by the Moran family in 2008 and has since been leased to the Sir Henry Royce Foundation, a charitable trust run by Rolls Royce and Bentley enthusiasts.

As we write, the heritage building is fenced off from the public, windows boarded and doors barred in a convincing impression of a diabolical haunted house. The presence of workmen replacing the roof, however, indicates the Foundation is serious about returning this historic gem to its previous magnificence. Once completed, it is sure to be a showpiece worth visiting.

As well as reinstating Studley Park's heritage value, the Foundation is also committed to the preservation of its history, including the well-known ghost stories long associated with the home. Two young boys are believed to have died at the house: 14-year-old Ray Blackstone, who drowned in a dam in 1909 when the house served as a boarding school; and Noel Gregory, the 13-year-old son of one-time owner Arthur Adolphus Gregory, who died of appendicitis in 1939. The bodies of both boys are said to have been stored in the house's cellar until burial.

Although local folklore has long told of strange goings-on in the dilapidated mansion, it gained notoriety in 2001 when it was used as a location in the reality/game show *Scream Test*. Four contestants were locked up in four separate locations in the house, including the tower and the cellar, and it was in here that several of the contestants had intense experiences, a dark presence blamed for the oppressive ambience.

Independent paranormal researcher Attila Kardy has conducted several investigations at Studley Park since 2006, and is convinced that 'something is going on' in the mansion.

'There have been a couple of occasions when we heard footsteps or shuffling,' he says. 'As a researcher I claim to be able to differentiate between structural creaking and what are actual physical footsteps, a heel pressed against a floorboard. We've heard that on a number of occasions.'

By far the most intriguing evidence Kardy has captured, however, was the visual manifestation of a vortex, caught by infrared night vision on a handycam.

'We use what's known as infrared LED amplifiers or fog lamps which improve your night vision camera capability one hundred-fold or more. If you have a black room and look through the eyepiece, you can see everything. And if anything is reflected in infrared light, we'd be able to pick it up,' he explains.

'Lo and behold, we did get something. This little vortex came through the door, goes into the middle of the room, whirls around in a circle, then takes off to one side. The cameraman actually got a bit upset, he started shivering and we had to take him out of there. He saw it all through the eyepiece.'

Barwon Park, Winchelsea, Victoria

With the public's thirst for tales of the unexplained seemingly unquenchable, the National Trust of Victoria has jumped on the bandwagon and now offers ghost tours in several of its most impressive properties. These days, ghosthunters can be found at Como House, the Old Melbourne Gaol and Barwon Park, a majestic 42-room bluestone mansion at Winchelsea, on the outskirts of Geelong.

'People look at the house and automatically ask the question, "Is it haunted?",' explains Trudi Toyne, the manager of Barwon Park. 'So the National Trust decided to run ghost tours on that basis – we hire the venue to Australian Ghost Adventures and they take people through once a month.'

This magnificent rural property has only ever belonged to two families: the Austins, who built the home in 1869 and hold the dubious honour of importing rabbits to Victoria for sport; and the Batsons, who lived in the house for 60 years before it came under National Trust control.

Built to be a showpiece on the Western Districts social circuit, the house never fulfilled its potential with the untimely death of Thomas Austin in 1871, just six months after he officially opened the home with a celebratory ball. Austin's widow, Elizabeth, continued to live at the mansion until her own death in 1911; and by all accounts, the grand old dame still makes her presence felt, particularly in the bedroom where she slept alone for 40 years.

While Toyne has had no personal experiences in the 18 months she has been managing the property, her predecessor Pat Collins speaks openly of the strange occurrences that punctuated everyday life at Barwon Park during her 30-year tenure.

'We were going to have a masked ball here, many years ago,' she recalls. 'As I drove down the driveway towards the house, a light appeared in Mrs Austin's bedroom. There was no power up there. Not long after, another volunteer arrived; she had seen the light as well. Later we went back to meet another gentleman who was coming to help with the decorations. We went in my car, and since I thought it might have been my headlights reflecting in the window, I asked her to look backwards to see if she could see anything. She did — the light was still there.

'After we met the other gentleman, he led the way back, and halfway down the driveway he jammed his brakes on. When we got to the house, we asked him why, and he said he'd seen a light on in Mrs Austin's room.'

Over the years, Pat Collins said, nearly every one of the National Trust committee members has seen a light on in that room at one time or another.

Another close encounter with Mrs Austin occurred when Collins and another volunteer were in the bedroom, placing a white bedspread on the bed. 'I was kneeling down to straighten it out to make it neat,' Collins says, 'and I just said to her, "Mrs Austin, I hope you enjoy this lovely new bedspread and I hope it keeps you warm."'

At the time, the other volunteer was standing near the door — certainly nowhere near a vase of flowers that suddenly went crashing down off a dresser in the opposite corner, strewing the flowers across the floor.

'We looked at each other in amazement,' Collins remembers, 'and I said, "Did you knock that down, Joyce?" and she said, "I'm nowhere near it!" All these things have happened and it's not just the one person who's experienced it.'

As well as the spirit of Mrs Austin, Collins believes Barwon Park is haunted by at least one other ghost, possibly that of a butler. She recalls another time when she heard the servant's bells ringing in the courtyard — despite the fact that the bells had been disused for years.

'I went into the courtyard and there were two of these bells just swinging and ringing. We thought it might be a possum tangled in the wires, but we had repairs done and those wires are all so seized up and tight, you'd never be able to move them.'

According to Pat Collins, there's nothing scary about the presences of Barwon Park — they are as much a part of the place as the furniture, and therefore due respect as permanent residents of the homes to which they were so attached.

Chapter 2

Terror towns

Picton, New South Wales

There are two places to be on a Friday night in the New South Wales town of Picton — at the pub or on a ghost tour. Both are rather scary.

The former is a seething mass of local humanity, mostly blokes singing homophobic ditties or removing their shirts to a chorus of 'man boobs!' The latter is an encounter with somewhat more sombre residents — restless souls that have chosen to linger after death. And it appears there are almost as many of them as there are breathing, drinking inhabitants.

Picton, located around 80 kilometres southwest of Sydney, has been named the most haunted town in Australia, a label officials reluctantly admit brings in much-needed tourist dollars. Its ghost tours attract around 35 out-of-towners every Saturday night and every second Friday, promoting weekend trade and giving locals something to do when the pub closes — hooning past tour groups, taunting them with a ghostly 'whoooooooo!'

Like other settlements surrounding Sydney, Picton developed in the early 19th century as the search for arable farmland took pioneers beyond the original colony of Sydney. In fact, its first non-Indigenous residents were cows that had escaped from up north, found thriving on the banks of the Nepean River. Fat, healthy and in good breeding form, the decision was made to leave the herd be, gazetting the region between the Nepean and Bargo rivers as Cowpastures and sealing it off to allow the cattle to continue their life of leisure.

Trouble soon followed these bovine interlopers, however, and in 1832, a man who had been employed to watch the bullocks was brutally murdered by a convict named Smithwicks. Later, the area became the lair of the notorious bushranger John Lynch, who would not only rob passers-by but hatchet them to death, disposing their bodies into bushes on the side of the road.

Meanwhile, the first official land grant in the area was made in 1822 to Major Henry Colden Antill, the former aide-de-camp to Governor Macquarie. Antill built a small cottage on a prime holding of 2000 acres, his son John later expanding his vision into a grandiose two-storey mansion. The subsequent development that grew around Antill's property officially changed its name from Stonequarry to Picton in 1841.

Six years later, the government offered up land just south of the private town, causing a fracas by also calling it Picton. Resentment between the two settlements festered, with the uppercrust Antill mob forcing the newcomers to change their name to Upper Picton, differentiating on the basis of wealth and power.

Town rivalries, murder and cattle wars may be the stuff of a colourful history — but Picton is really no different from any other Australian town born from violence and unrest. So what makes this fairly insignificant hamlet of just over 4000 living residents such a hotbed of paranormal activity? And why are its former inhabitants so restless?

The answer appears to lie with one woman, Liz Vincent, a dedicated and passionate local historian who, for more than 20 years, collected stories from locals about spooky goings-on in their homes. If someone had a strange experience, heard odd noises or felt unwanted presences, they turned to Vincent to recount their tale; she provided a willing, empathetic ear, backed by detailed research to verify historical accuracy. Vincent then recorded the tales in 20 published works, painting a colourful history of the town and bringing its past to life.

Historical tours of the town were also on Vincent's agenda – though she soon realised all anyone really wanted to hear about were the hauntings. In 1997 she decided to organise a ghost hunt, 'just for fun'; 12 years later, her weekly tours are renowned as the best of their kind in the greater Sydney region.

With Vincent sadly passing away in May 2009, the legacy of her work has been passed on to her daughter Jenny, who is continuing the ghost tours in honour of her mother's passion. Filling Vincent's shoes as tour guide is spiritual medium Dannie Formosa, a former tour group regular personally trained by Vincent.

'Picton has a fairly stable population, which means stories don't get lost like they do in big cities,' Formosa tells us as we gather for a 'special investigation' near the graveyard of St Mark's Anglican Church in Lower Picton. 'Picton may not have more ghosts than any other town, but we certainly have more recorded hauntings, thanks to Liz.'

As we wander along the main street of Picton, Formosa's stories come thick and fast: of the 'fresh air freak' who haunts the old post office, opening windows and doors at whim; of the creative phantom that rearranges the window display at an antiques shop; and of the librarian who never left his beloved workplace, even after death. With trucks roaring past and shop lights blaring, the tales are interesting though not the slightest bit spooky — it's hard to give credence to the litany of alleged occurrences under these benign conditions.

However, at the Wollondilly Shire Hall — reputedly the most haunted building in Picton — our large and rather straggly mob snaps to attention as Formosa recounts the misdemeanours of the spirits inhabiting the former schoolhouse, now home to the Picton Theatre Group. At least three ghosts make regular appearances here: Ted, a tall, bearded theatre critic who stands at the back of the hall watching the actors on stage; a little girl who is heard crying during rehearsals; and the apparition of a small boy seen running across the stage.

Like many theatrical spectres, the spirits of the Shire Hall appear to be pranksters, moving props, furniture and even lights set up for performances. House lights turn themselves on and off; disembodied footsteps echo off-stage; and many a passer-by has heard music and the laughter of children emanating from inside, even when the place is locked up and in darkness.

As we shiver in a huddled group outside, we hear, on cue, the sound of children wafting through the air. Everyone immediately reaches for their camera, firing off random shots in the hope of capturing paranormal evidence.

Further investigation soon reveals, however, that there is a rehearsal underway, and we all feel a little sheepish about our hasty leap to conclusions. Clearly, our tour group is anxious for something to jump out and say boo, and, charged by our close non-encounter, we head back to our vehicles enthusiastic to begin ghosthunting in earnest – at the notorious Redback Range Tunnel.

This disused railway tunnel is arguably the most haunted individual site in Australia. Word is that not a night goes by without something inexplicable happening. Tour groups, we're told, are almost guaranteed a paranormal experience – a claim that immediately sets off alarm bells in sceptical brains.

However, as we approach the tunnel up a long muddy track, a blanket of rural darkness enfolding us, there's a definite shift in mood. The previously unruly group is reduced to whispers, rustles in the surrounding bush cause even the most boisterous British backpackers to jump out of their pasty skins, while two cows resting in their paddock cause conniptions as they are mistaken for supernatural entities.

There is also a noticeable drop in temperature as we leave the town lights behind; and it's a shivering, subdued and – dare we say it – scared group of tourists who gather at the mouth of the tunnel and stare into the black, gaping void.

Opened in 1867, the Redback Range Railway Tunnel was the first to be opened outside of Sydney by NSW Railways, but was eventually closed to rail in 1919 when the new deviation line opened. During World War II, it was used to store ammunition or possibly mustard gas, with large wooden doors placed on each end of the tunnel sealing it off from the public.

After the war, the 592-foot tunnel was used as a commercial mushroom farm — its dank, dark interior providing perfect fungus-growing conditions — and subsequently became known as the Mushroom Tunnel. It is currently owned by the Wollondilly Shire and closed to the public due to safety concerns. Vincent's tour groups are allowed to visit on a special licence, under strict orders not to venture beyond the entrance.

According to local legend (and backed by Vincent's historical research), a local spinster named Emily Bollard made the ill-fated decision in 1916 to take a shortcut through to the tunnel to visit her brother who lived on the other side. Unfortunately she hadn't read the train timetable, and halfway through, she was struck and killed instantly by an oncoming train. While her body was apparently carried on the front of the train to the roadway, Emily's spirit remained at the point of impact — and is today one of the most active, anywhere, on record.

One look at Vincent's website proves just how frequently Emily makes an appearance. She usually manifests as a glowing light, often a white light but sometimes blue, orange or red. Shadowy figures are seen flitting around the middle of the tunnel, and she has even been known to manifest as a white-clad figure with long wavy hair.

In her book *Ghosts of Picton Past*, Liz Vincent writes of her first encounter with the fully realised apparition of Emily:

> The atmosphere in the tunnel was positively charged . . . As we watched, the white light flew down the left side of the tunnel and when it was about twenty feet in front of us it materialised into a woman in a long, flowing white dress. We

froze. All except the sceptic, who screamed, turned and ran. The rest of us watched as the woman floated down the right side of the tunnel and eased back into a distant white light.[1]

During our visit, however, Emily is a little shy – or perhaps deterred by the presence of such a large, talkative group. Under Formosa's instructions, we lose the chitchat and stare obediently into the blackness. Almost immediately, those in the front row shout with excitement – 'There she is, there she is!'

Unfortunately, our eyes cannot adjust beyond the white sweatshirt of the man in front of us, so we ask him to pop down, willing away any scepticism. Several moments later, we both see . . . something – flashes of light, like distant sheet lightning, flickering in the distance. A murmur rises through the group, and then an icy wind begins to blow, an oncoming breeze that chills to the bone.

Until now, it's been a perfectly still night – not a breath of wind. The breeze suddenly whipping through is uncannily like that which occurs on an underground platform as a train approaches. It lasts for several seconds, then stops as suddenly as it started.

Emily's light display continues for several minutes Our logical brains keep telling us it's a trick of the eye, or perhaps a phosphorescent bat or moth creating the colours. But try as we might, we have no explanation for what we are seeing – other than it is, indeed, something paranormal.

In her book, Vincent points out that looking west from the main entrance, there is nothing beyond the tunnel but paddocks and the main southern rail line – no signals, roads or houses. There is certainly no light source to explain what we later find in our digital photos – glowing orbs, approaching our group in subsequent shots. In one image, the orb appears to be in motion, flying towards us.

Finally, Emily's energy seems to wane; the lights dim as our tour group becomes more rowdy. In a final ditch effort to regain control, Formosa asks for another couple of minutes' silence as keen ghosthunter, Jason King, sets his digital voice recorder.

'Are you there, Emily?' King asks. 'Have you got anything to say?'

It's an invitation one British backpacker finds impossible to resist – he lets out a massive fart, reducing his companions to uncontrollable giggles. Clearly it's time to abandon the exercise, and head to the warmth of our final destination – the Antill Park Golf Club.

The following day, however, King calls us with great excitement, asking us to listen to an EVP recording he's posted on his website, www.jasonghosthunting.com. As our group splinters away, voices disappearing into the distance, King is heard asking Emily once again to make her presence known. 'Last chance,' he says. 'Bye bye.'

Then, clear as day, what sounds like a small child's voice echoes, 'Bye bye'. There were no children on our tour that night, and certainly no-one with such a high-pitched squeak. Once again, we are flabbergasted, with no logical explanation for what we are hearing.

Back at the golf club, we warm our frozen toes by an electric heater and thaw out with tea and cake. The group is abuzz with what they have just experienced; the night could very well end here with great satisfaction. But according to Formosa, the best is yet to come — a private investigation upstairs.

Don't let the bland RSL decor fool you — this is no ordinary clubhouse. It is, in fact, the original mansion of Picton, the former home of the pioneering Antill family. 'Jarvisfield', built in 1863, is said to host several phantoms from the past, including a man dressed in period clothing nicknamed 'The Footman' and spirit children heard running around the second storey.

According to Formosa, there is another entity living upstairs: an elderly man who is rather grumpy — and not at all happy with her. Several weeks prior, she visited the property with a group of mediums and 'released' a small child spirit into the light, much to the displeasure of the little girl's grandfather. According to Formosa, the old man now has it in for her, smothering her with an unbearable pressure any time she ventures upstairs.

While we sense nothing out of the ordinary, our friend Sam feels an ominous presence in the end storeroom where the old man is said to linger. Then two strange things happen which even we witness — a door squeaks open of its own accord, and a bathroom light switches itself on. Faulty wiring? Crooked floorboards? Or very active entities?

Picton's reputation as 'most haunted' may be due to documentation and a thoroughly researched history, but having experienced more spooky goings-on in one single evening than we have in years of ghosthunting, we believe Picton's paranormal crown is well-deserved.

In fact, even that scary pub is said to be haunted.

Canberra, Australian Capital Territory

With such a brief history of European settlement, an Australian town only needs a handful of crumbling sandstone buildings to warrant claims that it is haunted. With an absence of medieval castles, ancient ruins or battle sites to set imaginations alight, Aussie ghosthunters instead scour every dusty doorway, cracked pane of glass or deserted corridor in search of paranormal activity, conjuring up the spirits of a not-so-distant past. Ghost tours are also increasing in popularity as savvy entrepreneurs realise the public's insatiable appetite for spooky stories presented in an entertaining, informative manner.

An unlikely contender for a scary night out, however, is our nation's relatively modern capital, Canberra. But the Canberra Ghost Tour, led by one of Australia's most high-profile cryptozoologists and ghost experts, Tim the Yowie Man, is one of the most popular ghost tours in the country, booking out solidly weeks in advance. And with good reason — the tour is loads of fun, great theatre whether you are a believer in the paranormal or not.

It is the night before Halloween when we climb on board the cobweb-strewn Destiny Tour bus, driven by a blind, drunk driver (a joke, in case you are wondering). Inside, witches, vampires, pirate zombies and *Scream* serial killers pull faces at passers-by while Tim the Yowie Man and his kilt-clad mate Tinny share stories of floating coffins, vicious murders and havoc-wreaking poltergeists in buildings ranging from seats of power through to pubs.

The flippant tone, however, becomes a little more subdued at one of the Australian Capital Territory's oldest stone buildings,

Something is Out There

Blundell's Cottage on the north shore of Lake Burley Griffin. Outside this cute little building, Tim tells the story of Florrie, a young girl burnt to death in 1892 when her nightdress caught on fire; consequently, a terrible stench is often said to waft along the outside verandah. Meanwhile one of our party — who we later discover is a well-known medium and mystic — photographs what appears to be a hanging body as well as several orbs in a tree outside the property.

We attempt to take a similar photo — but our camera, as it often does in places of high paranormal activity, freezes. Medium Anthorr, whose business card reads The Wizard of Australia, advises us to ask permission before taking a shot; and while this seems to appease the spirits somewhat, our resulting shot reveals no anomalies.

The tour continues with a fascinating parade of unlikely haunts: the National Library, said to be inhabited by a pilot who crash-landed during a ceremonial fly-by; the National Film and Sound Archive, which was once a morgue and has high levels of poltergeist activity; and the Australian War Memorial, which boasts a phantom horse as well as the ghost of a Japanese POW.

Even Old Parliament House has several ghosts, which of course leads to the inevitable jokes about politicians dying of boredom — or perhaps corruption. Most reports of paranormal activity come from security guards, who report seeing strange apparitions during their nightly rounds. Some spirits have been sighted by more than one person at a time, and one guard even quit his job after a terrifying encounter.

But the Australian Capital Territory's most haunted place is not an old building or one where politicos clash head to head. It is, in fact, a memorial, built in honour of ten people who died in a plane crash in 1940. To get to the Air Disaster Memorial in Queanbeyan requires some effort; through a gate and along a rutted, dirt road in the middle of a pine forest. The memorial is simple and moving, just a granite boulder surrounded by a bed of gravel; but it's said that many strange things happen near this rock – intense cold spots, strange sounds and countless orbs, which appear in many a photograph.

In what appears to be a case of energy transfer, cars frequently stall at this location and refuse to start; when this happens, even odder things follow. Some claim to have seen the apparition of a nurse, attempting to break into their car any way possible – even smashing the windscreen. Others have seen a little girl, crying at the gate or watching as they try to start the car; while some even swear that they have been abducted by aliens at this site.

Just in case, Tim does a head count as everyone boards the bus. All present and accounted for.

Kapunda, South Australia

While organised ghost tours may bring tourism to allegedly haunted towns, some communities do not welcome the attention that increased publicity brings. Whether it's because of religious conservatism or fear of the unexplained, some neighbourhoods simply do not like news of strange occurrences leaking beyond their borders.

This seems to be the case in the tiny South Australian town of Kapunda, 77 kilometres north of Adelaide, which gained notoriety in 2001 after the release of a documentary hosted

Something is Out There

by gravel-voiced TV personality Warwick Moss. *Kapunda – Most Haunted Town* implied that the former mining town in the picturesque Clare Valley was a hotbed of paranormal activity, with a dark and dubious past centred around the town's Reformatory, a derelict building that once housed orphans and wayward girls. Immediately, curious visitors began to flock to the town, poking around its buildings, asking questions and investigating its history – much to the chagrin of the locals.

Whether due to coincidental timing or as a deterrent to the reported low-life that followed in the wake of the documentary, the Reformatory was bulldozed by the church in 2002, the loss of an important historic site a small price to pay for peace and quiet.

Despite the building's demise, however, the site still attracts the attention of ghosthunters keen to investigate the story behind its most famous apparition, Ruby Olive Bland, who is often seen flitting around the headstones in the neighbouring graveyard.

While official records state that 18-year-old Ruby died of complications from gallstone surgery, local legend has it she was raped by the cruel and overbearing priest at the Reformatory, dying at the hands of her abuser during an abortion-gone-wrong. Whether this story is true or not, what has been verified is that the school closed down not long after Ruby's death in 1909 amid reports of improper treatment and concerns for Reverend Martin's questionable state of mind. He subsequently lived alone in the building, growing increasingly insane until his death 12 years later.

Although buried in an imposing grave in St John's Cemetery, it seems Father Martin's spirit also refuses to rest in peace, looming as a dark shadow, grabbing women by the hair or moaning the word 'sinner' into the wind. The bricks and mortar of the old Reformatory may have been torn down, but it seems the energies of those who lived and suffered there will linger for all eternity.

Richmond, Tasmania

Unlike Kapunda, the village of Richmond in Tasmania is at peace with its dark past, celebrating its links to a less tolerant period of human history. The blood, sweat and tears of convict labour is evident in nearly every structure in this perfectly preserved Georgian town; from the ominous walls of its gaol, to the clock tower of its church, to the arches of the pretty bridge spanning the river. Daytrippers from nearby Hobart flock here to wander the charming streets, visit galleries and craft shops, and soak up the olde worlde ambience in what has become one of the most popular tourist attractions in the state.

But the history of Richmond is not just presented as a static collection of bricks and mortar; it is brought to life with stories of real people, lovingly researched by locals who embrace the town's inglorious foundations. And what better way to spark the imagination than through tales of former residents who chose never to leave town, even after death?

Alan Jennison's Richmond Ghost Tours meet at dusk outside what appears to be a rather benign building – the town's lolly shop. But having lived above this shop for 12 months, Jennison's firsthand account of its paranormal occupants starts the tour with a rather spooky bang.

'The first night I moved in I was laying in bed reading when, at 11 o'clock on the dot, my cat went berserk in that room, absolutely mad,' he tells us. 'It ran up the curtains, down the curtains, under the bed, across the bed, out the other side of the wardrobe – then it stopped, walked out of the room, curled up in a chair and went to sleep. It then proceeded to do that every night at 11 o'clock, the second night, the third night, fourth night . . . every night for about nine months.'

But it was not just Jennison's cat sensing an otherworldly presence – Jennison himself has experienced some unexplainable events. 'I'd go to bed and hear every door slam shut; I'd get up and every door would be wide open. I'd hear footsteps coming down the fire steps; that was a bit disconcerting, but I got used to it,' he says.

He has also seen a man whom he believes was the first owner of the premises, formerly a honky-tonk hotel. 'I'd been there a few months when I saw a man in a brown suit and bowler hat walk from the top of the stairs, across the landing and into my lounge room,' Jennison recalls. 'Three weeks later, a clairvoyant walked in the door and saw the same thing, a man in a brown suit. She said his name was William, and that he was shot on the front verandah by a man on the other side of the road with a rifle. I haven't been able to verify that, but the first owner was a man called William Wise.'

From the shop, we continue down the hill to Richmond's most famous landmark, the bridge over the Coal River. With its grassy verge, picnic tables and quacking ducks, this picturesque location belies the grim story behind its construction. Dating from 1823, this is the oldest bridge in Australia, built block by block by convicts bound by chains and whipped into submission by cruel and heavy-handed overseers.

According to local legend, a convict who died during construction was bricked up into one of the centre piers on the south side of the bridge – an inglorious resting place even for someone considered of low social standing.

'Why do I think he was put in there?' Jennison asks our group as he points to the middle of the bridge. '1978, 1989, 1999, 2003, 2006 – there were car accidents each year at the midpoint of the bridge. Seventy years ago, a man was bringing a horse and cart into Richmond from the Sorrell direction. At the midpoint, the horse reared up, the man fell out and broke his neck and died. A lot of locals won't walk their dogs across the midpoint of the bridge.'

Another legend associated with the bridge involved the death of a nasty piece of work called George Grover, a chain-gang boss who earned the nickname The Flagellator through his overuse of the cat-o'-nine-tails. Himself a former convict, George Grover is said to have delighted in his underlings' suffering, riding on the heavy hand-carts full of stone dragged along by the convicts and beating them until their welted backs oozed blood.

In March 1832, the workers could take no more, pummelling Grover to a pulp on the bridge before hauling his body over the parapet. His ghost is said to appear on the bridge at certain times, particularly as the sun descends over the village.

As darkness embraces us, we sit beneath the curved arches in silence, waiting, waiting . . . Will the ghost of The Flagellator appear tonight? Several of our photographs reveal bright orbs – but are these truly an indication of spiritual activity or just insects and dust captured in the flash? A lone walker passes by; we say our 'good evenings' before realising the figure has disappeared from sight. A ghostly presence, or simply a fast-moving pedestrian? In the rural silence under a full moon, it seems anything is possible.

Passing churches and graveyards, the tour continues through the town, our footsteps and chatter echoing through the night. But silence and a distinct chill once again engulfs us as we gather outside the Old Richmond Gaol, Australia's oldest existing lock-up, to hear tales of desperate characters, intolerable cruelty and living conditions beyond the realm of human endurance.

Built in 1825, the gaol has been left largely in its original condition, its dank, gloomy cells evoking fear and trepidation. Many visitors testify to hearing moaning sounds and sighing coming from the windowless Men's Solitary Block, where prisoners were confined in total darkness to strip them of dignity and sanity alike; and many ghost tour participants claim to see an evil face staring from the top window of the main building.

While current managers Kerry and Veronica Dean never experienced anything unusual in their years living in the adjoining Gaoler's House, their four-year-old daughter swore to have seen a lady wearing a pink dress standing near the fireplace in the lounge room. 'She still claims what she saw was real,' Veronica tells us. 'She couldn't understand why her parents couldn't see the woman too.'

Despite this encounter, Veronica says the experience of living at the gaol didn't faze their family. 'It was always just home,' she said. 'And when a home is a happy place, the things of the past don't seem to matter.'

Wandering through the deserted streets of Richmond on a cool Tuesday evening with a dedicated bunch of ghosthunters certainly begs the question — why Richmond? The answer, according to Jennison, lies not only in its history, but in its preservation.

'It has the most old buildings still standing in Australia,' he says. 'Sydney is 30 or 40 years older, but a lot of the earlier buildings in Sydney were bulldozed. Richmond has the oldest Roman Catholic church, the oldest schoolhouse, the oldest bridge, the oldest post office, the oldest supermarket. If old buildings are traditionally haunted, Richmond has got them.'

Chapter 3
Creepy convict colonies

Port Arthur, Tasmania

The charmingly monikered Comfort Inn perches on a hill overlooking the historic convict settlement of Port Arthur, just an electric gateway separating the two. Hotel guests are privileged to 24-hour access to the site – a quick wave of a black token, and the gate magically slides open, a Narnia-esque portal into another world.

Crossing this threshold at dusk, however, requires a little courage – there's something ominous about what lies beyond. As the door slams shut, we can't help but shiver as we begin our descent down the gravel driveway, the highly charged air cutting to the bone and a sombre pall casting shadows in the fading light.

Superficially, our trepidation seems unjustified. On this cool summer evening, there could be no prettier place to wander, past cottages surrounded by hollyhocks and roses, along deserted avenues of oaks bursting with joyous birdsong, through village greens surrounded by picket fences. For all intents and purposes, we could be taking a sunset stroll through a quaint English hamlet, idyllically nestled by the shimmering sea.

That this tranquil site was once called 'hell on earth' seems unthinkable; that it was the scene of one of the most brutal, violent crimes of recent memory even more incredible. But in reality, Port Arthur has witnessed more horror than any other location in the nation, its very name holding overwhelming connotations of evil and sadness for many Australians.

Yet that is exactly why this place was conceived – to be a hellhole of punishment, exile and misery. Located at the far reaches of the British Empire, cut off from civilisation by sea and wilderness, Port Arthur was born in 1833 as a secondary prison, a place for repeat offenders from all Australian colonies. It was to be a dumping ground for the worst of the worst, an inescapable fortress for those banished from society.

That many of the 12,500 men and boys interred during its 40-odd years as a penal settlement had committed relatively minor offences is a fact often overlooked. Transportation to the colonies was the punishment for any number of paltry felonies – stealing a loaf of bread, forgery, even implication in a crime or association by default was enough to see wretched souls loaded onto overcrowded brigs and carted to unchartered corners of the globe for a minimum of seven years. This hapless underclass was to form the labour force that powered colonisation – it was, in effect, a slave society, operating under the guise of reformation.

Something is Out There

Between 1803 and the cessation of transportation in 1853, around 73,000 convicts were deposited in Van Diemen's Land, as the southern state of Tasmania was then known. They were set to work clearing land, building bridges, houses and roads, preparing the way for free settlers. Having come from the filthy, festering stinkhole of Britain, the clean air and relative space must have been a blessing in disguise; but any further rumblings of discontent or crime of any description resulted in punishments of unimaginable severity — floggings, secondary transportation, or in the worst cases, execution.

Port Arthur was not the first or by any means the most notorious of Van Diemen Land's secondary prisons. That title belonged to Macquarie Harbour in the far-western reaches of Tasmania, which according to author Hamish Maxwell-Stewart in his definitive history on that settlement was a place associated with 'inexpressible depravity, degradation and woe' where 'man lost the aspect, and the heart of man'.[1]

By comparison, Port Arthur was a model of reformation, a place where discipline and punishment operated hand in fist with education and training. The English prison reformer Jeremy Bentham described his penitentiary as 'a machine for grinding rogues honest' — and while its methods may seem cruel by today's standards, there was at least a glimmer of hope for inmates who managed to survive the hell of imprisonment and crawl clear of the penal system.

Port Arthur was also the location of the British Empire's first juvenile detention centre, located opposite the main settlement at Point Puer. Housing boys aged between 14 and 17, its intention was to protect street kids from the evil influence of older men, to teach them to read, write and gain skills that would equip them for a law-abiding future. It wasn't an entirely successful experiment – punishment was relentless and draconian – but some of Governor Arthur's 'little depraved felons' did manage to beat the odds and lead successful lives on the outside.

By 1840, Port Arthur had established itself as a major industrial settlement, fuelled by convict labour. Dozens of buildings, including a church, massive gaolhouse and various private homes had been constructed; and it featured the largest dockyard in the southern state, with a booming trade in shipbuilding. There were workshops housing carpenters, painters and blacksmiths, as well as steam-powered sawmills and foundries – everything required for a self-sufficient industrial settlement.

Life in this southernmost community, however, was far from easy.

Exposed to the fury of the Arctic winds, Port Arthur was bleak and bitterly cold; living conditions were primitive, disease rife and discipline harsh. Flogging, working on the treadmill, and solitary confinement in total silence were common punishments; while prisoners considered 'the worst class' were sent to nearby coalmines to work day and night in underground pits that were described as 'sinkholes of vice and infamy'. Under such conditions, convicts were to contemplate their sins and 'change the evil tendencies' of their minds – that's if their spirit wasn't broken in the process, leaving them pathetic shadows of their former selves.

Some inmates were even driven to escape – an act of brazen desperation, considering the site was virtually inescapable. Located on an isolated isthmus surrounded by water, the only land route was via a narrow sliver of land, heavily guarded by armed soldiers and a line of 19 vicious, half-starved dogs. But try some did: One audacious convict dressed himself in kangaroo hide and tried to hop past guards, while others attempted to swim the shark-infested crossing.

During its years of operation, around 1100 people died at Port Arthur, many of them buried in unmarked graves on an offshore island known as the 'Isle of the Dead'. Even the military and free settlers, whose graves occupy the high side of the island, fell to diseases such as scurvy, pneumonia and dysentery. Children were ravaged with whooping cough, measles and scarlet fever, while women died in childbirth. Convicts suffered industrial accidents, or died from medical misdiagnosis. Others became victims of vicious crime and murder, the perpetrators themselves facing certain execution as the ultimate form of punishment.

Today, Port Arthur resonates with these lost souls, echoing through its crumbling ruins or written on the headstones in the island graveyard. And it is these nocturnal whisperings, the cries of despair of spirits trapped in time, that we are heading down to investigate, as we join one of the site's nightly ghost tours.

We are clearly not alone in our morbid curiosity of this dark underbelly – in peak season, up to 15 groups of 30 wander Port Arthur each night, hearing tales of murder, mayhem and unthinkable brutality. Whether it's the fact that such tales bring history to life, or just that people love a good scare, there's no underestimating the public fascination with ghosts and the afterlife, particularly in such an evocative and infamous location.

By all accounts, Port Arthur's ruins are rife with paranormal activity. Reports have been flooding in since the site was closed in 1877; and during the 20-odd years of official ghost tours, more than 1800 accounts of unusual occurrences have been collated, stashed in 14 folders in managerial offices. Visitors from all over the world have written of apparitions, strange sounds, invisible touches and disembodied voices; photographs reveal countless orbs, slashing vortexes and strange mists; while several paranormal groups and television programs, including the popular US reality show *Ghost Hunters*, have verified hauntings during intensive investigations.

Despite the spooks of Port Arthur creating big business, our guide Caitlin Vertigan is refreshingly forthright, dismissing many longstanding tales as outright myth or ridiculous embellishments. 'Half of it was made up just to bring in the tourists,' this self-confessed paranormal enthusiast admits. 'Over time, the stories have just become part of the fabric of the place. Never let the truth stand in the way of a good story,' she laughs.

Instead, our lantern-lit meanderings through churches and chapels, into private homes and along echoing gaol corridors, are accompanied by yarns verified by repeat experiences and historical accuracy – all presented, of course, with enough theatricality and drama to entertain the masses.

Interestingly, most of the alleged hauntings are related not to convict miscreants, but instead to free settlers, military and family members. We can only assume that some prisoners, finally free of their shackles in the afterlife, chose not to linger in the 'inescapable prison', leaving the sandstone ruins to the restless spirits of their captors.

Something is Out There

One of the most frequently recorded spectres is an unlikely candidate – that of the settlement's chaplain, Reverend George Eastman. Highly esteemed by officers and known as the 'good parson' by prisoners, Eastman served at Port Arthur for 15 years, living at the Parsonage with his wife Louisa and ten children, said to be holy terrors with a penchant for running riot through surrounding farmland.

In April 1870, Eastman left his sickbed to attend to a prisoner dying at an outstation. He himself developed pneumonia, and passed away two days later at the age of 48. He is buried on the Isle of the Dead, occupying prime real estate on the highest ground of the free settlers' cemetery.

Legend has it, however, that Eastman didn't leave his congregation readily. A portly man, his coffin was too heavy to carry down from the upstairs bedroom where he died – instead it was lowered out the window by rope. Unfortunately, the rope snapped – spilling his rotting corpse into the gutter outside.

Almost immediately, strange occurrences were reported in the Parsonage – foul smells, strange lights and an apparition of a large, bearded man threatening unwanted visitors. During the 1980s, the hype reached fever pitch when builders working at the Parsonage ran out screaming, claiming an apprentice had been pinned down and assaulted by an unseen force. The incident even made headlines in the local paper – though later some of the men admitted they had exaggerated to further terrify the boy. Regardless, the youngster never did return to the job, having experienced something he believed was truly horrific.

Many of Port Arthur's ghosts are said to be children; and while this seems far removed from the prison environment, it must be remembered that many families dwelled here, with countless births, deaths and marriages on record. The spirit of a little girl with blood trickling from a gash in her forehead is said to inhabit the commandant's house – some say she is Amelia, the daughter of Commandant Booth, though there is no record of a child dying in the home. There are also several young ghosts witnessed in the Junior Medical Officer's house where at least 11 children lived – two little boys are sometimes seen playing on the roof, of all places.

As if to illustrate, we photograph some large orbs during our investigation, hovering just over the shingles where the boys are often sighted – and while we are sceptical about orbs as a manifestation of spiritual entities, we can't help but ponder the size, brightness and intensity of these particular anomalies. Did we capture the little boy ghosts at play?

A far darker scenario greets us, however, in the bowels of the house once occupied by the senior surgeon. In the dank basement is a particularly loathsome room reeking of mildew, its sandstone walls illuminated by a single slender shaft of daylight. During our visit, some of our party complain of the stench of smoke; others in the past have felt weak from the fumes of formaldehyde. Not surprisingly – for it is believed this room was used for dissecting corpses.

Of all the allegedly haunted buildings in Port Arthur, it is this enclosed space that elicits the most fear. Some claim to have seen a hideous face peering out of the hole in the wall, connected to the upper level by a chimney flue; others have sensed the shadowy presence of a man dressed in a white coat standing in the corner. Others – including, on one occasion, our guide Caitlin – have had trouble breathing, suffering symptoms of a panic attack.

While it has not been historically corroborated that dissections took place in this basement, it is highly plausible – after all, the mid-19th century was a time of medical experimentation, with curious physicians eager to delve into the workings of the human body and mind. And what better place to find organ donors than in a colonial prison, far from the emotional ties of loved ones?

With these gruesome thoughts fresh in our minds, we make our way up the hill to what is allegedly the most haunted building on the site – the Separate Prison. This fortress-like building was constructed in 1849, when radical ideas about rehabilitating criminals were sweeping the so-called civilised world. Suddenly, physical punishment – which Port Arthur had readily dished out in the form of floggings – was deemed to harden, rather than reform a man; far better to place him in a quiet environment where he could contemplate his sin and change his life for the better.

The result was a new building, based on Britain's Pentonville Prison, with four radiating wings and tiny cells designed for solitary confinement. Each new arrival at the settlement would spend four to 12 months in the Separate Prison before being assigned to work outside on the settlement. Prisoners were allocated a number, and thereafter spent 23 hours of the day in their cells, reading the Bible and working in solitude and silence. The other hour was spent in the exercise yard, heads covered in canvas 'silence masks' to prevent communication with other convicts.

Creepy convict colonies

In such an oppressive environment, it's little wonder that many men cracked; and the hopelessness, fear and resentment inevitably felt under these conditions has been etched into the very fabric of the building. There are countless reports of apparitions, balls of energy, whispers, clanging chains and shadowy figures in the corridors; while many visitors are overwhelmed with sadness or a heavy burden as they wander through.

On one occasion, a whole tour group complained about the disrespectful antics of an 'actor' dressed in prison garb, leering and making faces behind a tour guide as she talked. Of course, there are no costumed actors employed at the site – and to this day, no-one can explain what the group collectively witnessed.

It is in C Wing of the Separate Prison that our guide Caitlin shares several personal experiences, ones that still leave her rattled. The first involved members of a tour group, lagging behind the rest as they 'helped an old man' along the corridor and into the exercise yard. Later they identified this man from photographic records as a notorious prisoner, the child rapist John Gould.

On another occasion, a man listening to Caitlin's commentary felt a disembodied hand around his throat; as she talked Caitlin saw him clutch at his neck in panic. He later took her aside to ask if there were any marks on his neck – unravelling his scarf, he revealed fresh welt marks, as if he'd just been clawed by human fingernails.

Incidents of ghostly violence like this, however, are rare at Port Arthur – most of its otherworldly inhabitants seem content to share their realm with the hundreds of tourists who pass through gates each day. In daylight hours, it is an incredibly peaceful place, the quiet dignity of the ruins a reminder of just how far a nation forged from an oppressive, cruel regime has progressed in less than 200 years.

It is this tranquillity, however, that makes the most horrific moment in Port Arthur's history seem like an impossible, incomprehensible nightmare. On Sunday April 28, 1996, a troubled young man entered the site with a loaded AR-15 rifle, turning the weapon on innocent bystanders having lunch in the Broad Arrow Café. During his minutes-long rampage, the lone gunman killed 35 people and injured 21 more, with staff from the historic site amongst the victims.

Australia's worst-ever mass murder, the incident sent shockwaves throughout the world. Most chilling was Martin Bryant's apparent lack of remorse for his killing spree; newspaper reports claim he laughed hysterically when the court handed down 35 life sentences, without possibility of parole.

Why the gunman chose Port Arthur to mark his destiny may never really be understood, but the incident has certainly cast a permanent shroud over the site. Today, staff at Port Arthur are reluctant to talk about the tragedy and its implications; many lost friends and colleagues at the time, and the memory and pain is still incredibly fresh.

To commemorate those lost in the incident, it was decided to plant a memorial garden, incorporating the shell of the Broad Arrow Café, into a place of quiet contemplation. The result is tasteful and moving; the roofless building, now open to the elements, blending in with the other ruins subtly and poignantly. The memorial is not part of regular walking tours; instead, visitors are invited to the garden independently, spending time in personal reflection.

As the ghost tour draws to its conclusion just before midnight, the group disperses with new appreciation of Port Arthur's former residents and the conditions they endured. We are left alone to make the trek back up the hill to our beds, gravel crunching underfoot; but while we physically have the place to ourselves, we are both acutely aware of the lingering presence of those whose stories have kept us intrigued and entertained.

As the gate to the Comfort Inn slides open, we respectfully ask our supernatural companions to stay behind; after all, they have no place in the reality beyond this portal. It is their eternal choice to remain in their former homes, to keep their moment in history alive, to share their tales of life and death, of struggle and pain. They may have left this mortal coil, but their legacy endures, a permanent and precious gift for future generations.

Macquarie Harbour, Tasmania

> Rocks, caves, lakes, ferns, bogs, dens and shades of death,
> Where all life dies, death lives, and nature breeds
> Perverse all monstrous, all prodigious things.
> Abominable. UNUTTERABLE
>
> Colonial historian John West, describing the penal settlement at Macquarie Harbour[2]

Located at the very ends of the Earth, on the far-western reaches of Tasmania, 27 days by ship from the nearest city, Macquarie Harbour was the most feared of all secondary penal settlements.

The convicts interred here knew it as 'Pluto's Land', after the Roman god of the underworld,[3] while Quaker missionaries Backhouse and Walker reported that prisoners who passed through the heads of Macquarie Harbour 'despaired of salvation or hope'.[4]

Indeed, the narrow opening into this massive body of water — larger than Sydney Harbour and surrounded by dense forests and mountains — was known as Hell's Gates; it was described by writer David Burn as a place 'unblessed by man, accurst of God'.[5]

Conditions in the camp on what was then known as Settlement Island (now Sarah Island) were deplorable: overcrowded, unsanitary, with punishments such as multiple lashings frequently doled out for any paltry offence. Chain gangs bound by double-ironed shackles were put to work clearing timber, quarrying stone or constructing buildings, hard relentless labour beyond the realms of human endurance.

A dumping ground for murderers, rapists and thieves, violent crime was rife in the settlement — according to author Hamish Maxwell-Stewart, convicts killed other prisoners for no good reason, attacked guards and committed 'cool, deliberate and premeditated acts . . . to the disgrace of humanity'.[6]

Some saw these felonies — and the resulting death penalty — as the only way out, the only option of escaping hell on earth; others were considered monsters with no conscience, compared at the time to bloodthirsty vampires of Eastern Europe.

The fact that Macquarie Harbour was labelled inescapable also drove many desperadoes to attempt the impossible. During the life of the settlement, there were at least 150 escape attempts involving 271 individuals – nearly one in four of the 1200 transported there. Most escapees were captured or were simply swallowed by the wilderness, never to be heard of again; others lived to tell horrific tales, of attacks by Aborigines, starvation and even cannibalism.

Most notorious was the plight of Alexander Pearce, whose exploits have been fictionalised in print and film, most famously by Marcus Clark in his 1874 novel *For the Term of His Natural Life*, and more recently provided the inspiration for the classic Australian horror film *Dying Breed*. An Irishman who was originally deported for stealing shoes, Pearce absconded with six other convicts but was the sole survivor after several months on the run . . . having devoured the flesh of his fellow escapees. With no bodies as evidence Pearce was unable to be tried for murder, and he was subsequently returned to Settlement Island.

A year later, Pearce once again escaped, this time with just one foolhardy companion, a 24-year-old convict named Thomas Cox. Several days later, Pearce was found with half a pound of human flesh in his pocket. When questioned, Pearce claimed Cox had drowned and that he had sliced off a piece of his body as proof he was dead. This time, no-one believed him. His justification: 'No man can tell what he will do when driven by hunger.'[7]

Charged with Cox's murder, Pearce was tried and hanged in Hobart gaol in July 1824, his body dissected and skull presented to settlement surgeon Henry Crockett. This macabre medical souvenir was eventually smuggled to the USA, where it remains on display in the Pennsylvania Museum of Archaeology and Anthropology.

Tainted by tales of murder, cruelty and cannibalism, the ruins at Sarah Island are today an evocative reminder of an unthinkable past. While wilderness has reclaimed much of the site, many claim the island is haunted – some even say the headless ghost of Alexander Pearce still roams the surrounding blackwood forest.

Richard Davey, who runs an entertaining theatrical tour of the island as part of the Gordon River cruise experience, has spent many a night on Sarah Island, and generally finds it to be a benign, peaceful location. However, when he first started camping there, he was disturbed by what sounded like terrible groanings – a noise he later discovered was created by waves breaking into hollow logs.

Other campers, however, have reported the sensation of being crushed in their tents, unable to move as though shackled to the ground. A vindictive convict ghost, perhaps, or maybe the spectre of Alexander Pearce pinning them down, searching for his next feast.

Norfolk Island

Violence and bloodshed have also stained the shores of Norfolk Island, a former penal settlement located 1600 kilometres northeast of Sydney in the middle of the Pacific Ocean. With its white sandy beaches flanking sparkling sea, tranquil green countryside and towering Norfolk pines, this lovely jewel seems more like an idyllic island retreat than a penitentiary eliciting fear and trepidation. But during its incarnation as a secondary penal settlement from 1825 to 1855, Norfolk was known as 'Hell in Paradise', a place where convicts were broken with despair, misery and cruelty.

According to historical records, the Governor of New South Wales, Thomas Brisbane, had been instructed to send 'the worst description of convicts' to the settlement; his successor Governor Ralph Darling considered it 'a place of extremist punishment short of death'. Here, reformation was not an option – once transported, convicts were not permitted to return, working 'in irons . . . to deter others from the commission of crime'.

Conditions at the settlement were unimaginably harsh – inmates were forced to work in fields and quarries day and night, shackled by heavy chains and flogged to within an inch of their lives. For many, death seemed a preferable option, choosing to murder and hang for their crimes rather than endure a life of such degradation.

On three occasions, the convicts rose in mutiny. In 1846, ex-Port Arthur convict William Westwood burst out of the barracks shouting, 'Follow me and you follow to the gallows.' Fifty men were prepared for that fate, rampaging through the settlement in defiance before being caught and sentenced to death, their bodies dumped in a mass grave.

Visiting the colony in 1834 to comfort other mutineers waiting execution, Father William Ullathorne, vicar general of Sydney, found 'the most heart wrenching scene that I ever witnessed . . . each man who heard of his condemnation to death went down of his knees with dry eyes, and thanked God'.[8]

One of the most desperate acts of rebellion is the source for the island's most famous ghost story – the tale of the Bloody Bridge. The pretty little bridge was constructed by convict labour, their toil impeded by irons and the savage lash of the cat-o'-nine-tails. Driven beyond endurance, one labourer lost the plot, driving a pick through the skull of his heavy-handed overseer. The gang worked quickly to remove the evidence, bricking the tormentor's body into the bridge.

The following day, a relieving overseer noticed something oozing through the still-wet mortar – the blood of the entombed overseer. And by all accounts, the blood continues to seep through the very fabric of the bridge.

According to Maev Hitch, author of *Ghosts of Norfolk Island*, the most active haunting on the island takes place at the Convict Store, located near the pier at Kingston. This building, built in 1826, contained the crank mill, its massive grindstones turned by convict power. Records say the clankings and grindings of the mill could be heard miles away, the racket drowning the groans and curses of the men at their back-breaking work.

There have been numerous reports over the years of a greyish figure dressed in convict garb walking from the storehouse to the Kingston jetty, disappearing down a flight of stairs into the sea. The ghost is said to be a convict who drowned during the construction of the building.

Other haunted locations on the island include a whole street of convict-built homes in Quality Row, where every building has its own ghostly tale; the Military Barracks where disembodied footsteps are often heard; Rawson Hall, a post-World War II public hall where music is heard emanating from locked rooms; and there is even talk of a ghost who lurks in the main street.

In fact, so numerous are the spirits on Norfolk Island that tourism authorities claim it has more ghosts per square kilometre than any other place in Australia. This is quite a call – but in a place where bloodshed and misery were so prevalent, it's not surprising that negative energy of past atrocities has had a permanent impact.

Chapter 4
Paranormal prisons

Old Melbourne Gaol, Melbourne

Amongst institutions imposed upon and created by mankind, there is no more wretched place than a prison. Designed specifically to incarcerate and punish those who have wronged society, these are houses of angst and suffering, of misery and unhappiness. Few, if any, enter willingly, of their own accord; and negative energy inevitably abounds, embedded in impenetrable walls.

Little wonder, then, that so many gaols are said to be haunted, bearing the eternal imprints of lost souls, rejected and forgotten. And no Australian prison festers with more paranormal activity than Old Melbourne Gaol, Victoria's first purpose-built prison and the vestige of a bleak, sordid and sad chapter in this nation's history.

Located in the heart of the city on Russell Street, this austere and imposing bluestone structure is a symbol of harsh, unforgiving times. Construction commenced in 1841, its cells rapidly overflowing as the new colony of Victoria was swept up in goldrush fever and subsequent lawlessness.

At its peak, the Melbourne Gaol covered a whole city block and consisted of several cell blocks, a women's prison, warders' houses, a hospital, chapel and governor's residence; while tall towers stood silent sentinel along the wall, allowing guards to observe activity in the exercise yard.

With walls measuring more than half a metre thick and cells little bigger than a dog's kennel, Melbourne was a 'model' gaol, designed to house the worst of society's fiends – murderers, thieves, arsonists, baby killers and rapists. Also incarcerated, however, were those whose crimes today seem petty – drunks, vagabonds, prostitutes and even those of unsound mind. In the dark days of the mid-19th century, social deviants and misfits bore punishments far outweighing their crimes, with hard labour, solitary confinement and abstinence all considered the key to reform.

Conditions inside were unimaginable – prisoners were locked up for 23 hours a day, with the other hour spent exercising outdoors in a canvas 'silence mask' to prevent communication with others. Only a thin straw-filled mattress and one blanket protected inmates from icy slate floors; while sanitary conditions were virtually non-existent, the stench of dysentery overwhelming.

Disorderly prisoners were kept in chains and held in punishment cells on the ground floor; some cells were lined with timber and used as 'padded cells'. More serious crimes were punished with a lashing of the cat-o'-nine-tails; while the ultimate punishment was death by hanging.

Something is Out There

From 1842 until its closure in 1924, the Melbourne Gaol hosted the execution of 136 people. The earliest hangings took place on the road outside, large crowds gathering to watch the ghoulish ceremony. A nod to delicate sensibilities saw the gallows moved to their present location on the south wall of the octagonal tower in 1865.

Hangings were made with a traditional noose, the knot placed under the jawbone on the left side. If the job was done properly, the jerk of the rope broke the victim's neck immediately; if not, he was left dangling, slowly choking to a long, painful death.

After execution, the body was left for 30 minutes; it was then removed from the noose and wheeled to the Dead House — a small shed in the hospital yard — where an autopsy was performed. A death mask was then made of the victim's head, before a hasty burial in the gaol yard.

A quick glance over records reveals that most of the condemned were murderers, robbers, arsonists and rapists. Five of the first ten hanging victims were Indigenous men, an indication of the rampant racism of the day; while only four women had the noose pulled tight around their necks.

Of course, the most famous victim of Old Melbourne Gaol's gallows was Australia's most notorious outlaw and a folk hero in his own right — Ned Kelly. Captured after an epic battle with police in 1880, Kelly was brought to the gaol in a sad and sorry state, his legs (unprotected by his famous homemade armour) riddled with bullets. After two months in the gaol's hospital and another month in a holding cell, Kelly was publicly trialled over two days and found guilty of murder.

Legend has it that, after being sentenced to death by judge Redmond Barry, Kelly leant forward in the docks and growled, 'I will see you there, where I go.' Twelve days after Kelly's execution on November 11, 1880, Judge Barry himself left this mortal coil, Kelly's prophecy perhaps fulfilled.

One of the more macabre items currently on display at Old Melbourne Gaol is the death mask of the famous bushranger. While etchings of the hanging show Kelly being led to the gallows with full beard, the plaster cast shows him clean-shaven and his eyes closed serenely.

Unfortunately, this is all that remains of Ned's head – the skull, which was on display at the gaol until 1978, was stolen and its whereabouts still not known. A national campaign to retrieve the long-lost skull was recently launched by a group of concerned historians, who believe the relic should be part of the nation's heritage.

According to a report in the *Sunday Herald Sun*[1], a mass grave was uncovered at Old Melbourne Gaol in 2008, believed to contain Ned Kelly's skeleton sans skull. The other remains are undergoing testing at the Victorian Institute of Forensic Medicine at Southbank.

Despite the folklore associated with the famous bushranger and his inglorious death, it seems Ned Kelly may have found peace beyond the grave – or at least a more pleasant place to spend eternity than Old Melbourne Gaol. According to paranormal pundits, the ghost of Ned Kelly is noticeably absent from the prison corridors – much to curators' and the ghostseeking public's disappointment.

However, it seems there are plenty of other spooks lurking in the shadows, rattling their chains and terrifying staff members and visitors to what is now one of Melbourne's leading attractions. So frequent are sightings and supernatural experiences at the prison that the National Trust, who manage the property, now supports monthly paranormal investigations, held by the paranormal group Ghostseekers.

The idea of these investigations is to collect data, study the phenomenon scientifically and thoroughly, and to involve the public, providing them with an entertaining and informative experience.

And so it is that we find ourselves wandering the icy corridors of the gaol on a chilly winter's night, cameras, EMF meters and infrared thermometers in hand. We are part of a large tour group of 25, most of them local Melbournians under the age of 22, and all up for a thrill and perhaps a scare or two. Leading the night's proceedings is David, a self-confessed sceptic with a flair for the theatrical; while Ghostseeker cofounder Sylvia lends a more sincere intensity to the proceedings, quietly seeking evidence in a location she clearly holds dear to her heart.

Behind the scenes, a small band of volunteers monitors cameras and audio equipment, hoping to capture evidence of paranormal activity; while the tour group is also invited to record any experiences, each inexplicable moan and shiver padding an ever-increasing database of evidence.

After a brief introduction, the group is led in the dark to the most reputedly haunted areas of the gaol: Cell 17 on the third floor, where the energy of a woman is often felt; Cell 19, said to be the haunt of a violent phantom that terrorises women; the gallows area, where the original beam looms large; and the 'true condemned' cell, where prisoners were brought on their day of execution.

Of course, any self-respecting phantom will keep a wide berth from an unruly group of 25, so we are split into smaller groups with the aim of investigating each haunted location more thoroughly. We are warned that we are unlikely to have a *Most Haunted* experience (the UK television program where spirits seem to manifest every few minutes); and indeed, each half-hour spent on the icy slate floor of an airless cell drags interminably – perhaps emulating the incarceration experience?

Teamed with two Melbourne sisters (as the more 'mature' members of the tour group, we are wisely separated from giggling teenagers and tight-knit friends), we begin our sentence in Cell 17 on the top level of the gaol.

Inside this tiny cell is a perspex statue of a woman, a simple cut-out which inadvertently caused one of the greatest paranormal flaps of recent times. Dragged onto one of the overhead bridges for a photo opportunity, the transparent figure presented an eerie effigy; the resulting image was posted online, convincing true believers that this was indisputable evidence of paranormal activity. The fact that the round pedestal on which the statue stands was in clear shot didn't seem to register with those who kept the forum abuzz for almost three years, with more than 2000 postings offering opinions and animated discussion.

With the transparent lady standing over us, we begin our investigation just before midnight, our tools of trade including a thermometer, a crappy, ineffective EMF device which looks like it has come out of a cereal box, plus a set of divining rods. It is said this cell is the haunt of a female spirit – though why she resides in this male-only section of the prison is the subject of ongoing debate.

On previous investigations there have been reports of cold spots, icy touches and even the sound of voices. One team picked up an EVP recording of an Irish woman's voice saying, 'Get out'; while in 2003, Darren Done of Ghost Hunters Australia was monitoring activity in the cell when he and another investigator heard a woman's voice say, 'Help me':

> The following day, officials said this was impossible because there had been no female prisoners in that part of the gaol. Mr Done insisted they check again. 'Sure enough, they found there had been a prisoner, Lucy, who died in 1865 – on exactly the same day of the year, June 21, that we heard the voice,' Done said.[2]

Staff members at Old Melbourne Gaol also tell of the incident where a blind woman's guide dog refused to enter Cell 17, growling at the doorway, hackles raised.

It was in this cell that our group had the most intense experience of the night, whether or not it was the enthusiasm of our first investigation. Temperature fluctuations were quite marked; and during the session, the divining rods were incredibly active (but interestingly, only with two members of our party). From our questioning, we ascertained that the spirit in the cell was a female former employee (perhaps a cook) who was in love with a male prisoner. She indicated she had not died in the prison, and was quite emphatic that she was not a prostitute!

Our questioning of the female spirit, however, was interrupted by a loud kerfuffle coming from another cell, with a woman running screaming into the corridors claiming she had been touched on the shoulder by an unseen entity. While most of her companions put her hysteria down to an overactive imagination, the experience certainly put the rest of the group on edge, preparing them for the long night ahead.

Next up, our group was to spend time in the very cell where the woman had had her terrifying experience — Cell 19, or the 'growler room'. According to David from Ghostseekers, this cell is inhabited by the spirit of a nasty male spook with a tendency to pick on female visitors, growling like a bear before touching them or pulling their hair.

It's speculated that this particular entity may not be a victim of the gallows, but instead the inmate-turned-hangman, Michael Gately. This ugly, scarred misfit was described by John Stanley James as 'a frightful animal — the intense head, powerful protruding jaw, narrow receding forehead and deficient brain space, seemed fitly joined to tremendous shoulders and long strong arms, like those of a gorilla, which he resembles more than a man'.[3] After serving several years in the prison for assault, Gately, who was also known as Jack Ketch, Fagin or Ballyram, was 'promoted' to the role of hangman, an unpopular job notorious for attracting unsavoury characters. By all accounts, Gately was very ambitious, practising flogging and tying noose knots in order to impress the governor. It is also said he had a penchant for young ladies, marrying several times.

Despite the earlier hysteria in Cell 19, the hair-pulling fiend keeps his hands to himself during our group's visit. The only curious occurrence is the discovery of a puddle of water on our clipboard – not exactly a scary experience, but totally inexplicable. There was no water bottle in the vicinity, no other drinks, and no drips coming from the ceiling – and try as we might, we can find no logical explanation for how or why the puddle would have occurred. A message from a drooling Gately? It seems highly unlikely!

Adjoining the gallows is the 'true condemned cell', where prisoners were taken prior to execution. Although there are no reports of apparitions in this room, it is considered by many to be a place of extremely bad energy. Many people are overwhelmed with sadness in here; some say it reeks of fear and terror.

On the night of our visit, however, the true condemned cell appears devoid of any energy, positive or negative; and after a good half hour, we have nothing to report.

By this stage in the proceedings, however, it is well after midnight and we are tired, cold, and a little sick of each other's company. Six hours, we discover, is a long time to be in prison, especially when it's the dead of winter. It certainly made us appreciate what a horrendous experience it must have been to be incarcerated for years, with far more severe repercussions than numb backsides and frustration caused by inconsistent ghosthunting.

Dealing with spirits is a little like working with animals and children – fraught with annoyances. Ghosts do not appear on cue, or cooperate when you most want them to, and they rarely make an appearance when there are cameras around.

But that surprise element is also what makes ghosthunting so intriguing. You never know what to expect, so it's important to keep an open mind . . . just in case.

Hobart Penitentiary Chapel, Hobart

> As the Devil was going through Hobart Gaol
> He saw a solitary cell
> And the Devil was pleased for it gave him a hint,
> For improving the prisons in hell.
>
> T.G. Ford, describing the solitary cells under the Penitentiary Chapel in his 1932 book *Inhumanity*[4]

If there's a prize for spookiest, gloomiest and downright nastiest haunted location in Australia, then Hobart's Penitentiary Chapel wins hands down. Don't let the innocent façade of a church fool you — this was a grim and gruesome place of incarceration, and its history as a place of torture and death is evident in every crumbling stone, every creepy dark passageway and the ominous swing of a forlorn noose hanging over a bloodstained deck . . .

Today managed by the National Trust, the Penitentiary Chapel was built to serve several purposes — it was a place of worship as well as housing hardened criminals. Later it would become a courthouse and an execution chamber — in effect, taking care of all the requisite steps to heaven or hell. With the chapel located directly above the cells, those who wished to atone for their sins had a convenient stopping-off point before being tried and executed — all without having to step outside the front door.

Designed by colonial architect John Lee Archer, the chapel was originally built to service the adjoining gaol, known as the Tench. With the gaol already overflowing, Lee Archer incorporated 36 solitary confinement punishment cells, brick hidey-holes that support the inclined floors above. The smallest cell — called the Dust Hole — was only 70 centimetres high; convicts who returned from work drunk were cast through this opening to sober up.

While the chapel was never consecrated as a church, it was attended by both prisoners and the public, with an imposing tower built to welcome free settlers on Brisbane Street. Private pews, which could be reserved for an annual rental of 1 pound, provided seating for the public, while more than 1000 convicts were crowded into the east and west wings.

By all accounts, church services were often unruly. Linus W. Miller, an American lawyer who was transported from Canada as a political prisoner, described services thus:

> On looking about me, I could not discover more than 12, among 1200 prisoners, who appeared to be taking any notice of the service. Some were spinning yarns, some playing at pitch and toss, some gambling with cards; several were crawling about under the benches, selling candy or tobacco.[5]

Even more disturbing, however, were the groans, moans and shouting coming from the convicts chained in the cells below. Clearly, the system wasn't working; and in 1845, the chapel was closed to the public and only used by convicts, prison officers and their families.

In 1857, the Penitentiary was proclaimed a Gaol and House of Corrections, and an execution yard was added to the western wing of the chapel. Between 1857 and 1946, 32 souls were put to death here, including one woman, Margaret Coghlin, who hung for the murder of her husband John in 1862. The original beam, decking and trap door remain to this day; a noose hangs ominously, a grim reminder of those lost souls.

'We arrived here one night and found the noose swinging of its own accord,' ghost tour leader Brendan tells us. 'There wasn't a breath of wind.' A tall, skeletal type whose expressions remain stony throughout every gruesome story, Brendan is an unlikely tour leader, devoid of theatrics and embellishments. However, his deadpan demeanour suits this very spooky nocturnal investigation, allowing the paranormal activity to speak for itself.

In the 13 years he has been running lantern-lit tours, Brendan claims to have had hundreds of personal experiences, with countless other reports from tour participants. Most common is the sense of being followed in the tunnels; others have been overcome in the area beneath the gallows, complaining of the stench of blood; while some attest to seeing full-blown apparitions, particularly in the chapel itself.

During the mid-1800s, the nave and eastern transept of the chapel was converted into two courtrooms, the cedar pews utilised as jury boxes. Tunnels were installed underneath to connect each court to a central entrance; later, a cyclone-wire runway cage was put in to herd prisoners from holding cells.

The descent from the courtroom into the cell area down a tight spiral staircase is akin to entering hell itself, and downstairs the warren of tunnels and tiny cells is horrendously claustrophobic. The execution yard and gallows almost come as a relief when we finally emerge out of the mire – and we can't help but wonder if the prisoners confined here felt the same.

Chapter 5

Wards of woe

Quarantine Station, North Head, Sydney

'Don't be surprised if your camera plays up down here,' clairvoyant Antesia Leigh tells us as we descend into the bowels of the third-class dining area at Sydney's infamous Quarantine Station.

Sure enough, within 30 seconds of entering the icy kitchen, our camera whirrs shut, the batteries completely drained of power. Our spares — fully charged that day — are also dead as a doornail.

'It often occurs in areas of high spiritual activity,' Leigh later explains. 'I guess it's an energy transfer — it always happens down there.'

With a reputation as the most haunted site in the city of Sydney, the Quarantine Station challenges even the most sceptical visitor with unusually high energy levels and inexplicable paranormal occurrences.

Located amongst dense bushland on North Head, this rambling site — once used for burial and healing by the local

Gayamaygal clan — holds a unique place in Sydney's history as first port of call for ships bringing new arrivals into the colony. In all, more than 13,000 people suspected of carrying contagious diseases such as smallpox, Spanish influenza and yellow fever were interred here during its 150 years of operation.

Belying its peaceful harbourside location, the Quarantine Station was a place of isolation, suffering, loneliness and death. In fact, more than 570 patients perished here, many buried beneath its soil in unmarked graves.

And it appears some of those miserable souls chose never to leave. Since its closure in 1984, there have been countless reports of hauntings at the site — so much so that former caretakers, National Parks and Wildlife Service (NPWS), decided to run ghost tours to capitalise on its spooky reputation.

The NPWS visitors' book makes compelling reading, brimming with reports of strange shadows and sounds, flickering lights, running showers and self-slamming doors. Some guests claim to have been touched by unseen hands, while others report feeling physically ill on entering certain buildings.

Even NPWS staff members — many of them former non-believers — were not immune to strange occurrences. Ranger Peter Salt recalls entering the old wooden hospital wing (which burnt to the ground in 2002), only to be greeted with a stench that stopped him in his tracks.

'I was standing beneath the door frame when something caught in my throat,' he tells us. 'I stepped out and thought, "That's strange, that's a funny smell — it's the smell of phenol." Phenol is an old-fashioned disinfectant that was used here in the Quarantine Station. That evening it was like walking through a wall of phenol — only phenol has not been used here for 50 years.'

For regular ghosthunters relatively unfazed by paranormal activity, even we find the Quarantine Station unsettling. We have personally visited the site numerous times — sometimes on organised ghost tours, but also with film crews in the dead of night — with every experience presenting undeniable evidence of spiritual activity.

Prior to our batteries dying that night, we had captured several anomalies on our digital camera — strange mists hovering over tour guests, glowing orbs and odd face-like images in windows. In the past, we have also witnessed professional video cameras switch themselves off, had sound equipment inexplicably fail, and seen strange images captured on celluloid.

During the making of a pilot television program in 1999, we filmed television presenter Terasa Livingstone in the notorious hospital ward, recounting the story of a phantom matron who lingers around the beds. After Livingstone departs the frame, there is clear evidence of a strange figure loitering momentarily in a doorway — an anomaly Livingstone believes was the alleged ghost.

'There was no glass, there were no lights on — and the film crew were in a totally separate section,' she said. 'I have no other option to believe that it was the nurse — which scares the hell out of me, to be honest!'

At the time of this encounter, Livingstone had been telling the story of a sleepover tour guest who, during the night, had woken to find herself propped upright by an invisible force. Apparently, this was the treatment for Spanish influenza — with the ghost of the matron reliving her Florence Nightingale role.

The bed where this experience took place has earned the reputation as 'the haunted bed', with many other tales of ruffled bed covers, warm patches and unexplained dents in the mattress fuelling the legend.

According to some reports, the matron is none too happy with the intrusion of curious visitors, especially those cynical about the afterlife. One visitor reported making a rather unpleasant comment to his friend about the matron:

> Needless to say when entering the bathroom in that building, I was 'held' in the bathroom in the doorway by an unseen force ... Don't make any comments about the Matron whilst on the grounds or you will regret it like I did! (Dan, Chipping Norton)[1]

Resident medium Nikki Parsons-Gardiner believes matron also dislikes changes to routine, such as new scheduling for tour groups. 'We encountered that just the other night,' she tells us. 'We usually take tour groups through at a different time, but we changed the schedule – and she didn't like it. She wouldn't physically let people walk in the ward, they would get as far as the door and they felt someone was standing there blocking it. I'm thinking maybe for her, it was quiet time, rest time in the ward – and we were disturbing her.'

According to one rumour, matron's strict rules regarding patient visitations may have been responsible for a fire that destroyed the old hospital ward in 2002:

> The story that we were told goes something like this: The Matron had been very vocal for a long time about the NPWS

taking tours through her hospital as she believed it upset her patients. Apparently a few days before the hospital burned down, a guide took a tour in and saw the Matron there. The Matron told her that if the tour groups didn't stop coming through her hospital she would have to take drastic measures to stop this. The night before the building burned down, many people on the tour found the hospital ward uncomfortably hot, despite its high ceilings and good ventilation. After the fire investigators looked at the site, they concluded the fire was caused by an inexplicable electrical fault. The next day, the Matron appeared on the wreckage with her arms folded, smiling. (Jane Armstrong, Sydney)[2]

The grey nurse – a common apparition in haunted hospitals – is just one of the entities with a starring role at the Quarantine Station. Other frequently seen apparitions include that of a little girl, dressed in period garb with two long plaits (said to be the spirit of a child lost on North Head in 1900); several old Chinese men lurking around the Asiatic section; and a menacing face etched onto the window of the morgue.

Since commencing her role in October 2008, Nikki Parsons-Gardiner has come across roughly 55 different ghosts on site, as well as making contact with the Indigenous ancestral spirits in the neighbouring reserve. She claims to have a particularly close relationship with a girl named Martha Elizabeth Reynolds, a little blond ghost who plays in the autoclaves near the wharf.

She also regularly experiences a male entity wandering outside the morgue, possibly the ghost of a lab technician. 'He just appears as black to me, often standing under the telegraph pole there. I get people to stop and take photos there, and 90 per cent of the time an orb will turn up in the frame next to the pole. He doesn't say a word, he just stares at me as we walk past.'

According to Parsons-Gardiner, the most haunted location on the Quarantine Station grounds is the shower block, where new arrivals were made to bath in chemical solutions under the misapprehension this would actually kill germs. Set out in rows, each creaky doorway harbours ominous shadows, and the temperature in the block is always a few degrees colder than everywhere else.

Stories here include visitors being grabbed by unseen forces, doors slamming, unexpected thuds on the metal roof, and evidence of running showers – despite the water being disconnected. Many visiting psychics have stated that some sort of sexual abuse took place in one particular corner of the shower block, verified by cold spots and the sounds of supernatural screaming.

During the filming of the television pilot, Terasa Livingstone was visibly shaken by a loud bang and a dark shadow appearing above her during her solo investigation of the shower block.

'There was a definite banging on the galvanised iron and a dark figure,' she recalls. 'It wasn't a torch, it wasn't a trick of the light, there was no white light . . . just a dark figure that moved above and a sound . . . right there!'

With its rich history and prime harbourside location, it was inevitable that the Quarantine Station would eventually attract commercial interest and face redevelopment. In 2008, after a $17.3 million renovation, the site reopened as a boutique hotel; the old Boiler Room is now a swanky restaurant, and an immersive theatre experience occupies the building next to the shower block.

The eerie atmosphere of the shower block courtyard has been tempered somewhat by a blinding floodlight, while inside, the addition of infrared lights makes nocturnal investigations about as scary as wandering down a supermarket aisle.

However, according to Parsons-Gardiner, improvements at the site have not resulted in a downturn of paranormal activity. Her Spirit Investigator tour — an interactive 'ghost hunt' where punters get to play around with ghosthunting equipment — is hugely popular, with the use of the hi-tech gear enhanced by the medium's ability to communicate with wandering spirits.

And with the tours attracting around 20 people a night, it seems the lost souls of the Quarantine Station will not be resting in peace any time soon.

Aradale, Ararat, Victoria

In centuries past, the cycle of life generally ended where it began — in the warmth of the family home, surrounded by the hushed presence of loved ones. But as society became more industrialised and medical procedures more complex, so the most inevitable of nature's processes was transferred from the personal to the institutional, with death a taboo dealt with largely by medical professionals.

With the exit sign permanently alight in hospital wards, it is no surprise that they are considered extremely haunted places, abuzz with the residual energy of those recently and not so recently departed. Nearly every hospital, old or modern, harbours rumours of paranormal activity; but as places that are open 24/7 with a constant stream of human activity, opportunities for ghostbusting are next to impossible.

It is only when a hospital is decommissioned or converted to another function that researchers can actually investigate claims of hauntings. For this reason, the majority of Australia's most notorious haunted hospitals tend to be associated with the field of medicine that has undergone the biggest revolution in the past 50 years – that of mental health.

Misunderstood, feared and stigmatised, patients suffering common conditions such as depression, schizophrenia, epilepsy, alcoholism and even homosexuality were in the not-so-distant past locked up away from society in lunatic or mental asylums, an often permanent sentence where repression, cruelty and isolation were accepted forms of treatment.

Changes to mental health acts during the late-20th century, however, resulted in many of these facilities being closed, with patients transferred to community living or incorporated into general practice in an attempt to ease the stigma associated with mental illness.

One such facility was Aradale, an imposing white building overlooking the town of Ararat in the goldfields region of Victoria. Decommissioned in the late 1990s, the sprawling complex on what locals called 'Madman's Hill' stood empty for several years after the last patients were transferred in 1997, but has recently being taken over by Northern Melbourne Institute of TAFE (NMIT) as a wine and hospitality training facility.

In its heyday, the Ararat Lunatic Asylum, as it was known until 1958, housed more than 1000 mentally ill patients, tended

Owner Reg Ryan on the verandah of Monte Cristo. Despite discovering within days of moving in that the house was haunted, Ryan went on to raise his family within its walls. Along with his wife he continues to make it his home. (Julie Miller)

The foreboding Monte Cristo of Junee, New South Wales viewed at night. Marred by a tragic history, it is widely reputed to be Australia's most haunted house. (Julie Miller)

The notorious Studley Park mansion in Camden, New South Wales, whose cellar and tower are said to house ghostly presences. (Julie Miller)

An orb moving through the Redbank Range Railway Tunnel at Picton is a good indicator of spiritual activity. (Julie Miller)

The graves of convicts and military lay side by side on Devil's Island at Port Arthur, Tasmania. (Julie Miller)

Orbs hovering over the roof of the Junior Medical Officer's house at Port Arthur where the ghosts of little boys playing on the roof are frequently reported. (Julie Miller)

Old Melbourne Gaol's most notorious hangman, Michael Gately, believed to be 'the Growler' haunting Cell 19. (Old Melbourne Gaol)

The Quarantine Station's resident medium Nikki Parsons-Gardiner walks through the haunted shower block, one of the site's most active locations, at North Head, New South Wales. (Julie Miller)

Aradale Lunatic Asylum looms large over the town of Ararat, a spooky reminder of a grim past. (Julie Miller)

In Melbourne General Cemetery lies the grave of Frederick Baker (stage name Federici), a noted actor of his day who died descending to hell on stage in the role of Mephistopheles, and who returned to tread the boards as a ghost. (Julie Miller)

The Devil's Coach House at Jenolan Caves, New South Wales, earned its sinister sobriquet in the late 1800s when a man claimed to have seen the devil pull up in a horse-drawn carriage under its cavernous roof. (Julie Miller)

A mysterious mist on the haunted stretch of Mount Victoria Pass in the Blue Mountains, New South Wales. (Julie Miller)

The bar in The Gearin Hotel at Katoomba, New South Wales, where the ghost of Mrs Gearin looks on disapprovingly. (Julie Miller)

Jenolan Caves House – Australia's most haunted hotel, or just falling into disrepair? (Julie Miller)

The subterranean passageways of The Drives at Seppelt's Great Western winery are possibly haunted by winemakers of yesteryear. (Julie Miller)

Towering figures at the 2010 Fisher's Ghost Festival street parade in Campbelltown, New South Wales, represent murdered settler Frederick Fisher's ghost, which allegedly pointed out the location of its own missing corpse, and the Indigenous tracker who finally found it. (Grant Osborn)

by 150 staff. Modelled on English-style asylums, it was a classic example of Italianate conservative architecture, with 63 buildings featuring linking bridges, arched gateways and towers on 100 hectares of arable land. The complex was surrounded by a 4-metre high boundary known as the 'ha ha wall' — so called because from a distance, it appeared lower and more scalable than it was in reality.

In addition to the main complex, a secondary annexe housing more dangerous inmates was established in the old bluestone gaol in town, a facility known as J Ward until its closure in 1988. J Ward now operates as a museum run by volunteers highlighting the historical incarceration of the criminally insane.

During its years standing vacant, word began to filter out that Aradale was haunted; local kids broke in to scare themselves silly, daring each other to spend the night communing with the anguished souls of patients past. And by all accounts, they got what they bargained for — looming dark figures, phantom nurses dressed in white, moaning, crying, disembodied footsteps and slamming doors have all been cited.

Verifying these encounters are the experiences of several investigative paranormal groups whose overnight vigils record compelling evidence of supernatural activity. A group known as Ghost Research International, for instance, has conducted several investigations at both the main Aradale complex and J Ward; and while the results from the latter were deemed 'inconclusive', the report published on the group's website lists temperature fluctuations, strange shapes, whistling and tapping sounds amongst anomalies suggesting paranormal activity.[3]

Such tantalising results certainly warrant further investigation, and needless to say the spooky white asylum looking over the town of Ararat is high on every paranormal investigator's list of must-visit locations.

The grey nurse

One of the most common apparitions found in hospitals across the globe is that of a 'grey nurse' – the phantom of a dedicated medical professional so attached to her workplace that she chooses never to leave, even after death. This tall, thin, transparent figure is often seen in wards hovering over patients in the dead of night, checking equipment and smoothing down beds. She has also been known to prop patients up in their sleep, usually scaring them half to death.

Some paranormal pundits speculate that the grey nurse is a former staff member who underwent a traumatic experience during her working life. Perhaps she made a fatal mistake, and forever lives with the guilt. Often the figure of the nurse appears to current staff members, perhaps as a harbinger to tragedy or to caution them about possible errors of judgement.

One such apparition was Matron Gracie, who was said to roam the wards of Sydney's Prince Henry Hospital until it was decommissioned in 2002. In life, Gracie was said to be a neurotic woman with compulsive attention disorder; when she'd bump into someone, she'd immediately wash her hands (perhaps just the sign of a dedicated professional?). She is said to have fallen down a disused lift shaft in B Block under mysterious circumstances.

Patients often reported being tended by a nurse in old-fashioned garb; staff also noted that mess they left in kitchens was cleaned up by a silent stranger. Gracie was said to be particularly active around 2 a.m., when clocks would often stop working.

Closed after 122 years of service to the sick, Prince Henry Hospital, located in a beautiful oceanfront location at La Perouse in Sydney's eastern suburbs, was recently redeveloped into luxury homes, shops and offices, with some of the heritage buildings retained and restored.

Whether the grey nurse still lingers in her former workplace, only time and anecdote will reveal; but in the meantime, her legend lives on, another classic example of how an evocative ghost story can keep history alive.

Chapter 6
Theatres of fear

Brisbane Arts Theatre, Brisbane

Actors are passionate creatures; their job is to portray emotion, heighten drama and create an atmosphere of tension. On the stage there are tears, melodrama and laughter as every gamut of emotion is played out, drawing in the audience and encouraging a response.

A theatre thus becomes a place of compressed human emotions, absorbed into the very fabric of the boards, curtain and stalls. Little wonder they are notoriously haunted, with ghosts or spirits fuelled by this highly charged energy.

The majority of theatres have at least one spook to contend with. It is often a friendly phantom, bringing luck to the players, though they also tend to be a convenient scapegoat if the production is fraught with problems.

Some alleged theatre ghosts are former actors whose careers have either lit up the stage or died a metaphorical death as they tread the boards. Others were people associated with the theatre in other ways, passionate about the stage to the very end and beyond.

One such person was Jean Trundle, the dedicated actor, drama teacher and director who founded the Brisbane Arts Theatre with her husband Vic Hardgraves in 1936. Described by the *Australian Dictionary of Biography* as 'flamboyant and stylish',[18] Trundle died in 1965; but by all accounts she continues to keep an eye on productions, making her presence felt in countless ways.

The current president of Brisbane Arts Theatre, Alex Lanham, had his first brush with Jean in 1990 during rehearsals for his first show at the theatre. 'We were in the second last rehearsal when I heard someone moving around in the balcony, making lots of noise,' he tells us. 'I had a bit of a whinge, and they asked me where this person making the noise was. I pointed to the chair, and they said, "That's Jean's chair". That's the first time I had any knowledge of the theatre having "visitors".'

Jean, Alex tells us, was very attached to one particular seat in the theatre; and over the years, many staff members have encountered her there, a quiet presence overseeing rehearsals. During a recent investigation by the Queensland Paranormal Society, a thermal imaging device detected unusual warmth in this particular seat – even though no-one had been sitting on it.

On another occasion, members of the paranormal society asked Jean to give an indication she was present in the dressing room where they were gathered. 'All of a sudden the coathangers along the rack all moved as if someone had run their hands along them,' Lanham says. 'There were no windows that open and the door was closed, so there was no breeze.'

Something is Out There

A perfectionist in life, Jean had a habit of pacing the corridor outside the green room, going over her lines before hitting the stage. Over the years, many people have heard disembodied footsteps outside this room, while her meticulous spirit also continues to play a hand in others' performances.

'I was rehearsing a play once and struggling with my lines. Everyone else left the stage and went down to the green room, but I stayed upstairs, sitting on one of the sofas and going through my lines. Frustrated, I threw down my script and went f***,' Lanham laughs. 'I had the feeling I was being watched, and I looked over my shoulder and saw standing in the wings the shape of a female in what seemed to be character clothing; this shape was shaking its head. I took off very quickly and raced down to the green room.'

While Jean is usually sensed in the balcony or dressing rooms, at least one other phantom is said to haunt the theatre, lingering in a storage area under the stage. Lanham became aware of this presence while he and another staff member were packing up one night after a show. Lanham recalls they were carrying flats (wooden-framed background scenes) down to the storage area. 'We both stopped at the same time, and I said, "Ummm, I think this will do." He agreed; and as soon as we put the flat down, he bolted. Neither of us went down there again that night; it was an ill feeling, an uncomfortable feeling. It's the only part of the theatre that at times I find awkward, uncomfortable.'

According to Lanham, this is a darker, more malevolent spirit than Jean. 'I don't like him and he doesn't like me,' Lanham says. While he's not sure who this ghoul may be, he theorises it may pre-date the theatre, when the building next door was a doss house for homeless men.

Prior to starting at the Brisbane Arts Theatre, Lanham says he was oblivious to the paranormal world – possibly a believer, but without evidence: 'Since then I'm absolutely certain there are spirits or entities around.'

Theatre Royal, Hobart

The oldest continually working theatre in Australia, Hobart's Theatre Royal is said to be haunted by a ghost named Fred. There are several theories about Fred's connection to this historic 1837 building: some say he was an actor who died during a performance in the 1880s and was never able to take his final curtain call; others believe he was killed in a fight in the theatre's basement, formerly a seedy tavern called the Shades.

With direct access from the Shades to the theatre, performances in the early days were rowdy affairs, as described in a history compiled by the Friends of the Theatre Royal Hobart:

> Sailors, prostitutes and general riff-raff would enter the pit with their full tankards and create their own drama, and during intervals prostitutes could be seen bounding across the seats making a bee-line for conveniences – all much to the displeasure of the gentry in the boxes.[19]

Fred, it is said, haunts both backstage and the gallery, overseeing rehearsals and performances. Many staff and cast members claim to have seen him over the years; and when the theatre was ravaged by fire in 1984, it was Fred who saved the day, lowering the fire curtain over the stage to protect his realm from total destruction.

Perhaps Fred was just reflecting on the words spoken by Sir Laurence Olivier after his final performance at the Theatre Royal in 1948: 'It's a beautiful little theatre. Your parents and grandparents have acted on this stage. In all the years it's been played in, it's built up a lot of atmosphere. The secret of atmosphere is antiquity. Never let it go.'[20]

Princess Theatre, Melbourne

The Australian theatre world's most infamous haunting is a consequence of one of the most macabre events ever to occur on its stages. The tragic drama unfolded on Saturday March 3, 1888, at Melbourne's grandest playhouse of the day – the Princess Theatre.

On that evening, the highly anticipated premiere of renowned French composer Charles Gounod's opera *Faust*, based on the classic German legend, had just reached its climax before a packed audience. The opera ended with Mephistopheles descending into the bowels of hell with his prize Dr Faustus, the man who sold his soul to the devil, clutched in his crimson cape.

As the two key players were slowly lowered by an onstage trap door, vanishing from the audience in a sulphurous red glow of stage smoke, the appreciative crowd applauded rapturously – completely unaware the actor playing Mephistopheles, Frederick Baker, a popular English baritone billing himself as Federici, was in fact about to cross over to the 'other side' for real.

The trap door reached the cellar floor and Federici suddenly pitched forward into the arms of a stagehand, victim of a fatal heart attack at the early age of 37. Staff rushed the performer to the theatre's backstage lounge area known as the green room. But he never recovered. In a bizarre, ironic and fittingly dramatic fashion, the great Federici had made his final stage exit.

Or had he? The first omen the deceased actor was reluctant to leave behind the world of spotlights and greasepaint occurred only moments later. The cast was gathered after curtain call by the stage manager, to be informed of their costar's demise. But many refused to accept the tragic news; they insisted Federici had just been standing beside them — in full costume on stage, enthusiastically taking his bows.[1]

The next disturbing twist took place at the performer's funeral in Melbourne General Cemetery. According to the *The Argus*, the major daily newspaper of the time, Reverend Goodwin, who was conducting the burial service, fainted inexplicably as Federici's coffin was being lowered into the ground. Actor Charles Warner, one of the pallbearers, stepped into the breach and completed the service.[2]

Faust folded within weeks. As a writer for *Illustrated Australian News* succinctly put it: 'The venture proved somewhat unfortunate . . . [Federici's] substitute was not up to the mark.'[3] But if the stories are correct, one cast member lingered on after production wrapped. The next reported sighting of Federici's ghost was made by George Musgrove, one of the producers involved in staging *Faust*. During a rehearsal for his next stage show, he spotted a lone figure in evening dress sitting in the front row of the dress circle. Since the theatre was locked down for rehearsal, upstairs seating areas should have been vacant. But before someone could be sent to investigate, the figure disappeared.[4]

A slew of sightings were reported over the following decade. In 1917 a wardrobe mistress was working late backstage at the theatre to meet an opening night deadline. In the early hours of the morning her work was interrupted by the nightwatch fireman (employed in the days before automated fire alarms to punch a safety clock every hour on the hour). He informed her he had spotted somebody up in the dress circle. She accompanied him to the landing, where she claims she clearly saw a male figure in evening dress sitting as still as a statue and staring straight ahead at the stage.[5]

Other firemen reported similar encounters with the spectral thespian. John Gange also stumbled across the apparition doing his rounds – in the very same position it was reported previously. At first he thought a theatre-goer had fallen asleep in his seat. He called out but his efforts elicited no response. When he approached, he claims the figure slowly began to vanish before his eyes.[6]

On another occasion the fire brigade rushed to the Princess when the safety clock failed to be punched. Upon arrival they found no signs of smoke. But they did find the petrified nightwatch fireman cowering in a corner, claiming to have encountered the ghost of Federici silently treading the stage.[7]

According to Frank Cusack, editor of *Australian Ghost Stories*, up to 30 sightings of the Federici apparition were reported in the half century following the actor's death.[8] Then things seemed to settle down. When Federici finally staged a reappearance, it was not at the Princess.

In 1972 neophyte director Dr George Miller, the man who would go on to create *Mad Max*, *Babe* and *Happy Feet*, was filming a documentary about Federici. Called *The Devil in Evening Dress*, and produced by his former business partner, the late Byron Kennedy, it included dramatised re-creations of events from the actor's life and death. During a re-enactment of Federici's funeral, staged beside his actual gravesite in Melbourne's General Cemetery, cast member Russell O'Regan took some camera stills. Upon being developed one revealed a spectral figure, clad in robes similar to those a stage actor would don to perform the role of Mephistopheles, lurking in the background behind another grave, watching the goings-on.[9] Was it actually a photograph of the ghost of Federici in full costume? According to John Pinkney, author of *A Paranormal File*, O'Regan reported the find to his director:

> I rang George Miller and he scoffed . . . I arranged to meet George and Byron at the office. George changed his attitude immediately. Byron and George were so intrigued they went back to the cemetery. To try to prove the phantom was a trick of light and shadows. But no matter how many shots they took – from many angles – all they showed was a tombstone.[10]

O'Regan's photograph is now out of general circulation. But those who have seen it, ourselves included, agree it is one of the more chilling unexplained images captured by a camera.

Today the heritage-listed Princess is the distinguished old lady of Melbourne's theatre scene. Her exuberant Second Empire–styled architecture may seem a little frayed at the edges, but she is still able to pull in big crowds with popular stage musicals.

Over the decades, many performers claim to have had run-ins with Federici – most notably the late singer and actor Rob Guest.

Something is Out There

On the ABC television program *Rewind* in August 2004, Guest told of a strange occurrence during his run in *Les Miserables*:

> I was backstage . . . about to come on for the barricade scene. But I was supposedly seen at the back of the dress circle by one of the ushers. And as she went over to talk to me to say there was a problem, she was distracted by somebody else, and when she looked back, I'd gone. But, of course, it wasn't me. I didn't come to the dress circle at all.[11]

Guest surmised the phantom was taking on the persona of the lead character in the production and indeed, the spirit of Federici does seem to evince somewhat of a 'show must go on' ethic. When perennial TV face Bert Newton was starting out his career, he found himself working the graveyard shift as an announcer at radio station 3XY, then housed in a cluster of rented attic rooms above the Princess Theatre. During this period many staff members claimed to have seen inexplicable lights in the upper circle, including Newton, who described it as 'a yellow object, hovering and fluorescent'.[12]

Again according to author and researcher Pinkney, one night Newton wandered away from his booth while playing an old LP record on a turntable (apparently on the late shows in those days albums were played in entirety one side at a time). Losing track of time, Newton realised the first side must have finished: 'I rushed back upstairs, ready to apologise to the listeners. But then, to my amazement, I saw someone had turned the record over! The needle was in the first track on the other side.'[13]

The only other person present that night, an engineer down the corridor, denied having done the good deed. Despite being sceptical about ghosts, Newton still has no explanation for the uncanny event: 'I'm forced to admit something very weird happened that night,'[14] he was quoted as saying in *A Paranormal File*. Consummate showman Federici to the rescue, perhaps?

But it is not just celebrities who claim to have strange encounters at the Princess these days. Recently, cleaner Trina Dimovska was terrified when what she believed was a supernatural force laid hands on her as she was working in the corridors early one morning:

> It just touched my hair and my shoulders and my body on the back. And I was just, like, frozen . . . No-one was there. No human. Only me. Because the theatre was closed . . . I never believed before . . . Now I believe we have a ghost in this theatre.[15]

Even current owner, Elaine Marriner, whose family purchased the Princess in 1987, has witnessed strange goings-on, observing a similar spooky light to that reported by Newton and his cohorts back in the radio days. She saw it while showing some people around the theatre after hours:

> There [are] no windows. No light can come into a theatre auditorium. And when we were having a look at the theatre auditorium and stage, we actually saw a shaft of light come onto the stage. And it didn't sort of register with us until later on that how could it have happened? Other than perhaps our friend Federici was making his presence felt?[16]

Theatre types are a superstitious lot, and at the Princess Theatre they have always believed a Federici appearance bodes well for a production. For many years one seat was always left unsold in the dress circle, reserved for the phantom, lest he feel like stopping by to catch a show. But as far as the authors were able to ascertain, no theatre-goer sitting beside this vacant seat has ever turned to discover a strange gentleman in period evening dress occupying the spot.

Live entertainers are known to use the catchphrase 'dying on stage'. It refers to those excruciating moments when an actor realises a performance is failing to connect with an audience. The great Federici managed to create a literal manifestation of this adage, in a performance still unforgotten more than 150 years later.

Some even claim he actually foretold his own death. Theatre legend has it that just before Federici stepped on stage to tackle the taxing role of Mephistopheles, he turned to his stage manager and said, 'I will give a fine performance tonight. But it will kill me.'[17]

Chapter 7
Ghostly grottos

There are few natural wonders as hauntingly beautiful and utterly terrifying as a deep, dark cave. With sharp stalactites dangling menacingly from the ceiling and stalagmites thrusting from the floor, it's not a huge leap to imagine you're entering a maw of hell – a thought not far from our minds as we descend the sinisterly long and steep staircase into the Temple of Baal, one of the more disturbingly named and downright disconcerting grottos in the Jenolan Caves system.

Armed with electric lanterns and led by an experienced cave guide, we are on a nocturnal search for subterranean spirits. The deeper we go the darker the darkness becomes, conjuring deep-seated fears of being abandoned in the void, a trait of caves that makes them perfect environments to engender haunting tales of ghostly goings-on. And although well trodden, Jenolan Caves, on the far side of New South Wales's Blue Mountains, boasts more than a few . . .

Science has established our ancestors were not, as was once believed, cave-dwelling troglodytes. Instead, they travelled the landscape hunting and gathering, building shelter when they could, and occasionally taking refuge in caves. It is now accepted caves — as indicated by ritual wall paintings — were more commonly used for religious gatherings, potentially making them the oldest spiritual centres known to humankind.

On many continents they also served as burial grounds. As evidenced by the 9000-year-old mummy known as 'Spirit Man', discovered in a Nevada cave, and the 7000-year-old Three Amigos buried in a cave in Los Canes, Spain, they were regarded by many cultures as safe and sheltered resting places for the dead.

Although some Australian Aboriginal tribes chose shallow rock shelters to bury their deceased, generally they shied from caves, considering them places of fear rather than safety. The Jenolan Caves were no exception: to the local Gundungurra people they were known as Binoomea, meaning 'dark places', and were to be avoided.

Today Jenolan, the oldest cave system in the world open to the public, has more than 250,000 visitors a year. Guides lead tour parties daily through the more accessible sections of its 20 tortuous kilometres of underground chamber, from which a steady flow of ghostly stories has emerged over the years. Security gates rattle for no reason, display lights turn themselves on and off, and phantom figures mysteriously appear and disappear.

Tour guides have connected many of these tales with the spirit of James Wiburd, Jenolan's third caretaker who, commencing in 1903, was responsible for the maintenance of the caves for almost three decades. An environmentalist before his time, Wiburd was a controversial figure, doggedly opposing any development directly affecting the pristine nature of the caves. The rationale of guides who have felt Wiburd's presence is that he loved the place so much he just can't leave, and lingers around to keep an eye on things.

Most of Jenolan's caves have some scary story attached, but to guide Cory Camilleri the chamber known as the Temple of Baal is by far 'the creepiest'. It was discovered and named by Wiburd, a Freemason rumoured to have held Masonic rituals within its walls, and Camilleri calls it the 'I'm-not-too-sure-I-want-to-be-in-here-by-myself cave'. We cannot help but agree. Once the display lights are turned on to reveal its features, we find ourselves first gazing upon a broad, blunt-topped mesa-like stalagmite, spookily resembling a sacrificial altar. To our right an ethereally translucent stalactite formation known as a shawl, and resembling a funereal shroud, drapes from a cave wall. And as we crane our necks upwards we are chilled by the eerie sight of the stalagmite formation referred to by cave guides as Baal. He appears to be leaning over a cliff-like ledge near the cave ceiling, surveying his domain.

'What I find intriguing about Baal is he looks at you. He looks at you from the top platform, and when you're on the middle platform, he appears to have moved,' says Camilleri with a shudder.

In early Christian beliefs Baal was a demon, in some cases taking the form of Ba'al Zebub, or Beelzebub – the devil himself. But to the Canaanites, Baal was a more benign god of fertility. The reason behind references to him in Masonic rights remains clouded in the veil of secrecy that still surrounds the society. But the cave's ability to invoke the unsettling feeling of standing in an ancient pagan temple obviously impressed Wiburd enough to name it in the ancient idol's honour. Whether or not the formation above actually resembles the deity is a matter for debate. But it certainly casts a sinister pall over the chamber.

Camilleri has found herself nearly frozen with fear on the stairs. Another guide felt a presence halfway down and refused to go any further. Yet another guide always insists on being safely tucked in the middle of a tour group and never at the front or back. And while temperatures are surprisingly moderate in most of Jenolan's caves, the Temple of Baal is a chilling exception.

'It is always cold in the Temple of Baal,' says Camilleri. 'The hair stands up on the back of your neck. And I have been tapped a couple of times. You don't have to see a ghost to know it's there.'

Nevertheless, according to Rob Whyte, tour guide and writer of *The Ghost Tour, Jenolan Caves* — a pamphlet handed out to tour members and a fantastic primer on the caves' hauntings — the ghost of James Wiburd has been seen. Not in the Temple of Baal, but in a tunnel off what's known as the River Cave, where two shocked maintenance men stumbled across an apparition of the long-dead caretaker sitting near a tool box they had left behind.

Flowing into the River Cave is the Styx, a subterranean waterway named after the mythical river between Earth and the Underworld crossed by the dead in Greek mythology. The Styx manifests itself in several hauntingly beautiful underground pools. Most startling is the preternatural Pool of Reflection, where crystalline waters reflect the ceiling like a mirror. The resulting effect is that the pool appears to have no surface.

It is here recently that a guide standing at one end of the Pool of Reflection spotted a ghostly figure at the other. Before he could investigate, it soundlessly vanished. Whether or not the apparition was Wiburd was not determined. Ironically, considering the guide in question is one of several who twice-weekly lead ghost tours through the caves, he has staunchly refused to ever again enter the Pool of Reflection — the very site where he encountered a ghost.

One section of the adjoining Pool of Cerberus is permanently closed to the public. Previously known as Skeleton Cave, it harbours the remains of the skeleton of an Indigenous person. The skeleton appeared to have already been laying there a long time when found by Wiburd as he discovered the cave in 1904. Considering Indigenous attitudes towards Jenolan, it is unlikely the poor soul wandered in and got lost. Speculation varies from the victim being washed in during a flash flood, to drowning while swimming in the adjoining outdoor lake outside and being sucked in through a subterranean vent by currents. Once a ghoulish tourist attraction, the skeleton is now afforded the dignity of the dead, resting quietly and peacefully on the cave floor, metres from the pool's edge, forever ensconced in the dreaded 'dark places' of Binoomea.

But things are not always so quiet and peaceful in other parts of Jenolan. Of all the spooky goings-on within these beautiful limestone walls, those that spook guides the most are its notorious 'audio hauntings' — strange sounds supposedly with no apparent source. One of these is the 'phantom tour group'. Twice guides in the River Cave have heard the voices and footsteps of an invisible group of visitors shuffling by. In nearby Jubilee Cave, entire tour groups have experienced the same phenomena. In some cases the sounds have been so 'real', people have stopped to let them pass. Perhaps this could be put down to the unique acoustic properties of cave systems, but apparent checks on tour schedules revealed no other groups to be inside at the time.

Of course we can't help pondering at this point whether the caves are really haunted or whether the dark, winding, shadowy environment in which the guides spend much of their days is just plain freaking them out. But our appraisal from meeting several staff members is they are, on the whole, sincere and professional people who take their jobs seriously and are prepared to speak openly about experiences they are unable to explain.

In the opulently picturesque Orient Cave, also discovered by Wiburd, ghostly opera singing has been heard. But by far the most disturbing manifestation of this 'audio haunting' phenomenon is the so-called 'beast' of Chifley Cave. Several guides have experienced terrifying encounters. Alone in the cave, they hear a large moving mass scraping along the cave floor, as though following them. Some have described it as a slithering sound; as it gets louder and seemingly closer, guides will quicken their step and head for the gate. Then, just as the invisible creature seems upon them, they will make it through the gate, slam it shut and lock it, whereupon the strange sound abates immediately.

Drawing on Indigenous folklore, some guides have connected this inexplicable phenomenon with a creature called Guringatch, a giant fish-snake from the Dreamtime. Is the spirit of Guringatch sliding through the tunnels of Jenolan terrorising its new caretakers? And was it fear of the creature that led local tribes to shun the caves? It remains another Jenolan mystery.

As we exit, no eerie sounds follow save the echoes of our own panting breaths, having climbed up and down countless steps and ladder rungs in our long subterranean search. Flicking dank-smelling slime from our fingers and palms, which we have collected from the metal hand rails, we are relieved to learn it is just underground condensation — and not ectoplasm. Although we have neither seen nor heard anything supernatural, we have experienced heart palpitations, freak-outs in the dark, and certainly hairs standing up on the back of our necks. But no ghosts. At least not tonight.

However, we have one last opportunity to encourage a supernatural encounter before the sun comes up. We are led to the Devil's Coach House, a majestic open-ended arch off to the side of the Grand Arch — through which most visitors enter the Jenolan complex. The Coach House's ceiling is cathedral-like, and all the more breathtaking for being natural. It is also where one of the more spectacular sightings of James Wiburd has occurred, when a guide claimed to have seen the spectral caretaker rising in the air towards its 50-metre roof, trailing ash from his airborne feet. What Wiburd's ghost was doing up there, and why it was dropping ash, no-one is sure. It has not been seen since.[1]

But a more sinister tale regarding this impressive arch relates to how it earned its name. In the late 1800s, a cattle thief named Luke White, sleeping off a hangover beneath its shelter, was awakened by a clamour and looked up to see no less than the devil himself pulling up in a horsedrawn carriage. Despite his throbbing head, White fled the covered archway immediately. Although he may not sound like the most reliable of witnesses, the name Devil's Coach House stuck.² And who are we to say the vision was the alcoholic hallucination of a drunken local ne'er-do-well? Perhaps Baal was merely returning to his temple after a big night out himself . . .

As we traipse back through the Grand Arch and up the gentle slope to the relative safety of Caves House, we are still in two minds as to whether Jenolan deserves its fearsome reputation as Australia's most haunted caves. But we do seem to have been convinced, as the cover of its tourist brochure proudly proclaims, that 'magic happens here'.

Chapter 8
Hotels from hell

Caves House, Jenolan Caves, New South Wales

We open our door at midnight and step into a musty corridor, only to come face to face with a wide-eyed, ashen-faced vision. He jumps; we jump. Neither party is expecting to see the other – it is, after all, the witching hour and the hotel is next-to-empty.

'Working late?' we ask, having ascertained we are communicating with a flesh-and-blood person and not a ghost. It is, in fact, the night cleaner at Jenolan Caves House, tiptoeing along the creaky floorboards on his nocturnal rounds, vacuum cleaner in hand.

'Long night ahead,' he laments. 'And let me tell you, it's pretty creepy here in the middle of the night.' This, of course, sparks our curiosity – and before long, the cleaner is opening up about the alleged spirits of Caves House and the strange occurrences that happen here.

'There's a lady on the third floor, a little girl on the second floor,' Andrew elaborates. 'And as for the dining room – well,

I hate going in there — I try to avoid cleaning it till around 6 a.m., when it's getting light. It's seriously creepy — I'll let you in there later, see for yourself.'

Located in the middle of nowhere, at the end of a *Shining*-esque winding road, Jenolan Caves House — one of New South Wales's most famous heritage hotels, built in 1898 — is the epitome of a haunted house: old, mist-covered, remote and eerie.

Nestled amongst the trees and surrounded by dramatic limestone caves, its very appearance, with wooden gables, Tudor-style beams and an anthropomorphic stone galley, evokes images of the Victorian era, when the caves were first discovered by intrepid adventurers and even getting there was a long and arduous process involving days of horsedrawn travel.

Inside, the hotel — currently managed by the New South Wales state government — is in a dubious state of disrepair, with stained, worn carpets, peeling paint, tired guest rooms and less-than-desirable standards of hospitality. As we wander through its corridors on our nocturnal ghostbusting investigation, every door creaks and every floorboard groans under our weight — leading us to question if it is, indeed, haunted . . . or simply falling apart.

According to hotel legend — and verified by Andrew the cleaner and other staff members — there are several ghosts who refuse to check out of Jenolan Caves House. One of the most active spirits is a little girl named Marjorie, said to have drowned in the bathtub in our very room, Room 116.

According to cave guide Cory Camilleri, the playful spirit of Marjorie often tickles toes during the night, or is seen running through the corridors. She has been described by a medium as around six years of age, with straight brown hair and wearing period clothes. Although Marjorie and her tragic death has never been verified historically, sightings of this spirit are so common she is now accepted as part of Jenolan folklore.

Other stories do have their basis in fact, however, such as the spirit of the Gate House, a former staff member said to have been pushed out the window; or the victim of a vicious love triangle, another hapless employee stabbed to death during the 1970s.

Most of the ghosts of Jenolan Caves — both in Caves House and the caves themselves — are not necessarily people who died tragically at the site, but instead loved the place so intensely that they have an eternal connection. 'They may not have died here,' explains Camilleri, 'but they have certainly left their mark.'

This is certainly the case with Caves House's most beloved ghost, Miss Chisholm. The former dining room supervisor at Caves House, Miss Chisholm was a fixture for many, many years, a familiar presence for return guests before her departure in 1965. Fussy and particular, she is now said to inhabit the dining room named after her, drawing drapes, changing table settings and opening doors to allow invisible diners into the room.

Many current staff members, however — including Cory Camilleri — believe the ghost of the dining room is a case of mistaken identity. Spooky happenings are said to have taken place during Miss Chisholm's time, and the ghost is often described as wearing period dress, which clearly doesn't fit the image of a 1960s maitre d'.

Instead, some speculate that the wandering spirit of Caves House is in fact Lucinda Wilson, the wife of the caves' first caretaker, Jeremiah Wilson. With her husband spending every waking hour either exploring the caves or entertaining guests underground, it fell upon his wife to supervise the newly established Caves House in 1898. Her continued presence in the dining room would certainly make sense, particularly at times when the service is a little slack . . .

True to his word, we are ushered into Miss Chisholm/Lucinda's lair later that night by the night cleaner. He asks if we'd like the lights on or off – then promptly bolts, too terrified to stick around. Despite his fears, however, all appears quiet in the restaurant, cutlery staying firmly in place and no ghostly images appearing in our photographs.

So is Caves House haunted? While our findings were inconclusive, there's no denying it's a very spooky place – and something is putting the staff on edge. Nearly every employee, from the cave guides, to receptionists and even the cleaner, have a story to tell – of uncomfortable feelings, of strange shadows and things that go bump in the night.

The following morning, as we stand at the second floor lift in preparation for checkout, the lift door opens and a woman inside – this time the day cleaner – nearly jumps out of her skin at the sight of us. We can only apologise for startling her, blaming the ghosts as the door closes behind us.

Ghosts in residence

Our colleague Jane hobbles to the lounge, clearly in pain after turning her ankle in the garden an hour earlier. On describing how her foot had inexplicably given way under her, sending her flying down three stone steps, the manager of Grand Mercure

Mount Lofty House in South Australia's Adelaide Hills offers a possible explanation — that she was pushed by the resident ghost, George.

It's as plausible a rationale as any, and the conversation inevitably turns to all things spooky, and the historic hotel's most famous and persistent occupant. According to local legend, George was a groundsman who tended the exquisite garden more than 100 years ago, when Mount Lofty House was a private mansion, a summer house built as an escape from the extreme dry heat of the coast. So enamoured was George with the genteel residence that he chose never to leave, persisting despite extensions, renovations and even a tragic fire that destroyed everything but the stone walls in 1983.

Said to be a friendly ghost (and therefore definitely not the perpetrator in our friend's calamity), George is said to haunt the cellar and catacombs under rooms 7 and 8. Over the years, numerous guests have reported feeling his presence but feel he is a welcoming rather than a dark spirit.

George is not alone in his eternal desire to stay put at his favourite abode. Many an Australian hotel is said to be haunted by the spirit of a former staff member, a dedicated manager or a guest who never checked out. Historic residences in particular delight in their ghost stories, with dark tales of the past only adding to the ambience of roaring fires, creaking floorboards and antique furniture.

During the Canberra Ghost Tour, supper is held at the very posh Hyatt Hotel in Canberra — which can be a bizarre sight, especially if the crew of ghostbusters are wearing Halloween fancy dress! But this stop on the tour is more significant than just tea and cakes – the hotel is actually reputed to be extremely haunted, with a plethora of eternal guests joining overseas diplomats, local politicians and visiting celebrities in its Art Deco lobby.

Built as a hostel to house public servants in 1913, the Hyatt once doubled as a hospital before being converted to a five-star hotel. Both staff and guests testify to strange occurrences and noises, particularly in the old, original wing – it's even rumoured that Qantas cabin crew, who used to stay in the hotel, checked out after a spate of paranormal experiences.

The hotel ballroom is said to be the haunt of a rather nasty spook who, during the refurbishment of the room, abused painters, tipped over their paint and shook the chandelier in order to scare them off. Another story often told is that of a little girl, burnt to death in the boiler room after she went in to retrieve a ball. The room is now a wine cellar, where the apparition of the girl wearing a long red dress flitting past is often seen.

With its imposing Art Deco architecture, rambling floor plan and spectacular views over the Megalong Valley, the newly renovated Hydro Majestic has been delighting visitors to Sydney's Blue Mountains since it was built in 1904. Conceived by retail baron Mark Foy, it was originally an upmarket health spa, with celebrities such as Dame Nellie Melba, Sir Arthur Conan Doyle, the Rajah of Pudukkutai and Dame Clara Butt coming to 'take the waters'.

One famous guest also met his maker in this hotel, with Australia's first Prime Minister Sir Edmund Barton passing away of heart failure while taking a bath in a second-floor suite. And there was at least one murder known to have been committed in the hotel – a young lady strangled with her favourite silk scarf by a troublesome male suitor in 1912.

Whether Sir Edmund still splashes in his bath or the young female victim still gasps for breath is debatable, but there are at least two other resident ghosts said to creep around the Hydro in the dead of night. Long after diners have returned to their rooms, staff often see a little boy sitting, bizarrely, in the dining room's chandeliers, while upstairs, a little girl in a blue frock with a white lace collar is seen running through walls.

According to Jasmine, an Indigenous elder, the very site of this grand hotel is haunted by spirits of local Aborigines, who were forced to their deaths off the sheer cliffs lining the property during violent clashes with early colonial settlers. Jasmine claims that the whole of the Megalong Valley resounds with the screams of dying women, children and warriors, a sad indictment of the European history of the region.

Paranormal experts call this type of spiritual activity a 'residual haunting' – when the imprint of a past tragedy plays out visually over and over again, like a scene from a movie stuck on repeat.

Another example of this type of haunting occurs at Cedar Creek Lodges at Thunderbird Park, an eco-friendly adventure resort on Tamborine Mountain in the Gold Coast hinterland.

Although the lodge itself is new, the land it's built on was the site of a former timber mill, with the history of the property living on through a pretty young milkmaid often seen walking across the bushland at first light.

According to local legend, Kate the Milkmaid, as she is known, was the common law wife of a logger. Her early morning walks are reported to be purposeful; she is heading off to milk the cows, swinging her milking bucket as she walks towards the flat paddocks, skirts swishing against the foliage as she brings in the breakfast milk for the property owners, her own family and a few favoured labourers.

According to the property owners, Judi and Bob Minnikin, more than half the staff members at the lodge have seen or heard Kate on her morning rounds.

'We have tried to establish an identity for this girl but it's difficult because settlers, particularly those of convict stock, reinvented their history as they moved up through the social strata,' Judi says. 'I am pleased our friendly ghost seems happy; it reflects the gentle ambience of the region as it was originally and is again now.'

Chapter 9
Possessed pubs

The Coach & Horses Inn, Clarkefield, Victoria

It seems to be no coincidence that many Australian pubs — particularly those with a long and volatile history — are said to be haunted. Hotels are associated with both the best of times, and the worst — the alcohol heightening emotions, inducing laughter, sorrow, drama. Australian pubs have been host to fights, murders, suicides — and of course, happy times. So if ghosts do exist, and linger in places where significant events take place, it's little wonder they choose a warm bar stool to spend eternity.

Claiming the mantle as the most haunted pub in Australia is the Coach & Horses Inn, an historic bluestone mansion in Clarkefield, Victoria. Located halfway between Melbourne and the Victorian goldfields, this pub was a Cobb & Co. staging post, its large stable block still standing as evidence of its importance.

The goldrush was a heady, lawless time — and local legends tell of murder, robbery and mayhem at the inn. At least three ghosts remain as testament to these wild frontier days, including the ghost of a Chinese miner who was involved in a fight for gold he had brought back from the field and was later found hanged in the stables.

An Irishman named Patrick Regan was also murdered for his gold, with rumours that his killers belonged to the local constabulary. The ghost of Regan is sometimes sighted fleeing from his attackers down the stairs, his apparition accompanied by a blast of icy air.

Former publican Frank Nelson had several encounters with the ghost of Regan; once as he was cleaning a window from the outside, he saw a hideous face staring out at him, while in 1984, he was bowled over by an invisible force on the stairwell, fracturing his ankle in three places.

He told Melbourne's *Herald* newspaper:

> My wife Sharon and I were asleep upstairs, when we were awakened by noises in the front bar. We could hear people walking around – bottles and glasses being rattled. Imagining we had intruders I tiptoed to the top of the landing and started down. Suddenly, from the bottom of the stairway, I felt a blast of icy cold air. Next, I was shoved in the back, with colossal force. I grabbed the banister, but the rail seemed to be gone. When I hit the deck, I turned to see who had pushed me. I couldn't believe it. There was no one there.[1]

The Coach & Horses' most tragic tale, however, is that of a young girl, said to have been thrown down the hotel's well by her father because she was autistic. The spirit of this sad little ghost is seen crying in the bathroom and at the top of the stairs, while the well itself is said to run dry, then gush with water within seconds. The current publicans claim they once found their mobile phones sodden with water; neither had been dropped anywhere near a water source.[2] Perhaps the little girl from the well had been experimenting with modern technology?

Over the years, licensees and staff have witnessed many strange, inexplicable things in the pub, with stories of broken glasses, stoves burning in the mornings, fires lighting when no-one is around, and cutlery and tables being moved. Staff have been pushed down the stairs, voices have been heard in the toilets, and children often report talking to a little girl in old-fashioned clothes.

Backing up these claims are the results of several investigations by Ghost Research International, which concluded that the spirits of the Coach & Horses, while currently quieter than they have been historically, are still restless, with definite indications of possible activity warranting further study.[3]

Hotel Gearin, Katoomba, New South Wales

'I can't open the door,' Jasmine mutters, fumbling with the keys. 'Come on, let me in.' Finally, the lock gives way, and we step inside Room 19 of Hotel Gearin, an old pub by the railway line in Katoomba, New South Wales.

Immediately we are hit with a blast of cold air. Jasmine grins – as head housekeeper, she's used to seeing the surprise on guests' faces when they come face to face with Mrs Gearin, the phantom said to inhabit these corridors.

Squeezing into a corner, we attempt to knock off a few photographs. The camera whirs, trying to focus; a second attempt, nothing happens. Another setting — still no action. The camera refuses to cooperate, despite the fact that lighting conditions are fine and the batteries fully charged.

But the second we step outside the room — it works. Clearly, Mrs Gearin doesn't want to be photographed — a trait which fits her image as a disapproving, strict landlady. Having opened the hotel as a boarding house strictly for women in 1910, it seems the old lady is none too happy about her alcohol-free policy being flaunted — nor the presence of men in the bar downstairs.

Jasmine herself has seen the spirit of Mrs Gearin on numerous occasions, walking up the stairs or disappearing around corners. She describes her as an elegant lady, dressed in frills and bustle, walking with her hand held regally behind her.

According to staff, footsteps can often be heard walking around the corridor directly above the back bar — when there are no guests in the building. Jasmine also complains that her freshly made beds are crumpled, as if someone has been sitting on them.

Bar manager Stephen Smith tells us the Hotel Gearin has been burnt down three times since it was built in 1881, most recently in 1954, when several deaths occurred. For this reason, he believes there may be more than one restless spirit in this drinking establishment, which is now owned by iconic Australian actor Jack Thompson.

Smith himself has seen the phantoms of four barflies, lingering over drinks at the front bar at 3 a.m. The image, he says, was captured not by the bare eye, but by CCTV cameras — the tapes from which have unfortunately since been erased.

The Bushranger Hotel, Collector, New South Wales

The Bushranger Hotel in Collector, on the shores of Lake George en route to Canberra, is an atmospheric old country pub with a violent history, thanks to the exploits of the infamous bushranger Ben Hall. On Australia Day, 1865, Hall's gang bailed up the pub, and youngest member John Dunne let loose with a volley of pistol fire when challenged by the local policeman, Samuel Nelson. Nelson died on the street outside the hotel, the murderers stopping to steal his belt before escaping. A memorial next door to the pub officially recognises Constable Nelson's sacrifice, stating he was 'shot dead on this spot whilst in the execution of his duty'.

According to ACT Paranormal Investigators, the ghost of Constable Nelson now haunts the hotel — he has been seen moving throughout the bar, with strange voices and knocks commonly heard.[4] And he's not alone — according to publican Guy Filmer, Nelson's just one of the many spooks that shake, rattle and roll their way through the afterlife in this historic hotel.

'There's a lot of activity occurs near the post where Nelson was shot,' Filmer tells us. 'And he's often felt in the beer garden — my mate has the house next door, and he's had a few things going on in his house too. He calls it "freaky devil shit",' Filmer laughs.

After two years in charge at the pub, former mortician and funeral director Filmer is totally unfazed by the racket the ghosts, who number at least four, make in the pub.

'They come in visitations – they aren't grounded spirits,' Filmer says, referring to the paranormal term used to define occasional hauntings. 'We have poltergeist activity, glasses have exploded and moved up and down the bar. We've had laughing upstairs, footsteps, touching on the shoulder. We hear them more than see them, they belt up and down the stairways all night.'

Patrons and staff also complain of cigar smells, quickly followed by the sweet scent of lavender. Filmer believes this could be the dual spirits of Thomas and Emma Kimberley, who built the hotel 150 years ago in 1860.

Joining this couple are former publican Tim Quirk, who is said to reside in the bar; a chambermaid upstairs called Catherine, believed to have either been murdered or committed suicide; and a little girl who runs around downstairs named Hannah.

Bar manager Leslie, who has worked at the Bushranger for eight years now, says she has personally seen the vision of a little girl walking through the window of the lounge room; she has also felt a hand on her shoulder while she's been working behind the bar.

For Filmer, it's all just part of working at an historic hotel. 'There's a lot of history here,' he says. 'We've had a lot of people pass through these doors.'

The Wisemans Inn Hotel, Wisemans Ferry, New South Wales

Colourful characters, villains and rapscallions make frequent appearances in hotel ghost stories. Solomon Wiseman was one of the early colony's most notorious entrepreneurs, pardoned for his convict past to receive a land grant on the Hawkesbury River. With an eye for business, Wiseman started a ferry service across the river in 1827, a money-making venture that would give the settlement its name.

The previous year, Wiseman had built an ostentatious sandstone mansion called Cobham Hall, lording over his servants and neighbours. Despite his dubious past, Wiseman was not a generous man, refusing to grant a ticket-of-leave to one convict servant due for release. When the young man complained, Wiseman is said to have put him to work on a chain gang, where he was forced to work on top of a huge ants' nest.

Eventually the boy escaped but, weighed down by his leg-irons, drowned as he attempted to swim across the Hawkesbury River. But vengeance was his — and every year, on the anniversary of what should have been his release, the spirit of the young man is said to rattle his chains on the stairs of Cobham Hall.

Possibly the most heinous of Wiseman's sins, however, has never been proven — the alleged murder of his wife, Jane. According to his great-great-great granddaughter, famous novelist Kate Grenville, family legend has it that Jane was thrown to her death off the balcony at Cobham Hall after a heated argument, cracking her head on the bottom step.[5]

Both family and staff at the hall, which now operates as the local pub and is known as Wisemans Inn Hotel, have experienced the spirit of Jane, wandering through her former bedroom and kitchen, often playing practical jokes like turning the dishwasher on and off or pulling undone apron strings.

Bar staff also talk openly of pianos playing of their own accord, and of doors opening and slamming shut, despite the fact that they are firmly locked.

As for Wiseman himself, he appears to be resting in peace, having been buried in top hat and tails to signify the social status he worked so hard to achieve. 'Because he was so much not a gentleman, he obviously wanted to pretend he was,' Kate Grenville says.[6] A lifesize bronze of Solomon Wiseman now stands just down the hill from the Wisemans Inn, a triumphant portrait of a man who made something of himself — at the expense of others.

The Overland Corner Hotel, Riverland, South Australia

It is in outback regions of Australia that pubs come into their own as social establishments — they are a hub for drinking, cutting loose, gossip, romance and local drama. And often, it seems, their patrons just can't bear to go home.

The Overland Corner Hotel is located in the Riverland region of South Australia, its isolation on the banks of the Murray River contributing to its importance as a staging house for mail coaches and steamboats in days gone by. Built in 1859, it has seen many births, deaths and marriages during its long history, a cemetery located on a nearby hill testament to the harsh realities of outback life . . . and death.

The hotel has a wealth of colourful stories associated with it, including a legendary tale of bushranger Captain Moonlight, who locked the solitary constable in one of his cells, shod his horse using government gear, then rode up to the hotel and straight into the old bar for a beverage.

But it's the pub's ghost stories that really fuel the imagination of patrons. According to current owners Andrew and Heather, there's one particular phantom who likes to make his presence felt – via his music selection.

'George likes to play the jukebox,' Heather tells us. 'He uses it as a way of communication. For instance, depending on the topic of conversation in the bar, George will play a song coinciding with the topic at hand. For instance, one particular day, the open fire was letting off a lot of smoke; within seconds "Smoke on the Water" started playing on the jukebox. Another hot summer day, the bar taps decided to seize up and we were unable to pour beer; and "Pub with No Beer" by Slim Dusty started playing.'

Who exactly George was during his lifetime hasn't been determined – but a visiting clairvoyant believes he may have been a drover with a particular attachment to the place. She also concluded there were several other ghosts residing at the pub, including a young man who is buried on top of the hill and a woman in the pool room.[7]

During their early days at the pub, Heather and Andrew often noticed knives go missing from the dining room; their cleaner also experienced the same mystery within minutes of setting the table. The visiting medium believes the perpetrator was a little boy with red hair who allegedly choked on a hot potato in the dining room (a story grounded in history, according to locals). This little ghost has since been seen playing with a ball up and down the hallway.

Something is Out There

Of course, alcohol can heighten senses and play tricks on the mind — but staff and patrons of the Overland Corner and other allegedly haunted pubs claim that more sightings occur during sobriety than inebriation. Hauntings are also not restricted to after-hours; strange things can happen any time of day. And when a stranger from the past is revealed in all their mystery, it's a moment that will stay with you forever.

Chapter 10
The banshee in black

Mount Victoria Pass, Blue Mountains, New South Wales

> You'd call the man a senseless fool, —
> A blockhead or an ass,
> Who'd dare to say he saw the ghost
> Of Mount Victoria Pass
> But I believe the ghost is there
> For, if my eyes are right,
> I saw it once upon a ne'er-
> To-be-forgotten night . . .
>
> 'The Ghost at the Second Bridge', by Henry Lawson

The road from Mount Victoria to the historic settlement of Hartley, on the western reaches of New South Wales's Blue Mountains, is a precipitous and dangerous descent, sharp curves dropping off into canyons of dense bushland and sheer rock faces. Known as Mount Victoria Pass, this convict-built road is the nemesis of many a large-vehicle driver, with an accident rate 53 per cent higher than the average crash rate.

In fact, you could call this a killer stretch of road, with eight fatalities and 74 injuries occurring during 156 crashes between 2003 and 2007. Twenty-four per cent of those accidents involved trucks — so it's little wonder that truckies face this stretch of road and its bridges with trepidation.

According to legend and history, however, it may not just be the gradient and road surface contributing to the problem. It is said that Mount Victoria Pass — and in particular the notorious crossing of Mitchell's Bridge — is haunted by the Lady in Black, a wild-haired banshee who clings to the back of vehicles as they cross the bridge, causing the vehicles to skid from the road.

Peter Clifford, who runs the Blue Mountains Mystery Tours, says this demonic spectre 'frightens the life out of the truckies',[1] causing them to swing right off the road. Although Paranormal Pete, as he likes to be called, has never experienced the ghost himself, many of his clients feel her presence on the stretch of road, and there have been a couple of sightings.

By far the most famous record of this crazed female ghost was penned by one of Australia's most beloved and famous poets, Henry Lawson. Having a long association with the Hartley Valley (his father Lars is buried there), Lawson travelled this road on many occasions, and was obviously well-versed in its legend. But did he ever see her? According to his poem, 'The Ghost at the Second Bridge', he did, providing a very vivid description:

> And as we climbed the stony pinch
> Below the Camel Bridge

> We talked about the 'girl in black'
> Who haunts the Second Bridge.
> We reached the fence that guards the cliff
> And passed the corner post,
> And Johnny like a senseless fool
> Kept harping on the ghost
> 'She'll cross the moonlit road in haste
> And vanish down the track;
> Her long black hair hangs to her waist
> And she is dressed in black;
> Her face is white, a dull dead white –
> Her eyes are opened wide –
> She never looks to left or right,
> Or turns to either side.'

So who is the Lady in Black who has been terrorising travellers through Mount Victoria Pass for more than 100 years and inspired a great writer to pen her supernatural exploits? According to popular legend, her name is Caroline Collits (sometimes spelt Collit, Collitts or Collett), a young woman from Hartley Vale whose murder in 1842 at the hands of a violent ex-lover shocked the nation.

Caroline James, aged only 16 at the time of her death, was married to William Collits, the youngest son of former convict Pierce Collits who built an inn at the foot of Mount York. Originally called the Golden Fleece, this lovely heritage building is today a private residence known as Collits Inn. The inn was a popular stop with travellers crossing the Blue Mountains en route to Bathurst; it's even mentioned in the journals of Governor Bourke.

William Collits was said to be somewhat of a wishy-washy character, with speculation he may have had Down's Syndrome. In a very public newspaper announcement, Pierce Collits proclaimed his son 'an idiot', cautioning 'any person giving trust or credit to his son', and stating 'he would not pay any debts he [William] may have contracted'.[2]

Adding to Pierce Collits's doubts about his son's ability to control his assets was William's child bride, who was said to come from an 'unstable family'. According to a report in the *Sydney Gazette*:

> After [Caroline] had been married about a year, in a fit of drunkenness her mother hanged herself in her own house; her husband was in the house at the time, but in such a beastly state of intoxication, as to be incapable of preventing her destroying herself.[3]

On suspicion of contributing to his wife's death, Caroline's father was put in gaol for six months, but was eventually released. Meanwhile, both Caroline and her younger sister are said to have become involved romantically with a man named John Walsh (sometimes called Welsh), an Irish convict transported to the colony in 1833.

Walsh appears of dubious character. After arriving in Australia, he was twice tried for murder – once for murdering a man, the other for bludgeoning to death a woman and her young son. On both occasions he was acquitted, using his Irish gift of the gab to talk his way out of sentencing.

Caroline, it seemed, was totally enthralled with this rapscallion, and at one point actually left her husband to move in with Walsh and her sister. For this reason, both girls were described as 'of loose and abandoned characters, which is totally borne out by the circumstances'.[4] However, after Walsh married the younger sister, Caroline returned home 'and was again on terms of intimacy with her husband'.

On January 31, 1842, Caroline Collits and her husband began the long trek up Mount Victoria Pass on foot to visit Caroline's sister at Blackheath, then heavily pregnant with Walsh's child. En route, they stopped off at the Coach and Horses Inn, a drinking establishment at the base of the pass owned by a man named Jagger.

There, Caroline and William had words – apparently over a pretty bonnet that had been given to her by Walsh. The situation was exacerbated by the appearance of the Irishman himself who, according to reports, had had 'two glasses of brandy'. Then the drama began:

> Soon after leaving the public house, without the slightest provocation, Welsh knocked Collit down, using the most dreadful imprecations; his victim [Caroline] interfered with the murderer, and by seizing his arms, at the same time shouting to her husband, 'Run, run, he has got a stone and will murder you,' allowed him to escape. These were the last words that Caroline Collitt was heard to utter, nor was she after that affray again seen alive.[5]

The following morning, Matthew Mall, a mail driver from Penrith to Hartley, found some clothes lying on the road midway between the top of Mount Victoria and Soldier's Perch, about 3 miles from Jagger's hotel. On further investigation, he discovered the body of Caroline Collit, her body and head covered with bruises, cuts and blood. A deep wound on the temple had penetrated the brain, no doubt inflicted by a sharp, jagged stone (which was found nearby, covered with hair and blood). It was said she'd been sexually assaulted before death.

John Walsh was arrested and tried in Bathurst. Despite claiming that the hotelier Jagger's son and several other young hooligans had set upon both him and his former lover after they left the hotel, he was found guilty of the most 'despicable and horrendous murder in the history of their time' and sentenced to death.

However, even the judge admitted that Walsh had been committed on circumstantial evidence, and that Jagger and other witnesses should have been called — that 'expense and inconvenience should have been disregarded in a case like this'.

Walsh was hanged on Tuesday May 3, 1842, at Bathurst.

While the case appears on the surface to be a cut and dried case of a ménage a trois gone horribly wrong, some people — including Hartley historian, journalist and barrister Marcia Osterberg-Olsen — believes the trial was badly handled, and that the wrong man was hanged for the murder.

'There was a group of young men, including Jagger's son, chayaking Caroline and her brother-in-law that night at the hotel,' she says. 'They had far more reason for the pack rape than he did.'

'Caroline had had a long association with Walsh,' she continues. 'He was her brother-in-law, who loved her well enough to buy her a bonnet. If Caroline was of loose morals, she might have had a play around with him before, but it would not have been rape. If he really was having a bit on the side with her and she was willing, why would there be a murder?'

Ms Osterberg-Olsen, who lives in the home where Caroline and William spent their brief married life, calls Caroline 'her ghost', and refutes her reputation as a wild, crazed demon. 'She's a nice ghost, a very gentle girl,' she says.

In life, according to family histories, Caroline was a kind and caring teenager who looked after her younger siblings after their mother committed suicide. 'She was also very caring of William Collits, as he was backwards,' Osterberg-Olsen tells us. 'She decided to marry him so she could look after him. That sort of girl is not like the girl the testimony of the witnesses would have you believe.'

According to Osterberg-Olsen, the spirit of Caroline Collits also inhabits her home, appearing to visitors but never to her. 'I used to be rather peeved that other people had manifestations but I never did. I was talking to a seer about it and she said that Earth-bound spirits bound to a place are curious about interlopers. They will appear to people they don't know anything about. She said they considered me part of the place.'

The ghost, it is said, appears to guests sleeping in the second bedroom, manifesting in the night as a gentle presence and sometimes stroking them on the forehead as they sleep.

This is certainly a far cry from the spirit said to haunt the road, a vengeful, demonic presence out for the blood of her betrayers. But just as in life, people have two sides to their personality – who's to say that a ghost can't appear in multiple locations, reaping justice as she sees fit?

Gentle ghost or screaming banshee? Perhaps the troubled soul of Caroline Collits is both, as misunderstood in death as it seems she was in life.

Chapter 11
Spooky cellars

Seppelt Wines, Great Western, Victoria

With its dramatic sandstone cliffs looming over wide bushland valleys, verdant farmland and quaint country towns, the Grampians region of western Victoria is a hidden holiday gem, an enticing escape for nature buffs and outdoor enthusiasts.

The region is also known for winemaking, its cool-temperate climate ideal for the creation of quaffable sparkling wines. Dating back to the mid-1800s, the historic Seppelt winery at Great Western set the benchmark for Australian bubbly, its cheap and cheerful 'champers' launching many a celebration in the suburbs of Australia over the past century and a half.

Today, the historic cellar door at the gateway to the Grampians offers a warm invitation to passers-by to drop in, taste some wine, absorb the history and wander its picturesque grounds. But for many visitors, the real attraction of Seppelt's is not in the old homestead or its tasting rooms . . . but what lies beneath.

Spooky cellars

With torch in hand and a steely resolve, Seppelt staff member Andrea is leading us through the temperature-controlled working winery, past massive vats of fermenting juice, through function rooms, then down some ancient steps, descending 8 metres into the very bowels of the Earth.

We stand before a large black and gold wrought iron gate, decorative yet somehow ominous, as if an entranceway to Hades itself. We are about to enter The Drives, 3 kilometres of underground tunnels, a dark and gloomy labyrinth where bottles of wine have been stored since 1868.

Excavated from decomposed granite by former goldminers, this maze of passages — the largest underground cellar system in the Southern Hemisphere — once stored 120,000 bottles, a stockpile which in recent days has been reduced to around 40,000. But it's not the dusty racks of alcohol lining the metre-wide passageways we've come to see, but spirits of a different ilk — those belonging to the realm of the paranormal.

If the energies of the dead do exist, these subterranean passageways are as good a place to find them as anywhere. Coated in a black fungus called *Aspergillus niger*, the corridors are cool and damp, the total absence of ambient light prohibiting any natural changes in temperature. Illuminated by hanging lanterns and exposed bulbs, the light is unevenly cast, flickering as though blown by a supernatural presence, with shadows looming around every corner.

Having worked at the complex for many years, Andrea knows The Drives intimately, but for first-time visitors, the maze of tunnels is disconcerting, suffocating, oppressive. Those prone to claustrophobia will find it an uncomfortable experience, and it's easy to let the imagination run riot in the windowless, clammy environment.

Partly inspired by Andrea's own enthusiasm for the paranormal, the winery has been running ghost tours of The Drives since 2008. With her own psychic abilities in tune, Andrea has little doubt the tunnels are haunted — a belief backed by many tour participants who report hearing whispers and tapping, seeing white mists and strange shadows, and experiencing inexplicable presences. There have also been countless photographs of orbs taken in The Drives, a phenomenon that can possibly be explained by the high density of fungal spores in the humid atmosphere.

Another tour guide, Colin, has personally heard the sound of two women talking in the passageways, despite no-one else being in the system at the time, while another guide saw a white fog floating through a dark tunnel. On two separate occasions, candles literally exploded like firecrackers, while Andrea herself has had her hair tugged by an invisible force.

Who the spiritual entities taunting visitors to The Drives may be, however, remains a mystery. There have been no recorded deaths in the tunnels, and there are no stories of untoward behaviour, cruelty or foul play during their creation. Andrea personally believes the ghosts may be those with an emotional connection to the winery — perhaps the original owners or family members with fond memories of the winery's heyday.

'Reports of paranormal activity have increased since they started shifting bottles out of The Drives,' she theorises. 'This used to be a bustling work environment — since they stopped bottling five years ago, it's really quiet down here. I don't think the ghosts like the change in the environment — I think they miss the old days,' she says.

As well as leading ghost tours into The Drives, Andrea has been present during two separate paranormal investigations conducted by Victorian research groups. In a report published on its website, the group known as Ghost Research International claims there is 'indication of possible activity' in the cellars, with unusual sounds and sensations, including touching, recorded during their nocturnal vigil.[1]

The group also found evidence of paranormal activity above ground in the old homestead built during the 1890s, another location where Andrea has had intense psychic experiences. At least two ghosts are alleged to dwell in Vine Lodge: an old man is said to pace the alcove in the bedroom known as the Sparkling Shiraz suite, and a woman in blue has been sighted in the front bedroom. Guests staying in the lodge have complained of the sound of stomping in the corridors, while the apparition of a man in a tailored suit with two suitcases in hand has been seen kissing a female presence on the cheek, as if bidding farewell.

It is in the nearby cemetery that we find the biggest clue as to whom the spirits inhabiting both the homestead and The Drives may be. This peaceful, eucalypt-lined graveyard is an historic snapshot of pioneer days, of men and women who followed their dreams, forging a new industry against the odds. Here lies Joseph Best, who planted the first vines on the property and died in a horseriding accident in 1887; also his brother Henry, who established the neighbouring property, Concongella.

The most prominent slab in the graveyard bears the epitaph of Henry Irvine, who purchased the Great Western Vineyard for

12,000 pounds in 1888. Irvine, who studied the art of champagne making in Europe, was responsible for expanding The Drives, filling them to capacity with the bottles of sparkling wine that would bring him fame, fortune and critical acclaim, including the coveted gold medal at the 1900 Paris Exhibition.

Somewhat of a social butterfly, Irvine counted among his personal friends the opera singer Dame Nelly Melba, who visited the winery on several occasions, opening a tunnel named in her honour in 1910. According to local legend, Melba musingly wondered what bathing in champagne would feel like; her wish was Irvine's command, with the vigneron drawing her a bath from 172 bottles of his bubbly best.

When Irvine's wife died in 1915, he sold the cellars to his friend Benno Seppelt and retired to Melbourne. After developing a gastric ulcer in 1922, he travelled to London to seek medical advice, but died on the operating table before a cure could be found. His body was shipped back to Victoria and buried in the Great Western Cemetery alongside his wife.

Wine was Irvine's passion; winemaking his life. Perhaps in death, the founding father of a great Australian tradition could not bear to leave the place where he made his mark, forging an empire that would bring happiness to so many people.

Chapter 12
Australia's most infamous ghost

Without a doubt the most renowned (and enthusiastically marketed) Australian haunting is that of Fisher's ghost – the story of the apparition of a murdered man who led police to his missing body. In October every year the community of Campbelltown in New South Wales celebrates this ingenious spirit with the major event of its social calendar – the Fisher's Ghost Festival. But what is the true story behind the legend?

Established as fact is that Frederick Fisher arrived in Australia as a convict aboard the *Atlas*. By 1826 he was a 'ticket-of-leave' man – a convict whose sentence had not expired but was conditionally at liberty. Amongst other properties, he owned 30 acres fronting on to Queen Street, which would go on to become the main thoroughfare of Campbelltown. It adjoined the farm of George Worrall, another ticket-of-leave man.[1]

On June 17 that year Frederick Fisher mysteriously disappeared. Worrall informed authorities Fisher had fled back to England to avoid a forgery charge. But when police discovered Worrall selling some of Fisher's personal belongings, they became suspicious of the missing man's nextdoor neighbour. Of course, to press charges, they needed a body.

It is at this point Fisher's story takes a supernatural bent. Months passed with no other leads, until one day local man John Farley ran into a hotel in a highly agitated state. He claimed to have seen the ghost of Fisher sitting on a paddock fence in the corner of his own property. Apparently the apparition had turned, pointed towards a creek flowing alongside, and vanished.

Initially Farley's tale was dismissed, but with no other evidence to move on, police decided to search the creek. On October 20, troopers assisted by Indigenous trackers found the battered body of Fisher concealed in a swampy section of its bank, precisely where his ghost had pointed. The decomposed corpse was described as 'a sodden death-like sickly white', its face and head shockingly disfigured.[2] Troopers also found blood stains on several rails of the fence where the ghost had supposedly perched. They surmised this was either where the murder occurred, or where Fisher's body had been hoisted over the fence.

Worrall went to trial in Sydney on February 2, 1827. Despite the evidence against him being largely circumstantial, the jury found him guilty within 15 minutes. He was sentenced to death and hanged three days later. He went to the gallows claiming to have killed Fisher accidentally. The sensational story spread not just across the colony but to England as well. It was mentioned in Robert Montgomery Martin's *History of the British Colonies*,[3] published in London in 1835, subsequently making its way into *Household Words*, a periodical edited by no less than Charles Dickens himself.

Of course there is one obvious question mark hovering over the veracity of Farley's story. Could he not have fabricated his ghostly encounter to cover prior knowledge of Fisher's murder? Although his alleged sighting was not mentioned at Worrall's trial, due to the fact that supernatural evidence was not permitted in a Court of Law,[4] he was generally considered a respectable citizen, and even employed as a special constable (a law enforcement officer who is not a regular member of a police force). Legend has it that on his death bed he was still insisting he had seen the ghost.[5]

Over the years the legend of Fisher's ghost became entrenched in the local folklore of Sydney's southwest and surrounding towns. In 1956, when a Sydney radio station broadcast a story on the Fisher's ghost legend to mark the 130th anniversary of the infamous murder, nearly 1500 people turned up at night to try and spot the ghost, jamming Campbelltown's Queen Street with cars.[6]

It was this public reaction that prompted the local chamber of commerce to name the town's recently inaugurated annual parade after Fisher. This is the parade that over the years has grown into the week-long Fisher's Ghost Festival. Yet despite the commercialisation of his name, Fisher does not seem to have shied away from putting in the odd appearance.

We arrive in Campbelltown on the occasion of the 2009 street parade of the Fisher's Ghost Festival, held appropriately on October 31 – Halloween. The buzz starts building early afternoon, as local punters line both sides of Queen Street, competing for prime positions, their folding chairs and Eskies forming a virtual makeshift barrier between pavement and street. We set ourselves up in the old part of town, at the end of the street where Fisher's farm was located, and supposedly the spiritual centre of the hauntings.

The parade commences and immediately locals get into the spirit of things. The first float is a skeletal 4-metre-tall Fisher ghost puppet, moved and operated at ground level by eager young volunteers. It is followed by a similarly sized mega-puppet of an Indigenous tracker. Next, a perfectly polished 1960s red MG passes, carrying a Casper-like ghost in the back seat. In such fashion the parade continues for more than three hours, as community groups, local businesses and car clubs make their way through the Queen Street throng, 'ghouled up' to the max. This parade is the heart of the festival, and the locals love it.

After getting a feel for what the street parade is all about, we slink into Campbelltown's Town Hall Theatre, which stands on the very site of Worrall's former property, right next door to Fisher's. It is here that members of the local theatre group have reported flickering stage lights, unexplained backstage footsteps and misty figures appearing on stage after rehearsals – all attributed to Fisher's ghost.

We meet with former theatre group president Greg Dillon, who has been involved with the troupe for more than three decades. Dillon is also honorary historian of the theatre, devotedly scrapbooking clippings of reviews and ghost reports. He has had two personal run-ins with the spirit of Frederick Fisher, both during his presidency in 1995, a period when the stage end of the theatre was undergoing renovation.

Around 8 p.m. one night he was working downstairs beneath the stage, in what is now the make-up room, when he heard footsteps above. This surprised him greatly, since he knew he was working alone and that the theatre was locked. 'They crossed the wooden floor of the stage,' relates Dillon. 'Then I could hear them on the concrete floor of the backstage area. They were headed for the stairwell that leads downstairs. I popped my head up expecting to see someone. But there was no-one there.'

A similar experience occurred shortly thereafter, when he heard phantom footsteps above the orchestra pit. 'We all think it's Fred,' he insists. 'But he's not out to harm anyone. Nobody's ever been injured.'

Neil Hatchman, who held the theatre presidency in the 1980s, also had a ghostly encounter. 'I was working there a lot at night by myself, taking away rubbish around the back, when the lights went off,' he recounted in a 1995 interview in the *Campbelltown-Macarthur Advertiser*.[7] He claims that after switching the lights back on he spotted a figure cross the stage and enter a back room. Hatchman followed, brandishing a piece of wood. Despite there being no other exit, he found the room empty. 'It was an odd experience to say the least,' he summed up.[8]

The only photographic evidence of Fisher's ghost comes from a woman who was passing the theatre one evening at twilight. She noticed what she thought was smoke in an upstairs window. Alarmed, she stopped to watch, but could see no red glow of flames. She assumed theatre members may have been practising with a dry-ice machine, used to create the effect of fog on stage. Before the swirling mist disappeared she took a photograph then knocked on the theatre door. No-one answered – the theatre was empty. Could she have witnessed the swirling spirit of Fisher in ectoplasmic form?

Something is Out There

Surprisingly, since it housed hardened news types, the former offices of the *Campbelltown-Macarthur Advertiser* were also home to haunted tales. In 1992, the newspaper's current editor Jeff McGill heard a chilling ghostly voice, 'clear, yet strangely indistinguishable',[9] from a vacant hall outside an upstairs storage space. When other staff members experienced the same spooky phenomena, the classic 1990s paranormal television show *The Extraordinary*, hosted by the craggy-faced Warwick Moss, came to investigate. The story was aired nationally.

The swampy creek where Fisher's body was finally found came to be known as Fisher's Ghost Creek. For many decades, the bridge across it was the main thoroughfare by which people passed through Campbelltown. These days commuters bypass the town completely on the South Western Freeway and the creek is now a stormwater drain. The sludgy waterway empties into a small concrete reservoir on the edge of Koshigaya Park, an enormous grassy space named in honour of Campbelltown's sister city in Japan. Directly above the drain's concrete pipes is a wooden rail. Some local historians say this rail is most probably located where Fisher's ghost allegedly sat on a fence, pointing out the location of its corpse.

Another local legend relates to the period when Fisher's body was still missing for four months in 1826. Some local men had waded into the marshy creek in search of him. Part way down they began to hear a rumbling sound. At first thinking it was emanating from the water, they soon realised it came from the ground. The earth was mysteriously groaning – spooking the search party enough to turn and head back when they may well have been only metres away from discovering the body.

Could the uncanny sound have been Fisher calling out from beyond the grave?

The 'groaning earth' legend became entrenched in local folklore. In another story it was famously put to the test. Across the road from where Fisher's Ghost Creek once flowed stands a currently disused restaurant, overrun by weeds. Over the years it was known by a gamut of names, including the Fisher's Ghost Restaurant. According to Jane Roman of Campbelltown Visitor Information Centre, a local man, perhaps in a bid to impress his mates, stood in front of the property one evening in the 1940s and called out, 'If there's a ghost give me a sign!' Allegedly a god-awful roar vented from out of the ground. The man's dog ran off. Witnesses were terrified. And no-one ever issued the challenge again. Whether or not this paranormal perplexity relates directly to Fisher's ghost no-one is sure, but the premises are certainly situated close enough to the central goings-on of the murder yarn. Today the former Fisher's Ghost Restaurant is permanently closed; blocked from entry by safety-fencing, and in the process of being consumed by a tangle of vines, it looks like nothing so much as a haunted house.

We are now at the far end of Queen Street, where the parade is winding to a close. Thousands have participated, and a family fair is set up on the edge of Koshigaya Park to entertain the youngsters. Parents and children alike wander the event in ghostly drag — faces painted like skulls and devil costumes on display in the soft suburban late afternoon light. The landscape of Fisher's tragic tale may have vanished with the onslaught of time, but thanks to the efforts of his ghost, his tale seems set to live forever. Amongst the festivities we can't

Something is Out There

help indulging the whimsical thought that possibly, up there on the rail, overlooking all the merriment, might sit the spirit of Frederick Fisher himself bemused by all the fuss and the fact that in death he truly found immortality – as Australia's most renowned murder victim and celebrated ghost.

Part 2
Ufology

Chapter 13

Wycliffe Well – Australia's UFO capital

The waitress at the Tennant Creek Hotel offers a word of warning as we prepare to hit the road: 'Be careful driving in the dark, anything could jump out at you – wild pigs, horses . . . even camels.'

She forgot to mention the lights.

There's one travelling behind us now, hovering over the white line 20 metres back – a single white globe, occasionally blinking on and off, keeping pace at 120 kilometres an hour. It's an irritation in the rearview mirror; at first we think it's a motorbike, hassling to overtake. But it soon becomes clear this is not a motor vehicle of any description – just an unidentified light source, haranguing us in otherwise pitch blackness.

Slightly shaken, we pull over to photograph our highway assailant, thoughts of serial killers flashing through our overactive imaginations. It too stops, probably 300 metres down the highway. We flick on our hazard lights; the behaviour of the light doesn't change, leading us to ascertain it's not a reflection of our tail-lights. We flick off the headlights; the light remains constant. We wait; surely if it's another vehicle, it will soon catch up and overtake. For several minutes we simply sit and watch; the light doesn't move.

Perplexed, we return to the vehicle and recommence our journey. Once again the light follows, resuming its position on our tail. We travel together for several kilometres; then, suddenly, it vanishes, disappearing into the ether as suddenly as it arrived.

The following morning, we recount our tale to Lew Farkas, owner of our overnight accommodation, the Big4 Holiday Park at Wycliffe Well. Farkas nods sagely as we detail the experience; clearly he's heard it all before.

'I've heard several cases of people being menaced on the highway,' he tells us. 'People pull in here, terrified – it's brought me business because they come in wanting a room to get off the highway. Others come in and have coffee, then want to leave as soon as possible.'

Although he has not been hassled by the highway light personally, Farkas has a theory about it – and his explanation takes even us by surprise.

'It's an alien probe. They send out these balls of light, like a remote thing, from the big craft. It probably has a camera in it – they send them to significant places or to follow people, they control these things.'

Oh. So it appears we are being watched. Perhaps 'they' know why we are here – to uncover the secrets of Wycliffe Well. After all, this is the UFO capital of Australia. Or so Farkas says.

Wycliffe Well – Australia's UFO capital

He's certainly made a successful business from such claims. Located in the middle of nowhere, 380 kilometres north of Alice Springs on the Stuart Highway, there's little reason to call into this lonely desert pit stop apart from fuelling up, grabbing a cold drink and moving on. However, with some entrepreneurial nous, Farkas has turned his roadhouse and adjoining holiday village into an alien theme park of sorts, complete with murals, a mini-museum with dozens of newspaper clippings, souvenirs and statues of little green men and spaceships.

It's Roswell, Aussie-style – and the tourists lap it up. During peak season, they arrive in droves – family groups, grey nomads and ufologists alike – to pull up a deck chair on the manicured lawns, grab a beer and stare into the night sky, brilliant in its intensity. Barely a night goes by without some report of an anomaly – strange flashing lights, weird shooting stars, glowing balls of light . . . even hovering silver craft.

Inside the roadhouse, two visitor books bear testament to countless sightings by guests and passers-by:

> Coming back from the toilet, I saw a flashing red, white and orange light, moving up and down, low in the N/E [over the Marbles]. Observed for 10 minutes. Travelled further east and low in sky until it vanished. (Mark of Melbourne, 2003)
>
> At about 8.15 p.m. I saw two lights in the sky with red flashing lights just sitting there. All of a sudden, a light [white] started to flash across the sky at a very fast pace. I could see it flashing every now and then, but before I knew it, it had disappeared, travelling at a tremendous speed. (Julie of SA, September 2009)

Farkas himself claims to have seen scores of alien craft in his 25 years at Wycliffe Well. Before that, he'd never even considered the possibility of UFOs — and he certainly had no idea that his new home would be an alien hotspot when he bought it. In fact, it was only recently he discovered that the previous owner had two close encounters during his years at the roadhouse.

'One Sunday night he heard a rumbling sound above him, and the whole building was getting red hot and started shaking,' Farkas recalls. 'The windows were lit up like daylight around him, so he got under the bed, he was so panicked. This went on for ten minutes or so, there was so much heat that they were actually cooking inside the building.'

On the other occasion, the previous owner witnessed a blinding light on the Stuart Highway and lost an hour and a half of time, snapping in and out of consciousness. Although he was heading south at the time, each time he regained composure, his vehicle was facing north — an experience that occurred three times before he bolted for the safety of home.

While Farkas himself has never been terrorised like his predecessor, he has seen UFO craft close enough to pick out the portholes, through binoculars.

'I was walking out through the caravan park and saw a traditional hat-shaped craft. It was close enough to see the actual shape, but it wasn't until you looked through the binoculars that you could see the portholes, about a dozen on the side. It was dusk, and I'd say it was silver.'

Employee Julie Zanker has only been working at Wycliffe Wells for a few months, but in that time she's seen around 30 unexplained lights in the night sky.

Wycliffe Well – Australia's UFO capital

'They're out there on a regular basis,' she tells us. 'One night I came out here and saw a white, red and blue one flashing – everyone stood around watching it for about 45 minutes or so. I went home and had a shower and went back out for a cuppa and I saw about ten in the sky, red, blue and white, flashing all around the sky. They were all around us.'

It's a scenario verified by every current staff member at the holiday park, including the Chinese cook and his young family. With limited English, Goo Fong can only point and say, 'UFO – there – yellow, red', but his message is loud and clear – something is going on in the skies of Central Australia.

As we are talking to Farkas, a local Aboriginal man, known as GB, wanders into the roadhouse, and tells us of his own experience several weeks earlier. 'I was coming home from the top of the hill, and I looked over this way and saw something. Flashing lights, quite low down, moving around. It was around sunset, six or seven o'clock – my whole family saw it. They were up there.'

Another Indigenous woman, June, from the nearby community of Neutral Junction, painted her encounter with alien beings, depicting five, silver bowler hat–shaped craft hovering above the desert, green rays radiating from beneath round portholes. On the ground below are three iridescent, lizard-like creatures, classic Hollywood aliens with enlarged foreheads, slanting eyes and no mouths. It's a beautiful, evocative and intriguing work of art – and, according to Farkas, 'exactly what she saw'.

Other desert communities vouch for unusual activity above their traditional lands. In June 2008, the small town of Marlinja, 730 kilometres south of Darwin, was left reeling after four UFOs descended around 8 p.m., hovering just metres above their houses.

'We thought it was a jet,' local resident Janie Dixon told the *Tennant & District Times*. 'I saw what I thought at first was the evening star . . . but then we saw three red lights in the distance, and the sound kept getting louder. The ground felt like it was shaking, so we ran inside and shut the doors.'

According to the newspaper report, the drama continued for several hours. At one stage, the phone rang, but went dead when Ms Dixon tried to answer it. 'Then the light in the house became so bright, it was like we were sitting in a football stadium.'[1]

While most of the laminated newspaper clippings on the Wycliffe noticeboards have been collected over the past 20 years, Farkas says that UFOs have been buzzing the region since World War II, when Wycliffe Well was an army market garden growing vegetables and servicing the stock route. A photograph on the wall of the roadhouse – given to Farkas by Alice Springs plumber Phil Martin – shows Australian soldiers posing at nearby Devils Marbles in October 1942, with a small silver craft hovering nearby, clearly in shot.

'My father was a transport officer during the war,' Martin tells us. 'He'd drive trucks up and down from Alice Springs to Darwin with ammunition. He was standing on the hill at Devils Marbles and took that photograph, and in the distance – that's where they saw them. The guys took off after them but their tyres were shredded by tree roots. They spent hours and hours looking for them but they couldn't find them.

'Dad said after the sighting they got this beautiful feeling. It was like the earth and sky were one. It was like a connection – nowadays you'd call it a natural high. He said the feeling was absolutely beautiful. And your hands were really soft. He never saw anything else – but he saw that craft.'

There are two significant things about this iconic photograph – the first being the location. Situated 25 kilometres north of Wycliffe Wells on the Stuart Highway, the Devils Marbles are a magnificent natural formation, huge granite boulders stacked high, as if by a giant playing a child's game. There's perfection in their randomness and beauty in their stark isolation, particularly at sunset when they are illuminated deep russet and indigo by the sun's final rays.

Known to Aboriginal people as *Kalwekalwe* (literally meaning 'round objects'), the Marbles were an important meeting place for the Kaytetye, Warumunga, Anmatyerr and Alawarr people. Each of these four tribes had strong connections to the place, and would stop to hunt here on their travels around the country.

According to a senior traditional owner, Indigenous people believe that beings from the Dreamtime live in caves under the balancing rocks:

> They're real people like us. You can see them. A long time ago I went with my billycan down to the creek here to get some water. One of these secret people came out and started playing with me. I couldn't go away. My mother came and got me, saved me . . . They're kind, these secret people, but they can make you mad. They can change you into one of them. They can say, 'Follow me', and you can't go back.[2]

Something is Out There

On reading this quote, written on the noticeboard at the Devils Marbles Conservation Park, we get chills up our spines, especially in light of the information Lew Farkas and his staff have shared with us. Could these beings that have existed since the Dreamtime be alien in nature? Could they be the very same creatures depicted in June's painting?

While pondering this information, we get caught up in conversation with a couple of 'grey nomads', a sprightly duo from Melbourne travelling around Australia in a campervan. Arriving at Devils Marbles campground the previous afternoon, they'd set up camp before heading off to explore the landscape at sunset, camera in hand. It was only later that evening, flicking through their images around their campfire, that they noticed something curious in one of the shots.

We are stunned to see a photograph spookily similar to that taken by Phil Martin's father more than 60 years ago — a beautifully framed shot of the Marbles as the sun is dipping, with what appears to be a disc-shaped craft flitting through the blue sky. We zoom in on the image digitally — it definitely appears to be a flat, round object, a classic 1950s flying saucer.

Stumped and stunned by what they have captured on camera, the elderly couple agree to let us publish the photograph in our book — on condition of anonymity. We agree, thrilled to have procured further possible evidence of UFO activity in the region.

But why would aliens inhabit this desolate part of the world? What is the attraction of the Devils Marbles? Is it because, as some suggest, that this significant geological landmark is a designated ley line, emanating a magnetic force through either natural alignment or design? Or could the Marbles be an inter-dimensional portal to another world, associated with matter transfer and time displacement?

According to many prominent ufologists, there's a less mystical but infinitely more sinister impetus behind the high levels of UFO activity in Central Australia — the presence of the military, as evidenced by Phil Martin's father's photograph taken during World War II.

With Darwin falling under Japanese attack in 1942, the central desert region soon became strategic to the defence of the nation — one only needs to make the trek from Darwin to Alice Springs on the Stuart Highway to appreciate just how many air bases, air strips and army hospitals — now designated 'historic sites' — were constructed during that tenuous moment in history.

After the war, our US allies retained a presence in Alice Springs, and during the 1960s, construction began on the Joint Defence Space Research Facility at Pine Gap, located 18 kilometres southwest of Alice Springs.

Officially a satellite tracking station, very little is known about this covert installation, a facility isolated from civilisation by a mountain range, fenced off from prying eyes, with road and air space access totally prohibited. It is said to employ around 1000 people, mostly from the CIA and the National Reconnaissance Office, and it's rumoured to be a massive bunker, 12 storeys underground with countless tunnels and barely visible entrances to the surface.

According to Keith Douglass, Director for the Northern Territory branch of the Australian UFO Research Network

(AUFORN), there is a definite correlation between the high number of UFO sightings in Central Australia and the military presence at Pine Gap. 'There have been a few alien craft coming and going from Pine Gap,' Douglass explains. 'They keep an eye on everything globally. They have been here for eons . . . To keep them secret, they give [the military] things to play with as a trade-off,' he says.

Douglass claims to have spotted both alien craft and US military craft based on alien technology lurking in the skies around Pine Gap. 'I saw three huge orange spheres,' he says. 'They were about 6 metres across and 100 metres away. They were in a vertical row, only about 2 metres apart. After about two minutes the top one started to fade but kept its shape, until it wasn't there. Then the middle one and the bottom one did the same until all three vanished. They were aliens, because the military have different triangle-shaped ones.'

There is also no doubt in Lew Farkas's mind that the UFOs hovering around Wycliffe Well are snooping around the military facility, keeping an eye on what is going on. He also entertains the possibility that many of the inexplicable lights in the sky are advanced military craft, designed to match their intergalactic counterparts.

'I think it's a combination of both, human experiments and extraterrestrial stuff,' Farkas states emphatically. 'I'm pretty sure we have human-made UFO craft, but when they are being operated they are being watched by actual UFOs. I definitely think there's a possibility there are aliens from another galaxy watching what they are doing.'

Like many people involved in UFO research, Farkas firmly believes Central Australia has taken over as the UFO capital of the world, surpassing even the secret military base in Nevada nicknamed Area 51, where an alien craft that allegedly crashed to Earth in 1947 near Roswell, New Mexico, is said to be stored.

'I think Area 51 has actually moved to Australian air territory,' he says. 'Area 51 has become very quiet the last few years, sightings have dropped out. Too many people were going there, stickybeaking up in the hills there, trying to get pictures all the time. Also, the air space in the States was starting to get restricted, so they moved over here.'

We ask Farkas if he's ever afraid he knows too much — and he replies he's already been under notice, an anonymous caller telling him to watch his back.

'I've been grilled — had calls, "Be careful what you're doing". You can tell they're government by the way they are going through the exchanges,' he says. 'But I'm not concerned — I don't get involved. I don't approach anyone; if anyone asks, I answer. That works in my favour; it doesn't put me in the limelight as someone they need to worry about. I'm not looking for publicity — all this stuff here is from other people; there's not a single item here I have generated myself.'

Despite the disturbing possibility of the men in black — government agents of urban legend who threaten UFO witnesses to keep them quiet — knocking at our doors, it's time to do what the locals do: find ourselves some deck chairs, crack open some tinnies, and while away the hours looking up, scouring the skies for evidence as we chat with new friends under the brilliant, starlit canopy.

Something is Out There

Under such clear conditions, the stars certainly twinkle with an intensity we city slickers have never before encountered; and we're excited to watch a shooting star trail through the atmosphere, dazzling like a firecracker before petering out. Our necks stiffen as we gaze up, commenting on every possible anomaly — 'Did you see that?' or 'What's that red light there?'

Suddenly, a lightning-like flash illuminates the bushes 100 metres away. At first we ignore it; then it happens again, a split-second flash from below the tree line, coming from where there are no buildings and no possible source of light. The phenomenon occurs at least four more times over a ten-minute period, until we feel we have no choice but to investigate.

Scouring the bush clearing by torchlight, however, we find nothing unusual — no evidence of intruders, and no possible cause of the flash. It's a perfectly calm evening, with no sign of a building storm; all seems at peace in the outback scrub.

The following morning we question Lew Farkas about what the strange flash could have been — if it was something that happened regularly, he'd certainly know about it. He seems perplexed — he's never heard a report like this, and reiterates that there should not have been any other people in the vicinity.

Once again, he provides a theory — that we are being watched, recorded and followed. We dismiss this with a laugh, but can't help but feel a little uneasy as we commence the long haul back up the Stuart Highway to Darwin.

It seems not only is something out there . . . but it's watching us, watching them.

Chapter 14
The UFO hunter

An irksome obstacle often encountered when investigating the UFO underworld is the secretive and paranoid nature of many research groups. Phone messages are not returned, emails remain unanswered, and personally written requests sent to anonymous postal boxes seem to wind up in the dead letter office. Collecting reports of UFO activity from witnesses via website and voice mail, these closeted organisations jealously guard their records with such unrelenting zeal; their behaviour tends to reflect the very government agencies they incessantly accuse of cover-ups.

It is a shadowy field, riven with mistrust and petty feuding amongst splinter groups, and breaking through the veil of suspicion reserved for outsiders is not necessarily an easy task. First, some ufologists needed to be convinced we were not covert government operatives bent on pilfering their secrets and shutting them down; and second, that we had no intention of discrediting them.

Fortunately, within this murky milieu, it is also possible to come across both groups and individuals committed to illuminating, rather than obfuscating, the UFO mystery. Most fascinating are those mavericks professing no allegiance to any particular organisation; independent operators searching the skies off their own bat, their one and only aim to hit the UFO world's equivalent of a six – incontrovertible photographic evidence of a flying saucer.

Such a man is the Northern Territory's Alan Ferguson. Like many Top Enders, Ferguson is an iconoclast – he does things his way. To the average UFO hunter his methods may appear crude and unconventional. But claiming as he does to have photographed more than 30 mysterious aerial craft, it is difficult to deny he is getting results. For Ferguson, UFO hunting is not a precise artform requiring the latest hi-tech gadgetry; in fact the key to his success seems simplicity itself: 'If you put in the time, you've got a better chance of seeing them. No-one else sees them because they aren't looking. I look for them. I'm always looking up. I'm out there until one or two o'clock in the morning. Just kicking back and watching.'

With his trusty Canon Pro Shot digital camera in one hand and a Strongbow cider in the other, Ferguson will perch happily on his well-worn canvas deckchair for hours on end, patiently and persistently scouring the Northern Territory skies for otherworldly activity. Since realising his calling in early 2008, his photographs have not only hit headlines in the Territory, but have created a stir both across Australia and throughout the world.

The UFO hunter

We first encounter alien-hunting Alan at radio station Buzz FM, a family-run venture operating out of a home in Palmerston — a satellite suburb southeast of Darwin. From a recording studio set up in a spare bedroom, Buzz FM narrowcasts through the suburb and streams live on the internet. Ferguson is their star announcer, his twice-weekly UFO reports the most listened-to segments on the network.

On first impression, he doesn't look at all like what we expect of a UFO hunter. He looks more like any another local. But when the tapes roll on his 'UFO Watch' program, and he lights up on his favourite topic, we see the verve and enthusiasm which has propelled this otherwise laidback and unassuming Aussie bloke into somewhat of a local hero and burgeoning celebrity.

After delivering a comprehensive report on flying saucer sightings from around the world, Ferguson entreats us to take to the microphones, whereupon we find ourselves interviewed about our own adventures. Then, after joining him in a chorus of his closing catchphrase, 'Keep your eyes on the skies!', we are whisked away to his favourite UFO hunting site — his 20-hectare property in Acacia Hills, beyond the outer limits of Palmerston.

Joined by Stress, his stumpy-tail cattle dog — whose whimpering can apparently herald the approach of a UFO — we kick back and relax on folding chairs in Ferguson's vast backyard. Facing west, where 'most of the UFO action happens', and opting for beers rather than cider to combat the intense November heat, we intently watch the skies. Today they are blue, with some cloud moving in, though not enough to indicate a storm. Bordered by lush but alien-looking tropical savanna, the milieu could indeed evoke another world.

Ferguson spotted his first UFO at the tender age of ten, from the back window of the family car. Convinced by his parents he was seeing things, he blocked the experience from his mind, living flying saucer–free for the next few decades. Then in 2003, his interest was again piqued after he caught sight of one hovering above a lagoon in nearby Humpty Doo (a town which attained national notoriety in 1998 after an alleged poltergeist haunting was exposed as a hoax). But what really set Ferguson on his current mission was the discovery of 'small black thingies' in the frames of photographs taken in pursuit of his other passion – lightning storm photography. Upon enlarging the shots, he discovered what he believes to be extraterrestrial spacecraft.

We examine Ferguson's photographic efforts. In some of them we can clearly see small objects floating in the sky. A cynical observer might raise the possibility they are out-of-focus birds or insects, flashing past the lens at the moment of exposure. But Ferguson is adamant the objects he has photographed are the objects he has seen with his naked eye – alien aircraft. This may be the case, but we are nevertheless perplexed by the lack of consistency in their form. Ferguson has a theory for this: 'They come in all shapes and sizes – just like cars. Some are probably older model UFOs. They sell the secondhand UFOs to lesser races. They're the ones that crash!'

We are delighted Ferguson has such a sense of humour about his vocation, a quality rare amongst UFO researchers. But it is crystal clear from his dogged determination he is on a serious mission. When conducting a UFO search, Ferguson will take up to 150 photographs per day over a two-week period, and

The UFO hunter

then spend the next week scanning them for evidence. On a hunting day, his camera rarely leaves his side — a habit honed by harsh experience.

'I've been burnt three times in the past because my equipment hasn't been right there when I needed it,' he says. 'There was one time when I was outside, leaning up against the ute listening to the footy on the radio. And this orange object came straight across the sky. A big orange light about 100 feet in the air.'

Racing inside the house for his camera, Ferguson found himself thwarted by a strange ethereal force: 'Everything went into slow motion. Usually when I see something coming, I think, "Hello, the boys are rolling up", and I whoosh straight into the house to get the camera. But when I came back out that time, it had already gone past and it was just a pissy little orange dot. It definitely affected my sense of time. I was slowed down. There's no two ways about it. I was caught out big time there.'

Nowadays Ferguson is always at the ready. And although he prefers the convenience of staking out his own backyard he does have other stalking grounds, including a bare patch of land a couple of kilometres down the road, and his mother's yard in Humpty Doo. It is there he experienced one of his more spectacular sightings.

'That is the one that scared the shit out of me,' he recalls, a quaver still detectable in his voice. 'I was sitting outside at the back table at the old lady's joint. Then this triangle-shaped craft just dropped from the sky straight in front of me. It was super close — about 500 feet above the top of the trees. It was brown and black.'

Ferguson considers this his closest call. Which begs the question: What would he do if a craft actually landed beside him? 'I'd shit myself!' he exclaims. 'I'd be changing my jocks. If they come down . . . I don't want to think about it . . . It's a bit hairy. Because I'm out there by myself in the dark.'

But being alone in the dark is not the only danger in the realm of UFO hunting. If one is habitually looking up, there is a tendency not to look down. Just over a year earlier, while holding a ladder for a friend fixing a solar panel on his roof, Ferguson stepped with his thonged foot on a western brown snake. Feeling 'the slimy bastard' wrap around his ankle before he saw it, he tried to kick it away. But the reptile bit him on the leg, injecting its deadly venom. Ferguson wound up in intensive care for two weeks. Nevertheless, a month later, he was back on the UFO hunt.

'If I hadn't been looking up the bloody thing wouldn't have bit me!' Ferguson exclaims, taking a calming sip of cider but conveying no sense of self-pity or of malice towards the snake. In fact he seems more concerned about human than reptilian threats.

'I'm waiting for the men in black to knock on the door,' he reveals. 'Some of my mates reckon they'll come and rip my eyes out because I'm revealing too much.' While his tone is jocular, we suspect he may well be half-serious.

But Ferguson remains undaunted, and his collection of UFO snaps continues to grow. Although almost all appear to have been taken during daylight hours, he claims to have made his clearest sightings at night – including the craft he describes as the Big Mac of UFOs: 'It's metallic with red, orange and white flickering lights. And shaped like a hamburger. If you take the meat out of the middle and put in some red lights spinning around, that's what it's like.'

Of course lower light levels can make UFO photography difficult at night. So despite the rising and balmy mid-afternoon heat, we are relieved there is still an hour or so of daylight remaining. But if our quarry is so furtive, and potentially so distant, how will we know when we spot one?

'You have to watch for flashes in the sky,' instructs Ferguson. 'That's what gives them away. I originally thought when you see the flashes it was the sun reflecting off them. Now I reckon they actually flash when they manoeuvre.' But as we crack open our second Coopers and Alan breaks into another Strongbow, nothing is apparent in the sky save a large flock of galahs.

This was not the case a few months back, when Ferguson claims the activity above his house was fast and furious. A video on which he captured one of the UFOs was released to local newspaper the *Northern Territory News*, resulting in him having to field phone calls from curious media all over the globe: 'It went on for three weeks! I must have done about three dozen interviews!'

We view the footage in question. In jerky freeze-frame motion, against a blue sky, a small black dot appears to zip past the top of frame. Seconds later a closer dot moves similarly and fleetingly past the bottom of frame. Not the kind of indisputable evidence to comprise the Holy Grail of UFO hunting, but certainly a very interesting video.

We wonder if Ferguson has a theory as to why the UFOs are buzzing his part of the world in particular. After exhaustive discussions with other researchers based in the Top End and central Australia, he has theorised it may have to do with US military presence. After all, Darwin is the location of the biennial Exercise Pitch Black, where RAAF members are trained alongside American forces. According to Ferguson, increased sightings coincide with Pitch Black: 'They roll up more during military exercises. They love it! Every time they're on – bingo!'

Ferguson puts this down to the curiosity of alien pilots, apparently keen to keep tabs on what the military is up to. But surely there's the possibility of airforce craft being mistaken for alien craft? Not so, according to the UFO hunter.

'Some people say they're just military. But planes have got all sorts of stuff and you can hear them. I've never heard a sound from a UFO. If they're military, they're doing really good,' he says, adding, 'Comparing a UFO to military craft is like comparing a V8 supercar to a scooter.'

Ferguson isn't the only one seeing strange things in the skies above Acacia Hills. In fact reports stretch back at least four decades. On a fishing trip in 1970, business owner Bob Kennon, along with a now-deceased friend, witnessed a glowing ball of light curve through the night sky and disappear behind scrub.

'We were sitting on the edge of a billabong,' says Kennon, the event still clearly etched in his mind. 'It was about eight o'clock at night. We were having a meal after being out there on the water fishing all day. We saw a bright yellow moon-shaped object. It was travelling in an arc at a low speed. Not high speed like a meteor. I've seen meteors before. It moved slowly, like a flare.'

Kennon and his companion watched the incandescent object until it vanished from sight, appearing to land about 2 kilometres away in the vicinity of Acacia Hills: 'It didn't make a sound. Everything went quiet in the bush. It was spooky. The hairs on the back of our necks stood up.'

Above Ferguson's place, the only thing descending in the sky is the sun. Momentarily teased by the prospect of a vivid violet sunset, we are disappointed when its glow dissipates amongst low-lying cloud on the horizon. Night is moving in, and along with it diminishing chances of snapping a UFO. 'The moon is your worst enemy when you're trying to get a shot of them,' laments Ferguson. 'It makes everything hazy.'

It is time for us to depart, but for Ferguson the night is still young — there are many potential hours of sky gazing left.

'There's something seriously going on. And there is definitely an official cover-up. I'm just trying to tell the truth. I'm trying to get it out in the open,' he declares emphatically. 'I want to get the best photo anyone can get. It's just a matter of time.'

As we leave Ferguson to his quest, our lasting impression is that of a man on a mission, reclining in a deckchair, faithful dog at his side. The fearless UFO hunter, eyes always on the skies.

Chapter 15
The great UFO flap of 1909

> They didn't fly like any aircraft I had ever seen before...
> As I described them at the time their flight was like speed
> boats on rough water or similar to the tail of a Chinese kite
> that I once saw blowing in the wind... As I put it to newsmen
> in Pendleton, Oregon, they flew like a saucer would if you
> skipped it across the water.[1]
>
> Kenneth Arnold, pilot, writing of his encounter with unidentified
aerial phenomenon in 1947

And so the term 'flying saucer' was coined, entering the English lexicon for the first time and capturing the collective imaginations of true believers around the world. But while American pilot Kenneth Arnold's encounter with a formation of nine strange aircraft 'as flat as a pie pan' and 'shaped like a saucer' is attributed as sparking the modern UFO phenomenon, it was certainly not the first time strange objects in the sky had created mass hysteria.

The great UFO flap of 1909

Almost half a century earlier, a well-documented series of sightings occurred in the Southern Hemisphere, a sequence that's now known as the 'UFO flap of 1909'. For a couple of months in the winter of 1909, hundreds of reports of 'phantom airships', as they were described in the headlines of the day, were lodged in both Australia and New Zealand. In fact, at the height of the frenzy, crowds would gather on streets looking to the stars, hoping to catch sight of one of the strange flying machines.

'A good deal of excitement was occasioned tonight by the appearance of a mysterious light or an illuminated body to the south-east of the town,' the *Sydney Morning Herald* reported on August 10, 1909, after strange lights were seen in the sky above the Southern Highlands town of Moss Vale. 'Quite a number of people gathered in the main street, and speculation was rife as to the meaning of the strange illumination.'[2]

The buzz had begun several weeks earlier in the South Island of New Zealand, when several school children from the town of Stirling claimed to have observed the lights of an airship hovering in the night sky. The *Clutha Leader* reported:

> On Saturday night some half-dozen boys were playing on the beach at Kaka Pt . . . and saw a huge illuminated object moving about in the air . . . The boys thought it was being attracted by their lantern and ran away and left it on the beach. The airship then glided around the rocks and nearly came in contact with them. It shortly afterwards disappeared. The boys said it was as big as a house.[3]

Dismissing the boys' story as the product of overactive imaginations, a couple of local gentlemen staked out the beach the following night, fuelled no doubt by a healthy dose of scepticism and a hip flask of whiskey:

> On Sunday night the mysterious object again made its appearance at the beach and was seen by Mr George Smith and Mr Poulter about 8.30. Mr Smith viewed it through a very powerful night glass . . . It glided high in the air and sailed north in the direction of Kaitangata, swooping west and east and finally disappearing over the horizon . . . As seen through the glass, Mr Smith said it appeared to be a fair size, dark superstructure with a powerful headlight and two smaller ones at the side.[4]

Reports then began to flood in from other parts of the South Island. In one of the most dramatic encounters, an airship was said to have bobbed over the local school at Kelso, terrifying a classroom of boys. The *Otago Daily Times* reported on July 25, 1909:

> On Saturday Mr Gibson, of Kelso, telephoned us stating that at noon on Friday the school children beheld in the air a strange machine, which they described as shaped like a boat, with what seemed like the figure of a man seated in it . . . The phenomenon was observed also by Mrs James Russell, of Kelso. Our Kelso correspondent telegraphed as follows: 'There is not the slightest doubt that the airship was seen at Kelso yesterday at noon. I have eye witnesses to prove this. It is cigar or boat shaped, and is pointed at each end . . . It was seen by at least five persons, and their statements are all in accord.[5]

Before long, the frenzy had spread to the North Island. 'It has come at last,' declared the *Thames Star*. 'We have been expecting the dreaded news for weeks.'[6]

So what was this flying mystery machine, an object from outer space? Even back then, many seemed to think so, including surveyor Robert Grigor, who wrote to the *Otago Daily Times* on July 29:

> We will presume that they have been able to make a machine capable of going through space – say an airtight cylinder supplied with compressed air from their own atmosphere, capable of keeping them alive for an indefinite period with radium as a motive power and for light. They arrive in our atmosphere in the vicinity of New Zealand and are hovering around to get accustomed to our atmosphere.[7]

Others were less convinced, comparing the hype to that which occurred ten years prior on publication of H.G. Wells's *War of the Worlds*. A sardonic correspondent from the *Southland Daily News* suggested:

> It seems to me . . . to be the beginning of an invasion from Mars. Water being scarce on that planet, the Martians are looking out for a new world to inhabit; and New Zealand being a conspicuous object on our globe, they will probably attack us first.[8]

Then there were others who thought the phenomenon to be a more sinister, terrestrial source. After all, one can't help but notice how closely descriptions of the aircraft match a zeppelin, which first made an appearance in Germany in 1900. This, coupled with a building distrust of the German empire prior to World War I, led to the 'scareship phenomenon', with fear of invasion by zeppelin taking hold in many nations across the Northern Hemisphere.

Had the Germans ventured Down Under to test their dirigible technology away from prying European eyes? Were German spies hovering across the countryside to survey New Zealand as a potential invasion target?

Others, however, believed the threat was more parochial — a bunch of Aussie smugglers up to no good. But this theory was soon debunked when, just as the frenzy began to peter out in New Zealand, sightings began to occur across the pond.

The first Australian reports came from Goulburn, NSW, on August 5, 1909, when several residents reported seeing a bright blue light moving across the night sky:

> A mysterious moving light has been seen over North Goulburn nearly every night since Thursday . . . One youth describes it about as big as a carriage lamp. One adult saw it last night at about half past seven for about a quarter of an hour . . . Four young men saw the light on Sunday night, it came from the east . . . it was pale blue in colour. The brightness of the light attracted the youth's attention. Only the light was seen, there being nothing to show the presence of a supporting body.[9]

With reports from New Zealand still fresh in their minds, reporters began to speculate on the origin of the mystery. 'The lights have been variously described as resembling "a ball of fire", "a buggy lamp", a "50 candle-power gas jet" and a "Japanese airship" (whatever that may be),' wrote a correspondent from the *Hobart Mercury*. 'Various theories have been advanced as to what it is. The most feasible appears to be that of the Aerial League, which claims to have investigated the matter, and discovered that the Goulburn light, at any rate, was nothing more than an illuminated box kite, and that the New Zealand mystery was a joke along the same lines.'[10]

Debate was rife; some claimed the military had been experimenting; scientific types believed they were looking at a convergence of Jupiter and Venus; while others thought the planet Mars had 'been playing pranks of late',[11] with the red planet particularly close to Earth at that time. The *Hobart Mercury* reported:

> All sorts of theories have been voiced in connection with the 'phenomena', a very few persons . . . expressing the opinion that Mars has been signalling to the Earth. If the Martian signals could reach so far they might just as well come a little closer to us . . . Were we living in the superstitious days of the past, it might perchance be thought that: 'Either there is a civil strife in heaven; Or else the world, too saucy with the gods, Incenses them to send destruction.' But nowadays we look for a natural explanation of everything, although we do like to mix up a little sensation with our facts.[12]

From the east coast, the buzz shifted across the continent to Western Australia, where lights were reported in the sky near Onslow on October 20, 1909. A customs officer's report states that the craft was spotted by Mrs A.J. Roe, wife of the manager of Minderoo Station near Onslow, as well as three stationhands:

> At 3pm on October 20 when at the Minderoo homestead my attention was directed by a native to a big object in the air several miles away. The object was travelling away from us in an easterly direction. It looked compact like a dirigible

balloon but appeared to be squarer, more like an aeroplane. The sun shone on it and flashes came from it as though reflected from something revolving or off metal work. The colour of the object was dark brown or black. It was too far away to distinguish its exact nature and size or whether any persons were in it.[13]

According to the report, Mrs Roe was positive the object was an airship of some description, but did not care to sign a statement as she had been too far away from the object to get a clear view.

The customs collector, Mr L.O. Timperley, went on to speculate that the object was an airship of some kind— 'the result of a Western Australian inventor who wishes to perfect his machine before making his invention public and has chosen this remote locality for his preliminary flight.' Another option was that the lights were emitted by a foreign vessel anchored off the coast, 'reconnoitring the country'.[14]

The suggestion that the mystery airships were the work of mad scientists certainly holds some weight — after all, this was the dawn of the age of aviation, with the first monoplane crossing of the English Channel taking place on July 25, 1909. It stands to reason that other enthusiasts were conducting similar experiments with prototype aircraft — even in colonial outposts Down Under. In fact, the theory that a mystery inventor was bunkered down in the Otago countryside in New Zealand, creating his own zeppelin, was so popular that a reward was offered for the airship pilot to come forward and publicly display his wonderful creation. The offer was never taken up.

The great UFO flap of 1909

According to some scholars, however, the rash of sightings in the Southern Hemisphere was simply mass hallucination. Robert E. Bartholomew from the Department of Psychology and Sociology Studies at James Cook University in Queensland states in his book, *UFOs and Alien Contact: Two Centuries of Mystery*, that the flap of 1909 was purely a moral panic, brought about by concerns over political tension in Europe.[15]

After dominating the press for several months, reports of aircraft sightings on both sides of the Tasman began to peter out. And then nothing at all; the skies were empty again. Whatever had menaced the two nations for several months appeared to have vaporised into the Southern Cross.

Extraterrestrials? German spies? A mad scientist? The mystery was never solved, but would certainly add historic fuel to sightings later in the century . . .

The Mystery of the Wandjinas

While UFOs are generally considered a 20th-century phenomenon, there is evidence suggesting that alien life forms have been communing with humankind for centuries, certainly well before our collective minds were opened to the notion of space travel.

The theory that ancient civilisations were visited and shaped by beings from other worlds was particularly popular during the early 1970s, when Erich von Daniken's *Chariots of the Gods* reached cult status. Von Daniken's claims that aliens were responsible for ancient engineering marvels such as the pyramids and Stonehenge have since been largely debunked, and UFO theorists today steer cautiously away from von Daniken's fanciful approach to intergalactic colonisation.

In the most remote corner of the Australia, however, beautiful and eerie rock paintings representing the most spiritual and sacred mysteries of Indigenous life continue to fuel the debate, with many pointing to the stylistic depictions of supernatural figures as visual proof of alien visitation.

Indeed, the beings represented in these amazing paintings do bear an uncanny resemblance to modern-day depictions of beings from outer space – human-like, delicate bodies, prominent black eyes, and haloes of radiating lines encircling oversized craniums, aura-like. Hauntingly, most of the figures do not have a mouth.

These are Wandjinas, Dreamtime ancestors of the Worora, Ngarinyin and Wumumbul people who collectively make up the Mowamjum community from the Kimberley region of Western Australia. It is said that these spirit beings are the harbingers of the wet season, shaping the landscape, maintaining the cycles of nature and bringing the rains.

All images of Wandjinas, both ancient and modern interpretations, come under the custodianship of the Mowamjum people – only a small group of selected elders have permission to paint the spirits, and any unauthorised representation is considered disrespectful, resulting in severe tribal punishment such as spearing. For this reason, we are unable to reproduce any images of Wandjina in this book; and any speculation about the meanings and origin of the original artworks must be respectful to the traditional owners.

It is therefore pertinent that we allow the Mowamjum people their own voice in interpreting the symbolism of the figures.

According to eminent Worora leader Sam Woolagoodja, the power of the Wandjina 'is so great that they don't need to speak, so they have no mouth. Their eyes are powerful and black, like the eye of a cyclone. The lines around a Wandjina's head can mean lots of things – clouds, rain, lightning.'[16]

Woonambal artist Lily Karedada is regarded as one of the most important visual interpreters of the Wandjina, with her work held in major collections in Australia and overseas. Lily believes the Wandjina are rainmakers living in the caves. If people go to a cave, they need to warn the Wandjinas beforehand, calling out, 'Hello! I'm not trying to disturb you. I belong to this country. Don't make big rain!'[17]

According to Sam Woolagoodja, the Wandjinas themselves were responsible for the ancient images on the cave walls, leaving their images in ochre and white clay on the rocks before returning to the spirit world. They are therefore more than just pictures – they represent the very essence of the spirit of the creatures depicted.[18]

Chapter 16
Tully saucer nest

There is no doubt crop circles are amongst the more questionable elements of UFO lore. Stubborn cultists continue to believe these artistically complex, overlapping ring patterns are either residual proof of UFO landings or created by aliens as symbolic messages to humankind. The truth is they are essentially pranks, perpetrated since 1975, originally across the English countryside by grown adults with nothing better to do than scamper in circles through grain fields under the cover of night.

In fact, despite unfathomable resistance from hardcore believers, crop circles have been widely known as hoaxes since 1991, when the chief culprits publicly admitted their trickery – even demonstrating for a television documentary crew how they created such perfect orbs in wavy grain fields with wooden planks and balls of string.[1] The brains behind these practical jokes were art school students Dave Chorley and Doug Bower, their aim simple and to the point – to make people believe a flying saucer had landed in a field.

There is no doubt their efforts had great impact on popular culture for considerable time. Nor can we deny some crop circles are ingeniously designed and stunning to behold. But the most interesting aspect about all the fuss is where this pair of pranksters may have found the inspiration for their scheme – an alleged UFO landing site in Queensland known as the 'Tully saucer nest'.

A high-profile report in 1966 revealed that a banana farmer was stunned to see a flying saucer take off from a lagoon, leaving behind a large circular indent in the reeds. The site became known as the Tully saucer nest, and in an era where cosmic bliss was all the rage and pop singers were about to send out the call to occupants of interplanetary craft, it became the centre of a media frenzy; after being plastered on headlines in Australia, it spread around the globe.

Bill Chalker, one of Australia's most respected UFO researchers and author of *The Oz Files*, has spent almost 40 years collecting and investigating UFO reports. With an honours degree in science, and having majored in both chemistry and mathematics, he is a man who takes a rigorous scientific approach to his investigations. Chalker has delved deeply into the Tully event, and has labelled it one of the top ten cases in Australian UFO history.

The events unfolded on the morning of January 19, 1966, when 28-year-old George Pedley was working his tractor on a sugarcane farm belonging to Albert Pennisi. The land was located just outside Tully, 25 kilometres inland from Mission Beach in far North Queensland and bordering a body of water called Horseshoe Lagoon, part of the Tully River wetlands. As

Pedley approached a timbered area rimming the lagoon he heard a loud hissing noise, 'like air escaping from a tyre'.[2] Searching for its source, he was shocked to witness a large disc-like object rising up from the swamp:

> 'When I glanced at it, it was already 30 feet above the ground, and at about tree-top level,' he stated in an interview with Chalker after the event. 'It was a large, grey, saucer-shaped object, convex on the top and bottom, and measured some 25 feet across and nine feet high. While I watched, it rose another 30 feet, spinning very fast. Then it made a shallow dive and took off with tremendous speed. Climbing at an angle of 45 degrees, it disappeared within seconds.[3]

What Pedley describes could not sound more like a classic flying-saucer sighting. Perturbed but curious, he proceeded to the spot beneath which he had seen the object ascend. In the waters of the lagoon, not far from the bank, he spotted a circular patch of flattened reeds within which water was eddying. When he returned to the site to show farm owner Pennisi, the water had calmed and the reeds floated in a matted circular mass about 10 metres wide. After Pennisi took photographs of the reeds, both men swam beneath, ascertaining they were free-floating.

Pedley reported his sighting to the police. Next morning a sergeant from the local station accompanied him to the site, took his statement and unable to proffer further explanation, contacted the Royal Australian Air Force (RAAF). The nearest RAAF base in Townsville opted not to send a representative to the site, but did suggest the police sergeant collect samples of

Little green men at Wycliffe Well, the Roswell of Australia, in the Northern Territory. (Julie Miller)

Lew Farkas, owner of Wycliffe Well Holiday Park, who has personally seen countless unidentified lights in the sky during his 25 years in central Australia. (Julie Miller)

Co-author Grant Osborn and friends watch the skies in nightly entertainment at Wycliffe Well Holiday Park, Northern Territory. (Julie Miller)

A unidentified flying object, snapped by campers at Devil's Marbles, Northern Territory, site of countless UFO sightings since World War II. (Anonymous by request)

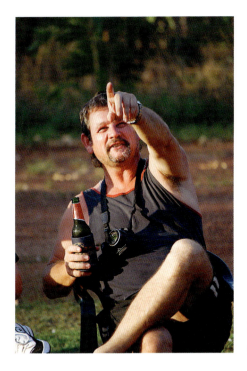

Alan Ferguson, fearless Top End UFO hunter, keeps his eyes on the skies. (Julie Miller)

One of many UFO photographs taken by Alan Ferguson, who claims flying saucers buzz his Northern Territory property on a regular basis. (Alan Ferguson)

Westall Secondary College (previously Westall High School) in Clayton South, Victoria, where in 1966 more than 100 students and teachers claimed to see between one and three flying saucers in the sky. (Grant Osborn)

According to a Westall UFO witness, this site is where one of the mysterious flying saucers briefly landed. Subsequently the site was examined and set alight by the military. (Grant Osborn)

Clayton South's the Grange, a tall stand of pines behind which the flying saucers were reputed to have bobbed up and down. (Grant Osborn)

Moorabbin Airport, from which pilot Frederick Valentich embarked on his fateful flight on 21 October 1978. Some believe he was taken by a UFO. (Grant Osborn)

The Min Min Lights have been embraced as an important part of the Queensland town of Boulia's identity. (Julie Miller)

Three glowing UFOs hover beneath tropical storm clouds in the outer Darwin suburb of Palmerston, Northern Territory. (Anonymous by request)

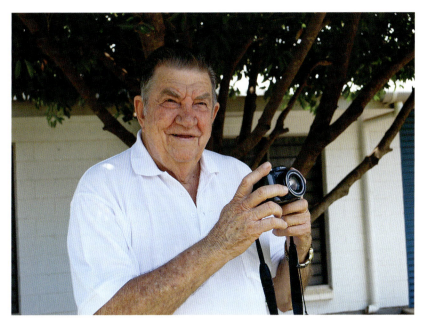

Top Ender Mark Schmutter, who at the age of 79 spotted and snapped his first flying saucer hovering over the city centre of Darwin, Northern Territory. (Julie Miller)

One of Schmutter's mysterious photographs of a blue 'muscle car' UFO, which made the front page of the local newspaper in Darwin, Northern Territory. (Mark Schmutter)

An unexplained glowing light floats over Echo Point in Katoomba, New South Wales. (courtesy of Ann Taylor)

Vernon Treweeke, the 'father of Australian psychedelic art', stands before one of his many 3D alien landscapes wearing 'prismatic Fresnels'. Treweeke theorises flying saucers may be time machines from the future. (Julie Miller)

plant matter from the site for testing. They also had Pedley fill out a 'Report on Aerial Object Observed' form, to which a cover note was attached confirming, 'There were no service craft or civil aircraft operating in the area at the time of the sighting.'[4]

By this time the photographs had hit the press, a media circus erupted, and the lagoon was swamped by news reporters. Three large indents were discovered in the muddy floor beneath the nest.[5] Could they have been made by a tripod-like landing apparatus? Then a local woman discovered a series of strange teardrop-like markings[6]— round at one end and pointed at the other — in loosely ploughed soil not far from the nest. Could they have been alien footprints?

The headlines grew as similar 'nests' were found in other parts of the lagoon. Reports of more nests flooded in from throughout the region, followed by a spate of UFO sightings. Previously undocumented sightings also came to light, such as that of another tractor driver who lived and worked close to Horseshoe Lagoon; Max Menzel claimed that in 1959 he had encountered 'a brilliant, large conical craft, approximately 30 feet long, hovering over a sugar cane field'.[7]

The plant matter samples taken from the initial nest were examined by the Queensland University's botany and physics departments. They were measured for radioactivity; one sample tested positive, and then only at very minimal levels, which university staff considered insignificant.[8]

The following week, a story in Brisbane's *Courier Mail* stated RAAF officials had discounted the possibility the nests had been formed by helicopters: 'The RAAF said that in depressions left by helicopters the grass usually ran in an anti-clockwise direction. The main nest found at Tully ran in a clockwise direction.'[9]

Two weeks later, the Secretary of Commonwealth Aerial Phenomena Investigation, Department of Air, released a statement including the following: 'There is no explanation for the visible phenomena reported but it could have been associated with the result of down draughts, willy willies or water spouts that are known to occur in the area.'[10]

This sounds unlikely. Down draughts usually require tight, steep valley walls to create the appropriate chimney-like qualities for them to manifest; water spouts generally appear above oceans and lakes, and need a much larger body of water than a lagoon to form; and willy-willies, or 'dust devils', tend to occur mostly in arid desert-like landscapes, none of which matches the terrain around Tully.

At the time local stock route inspector Alf MacDonald also refuted the willy-willy theory, pointing out such natural phenomenon usually leave behind a trail of dirt and debris.[11] Pedley also refused to accept the Department of Air's explanation: 'I've seen wet whirlwinds and I've seen dust whirlwinds . . . It wasn't a whirlwind.'[12]

Media interest in the occurrence eventually waned, but over the next few years UFO sightings continued throughout the area, including one from a pair of locomotive men who in 1971, upon stopping their train to investigate a strange light in a cane field, ended up under sedation in hospital suffering from hysteria.[13]

Sites similar to the Tully nest were subsequently reported from other parts of Australia. In 1972 in Tooligie Hill, South

Australia, after his neighbours had reported a strange red light in the sky the previous night, farmer Robert Habner discovered a 2-metre diameter ring in his wheat field.[14] A similar circle was reported from Navarre, Victoria, the same year.[15]

More recently, in 2004, a set of four mysterious circles was uncovered at Conondale, inland from Queensland's Sunshine Coast. Two local teenagers, Eli Colbran and Tom Braby, stumbled across the rings in dense blade-grass while mountain biking. Colbran recalls how taken aback he was: 'My guts sank as I thought about what they could be. And realised that they were. I was a little scared.' The boys reported their find to local paper the *Range News*, whereupon local crop circle experts or 'cereologists' turned up to study the site, determining the rings were not manmade.[16]

But the most spectacular discovery remains George Pedley's at Tully. In an interview with ufologist Chalker in 1981, 15 years after the event, he recalled the craft which created the circles as being 'something similar to . . . two saucers, face to face . . . it seemed a silvery grey – a blue grey . . . I thought it was a solid thing . . . I didn't see any portholes . . . antennas [*sic*] or anything like that.'[17]

The unassuming farmer, who both witnessed a UFO and stumbled across what was possibly the world's first 'crop circle', sounded as flummoxed by the encounter as he was the morning it occurred. Perhaps his comment to journalists directly after the event sums up his experience most succinctly: 'Had anyone asked me a week ago if I believed in flying saucers, I'd have laughed and thought they were nuts. But now I know better.'[18]

Chapter 17
The Westall UFO conspiracy

If there is one case which stands out in the annals of flying saucer folklore, it is the Westall UFO conspiracy. Still enshrouded in secrecy more than 40 years later, the Westall case was the close encounter to end them all: featuring mysterious craft, an aerial pursuit, crop circle-like landing sites – even an alleged cover-up involving shadowy men in black! And to top it off, the event was witnessed by more than 150 onlookers. In many ways, Westall may be one of Australia's greatest mysteries ever.

The drama started to unfold at approximately 11 a.m. on Wednesday April 6, 1966. The setting was Westall High School, located in the Victorian suburb of Clayton South, 20 kilometres southwest of Melbourne. Just before class broke for recess, a trio of domed silvery discs appeared in the skies above.

The first to notice was a PE class working out on the school's oval. Calisthenics came to a halting stop, as each member of the group gazed skyward in shock and awe. Within moments the entire class, including teacher Miss Muir, was nudging the fence at the edge of the sport field, staring agape at the inexplicable craft overhead.

Former school prefect Dr Ian Gordon remembers peering through a classroom window with other students and seeing 'a classic flying saucer shape',[1] silver blue in colour, hovering in the sky. Before long, most of the school had become aware of the disturbance and, as the recess bell rang, many rushed outside to investigate.

This is how one former fifth form (Year 11) student later described the events in Westall High School's journal – *The Clayton Calendar*:

> Suddenly, the school came alive with excitement. Everybody began running down toward where the girls were. I was among the surging mob. I had seen something that looked very unusual in the sky. As I looked up, I saw a dazzling, silvery object around some pine trees which grew on a ridge about a quarter mile directly behind the school.[2]

Amidst all that frenzy, it's difficult to assess exactly how many students and staff actually saw the craft, but researcher Shane Ryan, who has been collating information on the event since 2005, estimates the figure to be more than 60.[3] Former student Marilyn Eastwood remembers the object as being 'round, with a hump on top and round things underneath'.[4] One description given particular credence is that supplied to local newspaper, the *Dandenong Journal*, by science teacher Andrew Greenwood:

> It was silvery-grey and seemed to 'thicken' at times. The thickening was similar to when a disc is turned a little to

show the underside. The object was never really stationary. It seemed to move from side to side and up and down.⁵

Many witnesses were so fascinated by this object they failed to see two smaller craft hovering nearby. Those who did see them include Joy Clark and Suzanne Savage — both students in Greenwood's second form (Year 8) science class. Speaking to Clark today, it is clear she remembers the event vividly. 'I saw three craft. They were flying saucers,' she told us. 'They were absolutely what we saw in the comic books way back then — the saucer with the thing that spun around and a dome on the saucer. One was much bigger. And the other two were the same but smaller. Like two little escort vehicles. The big one was the one that really stuck in the brain.'

Suzanne Savage, however, suggests the size difference of the discs could have been due to perspective: 'One looked bigger than the other two. But the other two may have been further away.'

Let's just freeze the moment temporarily and relocate 2 kilometres northwest to Clayton North Primary School. This is where, also at recess the same morning, young pupil Dee Sardikay spotted a strange craft in the sky.

'I remember it clear as day,' she says. 'Like a shiny 20-cent piece. About the size of a bus. I used to watch *Lost in Space*. It was kind of like their spaceship. It was a clear day except for a few puffy clouds. At first I thought it was a plane. Then it went right over in front of me and I could see it was a disc.' Sardikay describes the flying saucer as having flown from Clayton South (the location of Westall High School) towards Clayton North (where her primary school was situated) then back again in the direction from whence it had come.

Along with a friend who also witnessed the flying saucer, Sardikay reported the sighting to a teacher, only to find herself reprimanded for making up stories. She subsequently kept the incident to herself, not even telling her parents. Decades passed until she happened upon a *Woman's Day* article in 2006, featuring Clark, Savage and another observer interviewed about the Westall encounter. With great relief she made contact with the ladies, thankful to have her recollection vindicated.

It is also worthy of mention that on April 2, 1966, four days prior to the sightings at the high school, a colour Polaroid photo was taken of a UFO above the Melbourne suburb of Balwyn. Preferring to remain anonymous, the man who took the photograph assumed the pseudonym 'James Brown'. Because of this, the copyright trail of his shot has unfortunately become impossible to trace. But according to Victorian UFO researcher George Simpson, the mystery photographer was both a respected businessman and member of the Jesuit community – not someone likely to fake such a photograph. We have viewed the shot and confirm that it shows a craft matching very closely the description provided by most Westall witnesses: domed and saucer-shaped, hovering over suburban treetops. Some ufologists suggest it may even have been from the same fleet of three that buzzed the school. Either way, the existence of the shot can't help but add credence to the Westall witnesses' claims.

Back at the Westall High School the crowd of curious onlookers had grown considerably. Substantiating Dee Sardikay's story, many claimed one of the mystery craft darted across an open paddock, in a northwest direction, before returning to its initial position above a stand of pines. Suzanne Savage recalls, 'They were hovering above the trees. And the bigger one went down. It dipped behind the trees. It went down for five minutes.'

This UFO is believed to have landed. Some witnesses also describe the other two saucers dipping below the tree line as well. Either way, their aerial manoeuvres drew the attention of light aircraft taking off from Moorabbin Airport, roughly 4 kilometres from the school, and several civilian planes approached the zone. Science teacher Greenwood describes how, flying at a low altitude, they began to encircle the craft, playing a kind of 'cat and mouse' game.[6] The amateur fifth form journalist from the Westall High School journal relates how the craft 'tilted on about a 45-degree angle and started to move into the distance, gradually gaining height. The planes increased their speed and began to follow it. But the object streaked away leaving the planes behind.'[7]

Savage's recollection is eerily similar: 'It banked on its side and took off real fast. I remember when it turned on an angle it was like when the sun hits a mirror. It shone. It flared. And then it took off really quickly.' The other mystery objects followed.

At this point we have a fleet of three UFOs hovering in the sky, witnessed by teachers and students of two schools – Westall and Clayton North. When seemingly menaced by other aircraft, they soar off into the wide blue yonder – never to be seen again. The drama plays itself out over a 20-minute period, culminating just before the bell rings to mark the end of recess.

But more strangeness was yet to surface. According to a report in the *Sunday Age*, the first witness to spot a ring of flattened grass – speculated to have been the UFO's landing site, and in size and shape not unlike the Tully saucer nest uncovered in Queensland four months earlier – was out-of-towner Shaun Matthews, whose family leased land for their horses nearby. He rushed excitedly to the location, perplexed at what he had stumbled across: 'There was a circle in the clearing . . . like it had been cooked or boiled!'[8] Within minutes this marking was itself encircled by curious onlookers, Matthews recalls, as 'a heap of kids . . . came charging through to see what happened'.[9] The errant students were herded back to class by teachers, and we can only imagine the discussions during fourth period in local classrooms

The military showed up at lunchtime, although no witness is absolutely certain which wing of the armed forces they represented. 'They were in khaki in jeeps with camouflage,' recounts Joy Clark. 'To me they were the army. They pulled up in their jeeps and jumped out of the back.'

Shortly afterward the school was also swamped by media and Clark found herself, along with two other students, being interviewed on-camera by Channel Nine News: 'When we were talking to the reporter a strange man appeared from nowhere and put his left hand on my shoulder. He said, "You stop talking and go back in school." I presumed at the time he was a police officer because he was in a blue uniform. But he may have been air force. He turned to the cameraman and told him to go away as well.'

Clark and her cohorts wound up in detention, but the television report nonetheless went to air that evening – including footage of the intrusion by the official. The original film has since mysteriously disappeared. One legend has that it was sent to Sydney at the personal request of Sir Frank Packer, who at the time owned the network. It has never resurfaced.

Amidst all the chaos an assembly was called by the school's principal, Mr Samblebe, now deceased. According to Suzanne Savage, 'He said he'd been hearing stories about flying saucers. He said it was a load of rot, that if anyone speaks of it again there'd be trouble, and we just weren't to speak of it again.'

Despite this warning, hordes of fascinated youngsters returned to the circular site for a closer look after school. There is a general consensus amongst these witnesses that the flattened ring of grass was approximately 9 metres in diameter. One ex-student, Jacqueline Argent, says the circle 'was not a swirl, but rather as if something had come straight down'.[10] This suggests that instead of being created by a rotating helicopter-like blade, it was caused by the weight of a heavy, circular object. Another former student, Kelli Rehberg, clearly remembers three tripod-like holes within the circle, suggestive of landing apparatus.[11] According to researcher Ryan the ring was probably viewed by more than 100 onlookers.[12]

It is at this point the cover-up conspiracy begins to take hold, with many witnesses speaking of another mysterious military unit showing up later to destroy evidence of the site by setting it alight. Today, the Department of Defence will neither confirm nor deny whether this took place — or even if they investigated the incident at all.

As we pull into the suburb of Clayton South on a clear, sunny autumn afternoon, it seems far from the kind of place where such a drama could have unfolded; in fact it resembles

The Westall UFO conspiracy

any number of quiet suburbs in the semi-rural belt outside of Melbourne.

Much has changed in the town over the past four decades. Many witnesses moved out as they moved on with their lives, while others have remained rooted in the area. Westall High School is now Westall Secondary College – home to the Westall English Language Centre, established to cater for the vast influx of immigrants to the area which started with the opening of migrant hostels in the 1970s. Nonetheless, as we stand on the edge of the oval where Miss Muir and her girls made their first sighting, some Pacific Island boys in baggy T-shirts amble by, enquiring sardonically if we're looking for flying saucers, and it quickly becomes evident to us the UFO incident has cast a long shadow over local folklore.

From here on our search becomes somewhat *Rashomon*-like, in that the facts become endangered of being obscured by the multiple perspectives of differing accounts. Some witnesses claim the UFO landed behind the trees, where a golf course is located today; others that it landed amongst tress; still others, such as Joy Clark, believe the site where it landed has been built over by suburbia. Adding to all this confusion, of course, is the tyranny of time.

We have arranged to meet one witness, who prefers for 'family reasons' to remain anonymous, and who remembers the landing site being amongst the trees. From the grounds of Westall Secondary College we can see, looming over nearby suburban rooftops, the stand of pines amongst which the UFO dipped. We head towards it, no more than a five-minute walk, finding it now sandwiched between a children's playground and a football field. It is as innocuous a spot as one is likely to find on the edge of any Australian suburb; yet in the late afternoon light, the trees seem to cast somewhat eerie shadows. They fall upon the entrance to the Grange Reserve, a stretch of heath protected by wire fence for the benefit of local wildlife and, according to some witnesses, the site of the alleged UFO landing.

The anonymous witness, who we will refer to as Dharma (in honour of the legendary unmade UFO conspiracy film 'Dharma Blue' planned by the late Hollywood producer Don Simpson), claims to have seen both the UFO and the landing circle. She recalls the site being cordoned off and, the day after the incident, Thursday April 7, 1966, military personnel showing up at a neighbour's home, demanding to be taken to the site. The neighbour was driven to the Grange and instructed to stay aboard the vehicle as soil samples and measurements were taken. Dharma also claims to have been amongst the dozens of witnesses who two days later, Saturday April 9, 1966, saw the unit return to the site and incinerate it.

We meet Dharma outside the gated entrance to the Grange and follow her inside, wending our way along a meandering but well-trodden dirt trail. The vegetation is low and scrubby, with intermittent patches of acacia. Eventually, we arrive at the site where some claim the UFO landed. A circular patch of green scrub grass is apparent, markedly more verdant than the surrounding vegetation. This would not be inconsistent with a small-scale burn-off conducted decades ago. As any bush firefighter knows, burnt areas tend to grow back with a vengeance; the flames consume tangled undergrowth, benefiting the habitat considerably by allowing in moisture to germinate fresh seeds. This is known as regeneration, and the roughly 12 metres in diameter area revealed to us by Dharma certainly seems to have benefited from such a process.

As we photograph the spot, we can't help but wonder who the mystery men were behind it all. Even the *Dandenong Journal* reported on its front page in the week following the event how 'military personnel had been in the area', and that 'witnesses reported being spoken to, or later visited by, these personnel'.[13] Journalists from the newspaper contacted the army, which flatly denied the claims.

The *Dandenong Journal* also complained how its efforts to report the story were hampered by the reluctance of Westall High School to permit interviews with eyewitnesses.[14] Rumours abounded that staff members were warned not to talk about the matter publicly, and that one teacher who had taken photographs of the landing site had the film seized and his job threatened by school authorities.[15] It was as though a wall of silence had been put up around the school — broken only by science teacher Andrew Greenwood.

Adding to the layers of conspiracy, Suzanne Savage contends Greenwood himself was put under extreme pressure by both the education department and other government powers to remain silent. 'He told me the headmaster Mr Samblebe gave him hell for the rest of the year,' she says. 'He was paid a visit and threatened by airforce officials. They told him that if he were to speak of the incident again publicly, they would discredit him and he would never teach again. He left Westall at the end of that year. He was more or less pushed out. He went to work for a private school.'

Savage is one of the few Westall witnesses still in contact with Greenwood, who since his comments at the time has reputedly shunned media and remained tight-lipped on the matter. 'I spoke to him two years ago,' she recounts. 'And he will not speak of it in public. He's still scared about what could happen to him.'

We have noted during our visit to Clayton South that because of its proximity to Moorabbin Airport, the constant drone of an endless procession of light aircraft can be heard in the distance, buzzing the skies like angry bees. Although such planes feature incidentally in the Westall drama, some cynics have put the entire event down to a case of mistaken aerial identity — suggesting light aircraft were simply confused for spacecraft. Joy Clark is quick to shrug this notion off: 'Because we were so close to the airport, we were used to the planes flying over. And we knew what planes looked like. These were nothing like planes . . . This big shadow came up over the playing field. And we all looked up. And oh my God . . .'

But this does make us wonder about the involvement of the other aircraft in the sky — the Cessnas apparently drawn to the alien craft like moths to a flame. Moorabbin Airport records showed several small planes taking off on the morning of the incident, but no flight logs made mention of UFOs. Similarly, no reported sightings were made to the Department of Civil Aviation.

But what of the elusive craft themselves? Were they of alien construction or secret military design? The aircraft most approximating the flat shape of flying saucers are those incorporating flying wing 'stealth' technology — although it should be pointed out they generally tend to be triangular rather than circular in design. The first true 'stealth' aircraft was probably the Gotha Go 229, developed in Germany during the last years of World War II.[16] As soon as the war ended, US military brass initiated Operation Paperclip – the recruitment of German scientists from Nazi Germany in order to obtain as much advanced German technology as possible before the Soviets did the same.[17] Attempts were also made to secure weaponry, and it is rumoured a Gotha Go 229 was transported to the US for evaluation. Either way, in 1988 Gotha Go know-how appeared to have been spectacularly resurrected in the flying wing design of the now-legendary B-2 stealth bomber (a US military 'black project' since 1979).[18] It is generally assumed throughout the previous three decades of the Cold War other 'black project' prototypes were also developed. But the notion of a secret US test plane making runs above an outer suburb of Melbourne in 1966 still remains unlikely. As Joy Clark puts it: 'If someone could tell me it was experimental craft then I would accept that. But I don't accept that it was a light aircraft. And I don't accept that it was a weather balloon. Because of how it looked and how it moved. It moved so quickly.'

It would be remiss of any investigator examining the Westall situation not to at least consider the possible role of mass hysteria. In a 2009 article in science magazine *Cosmos*, editor Wilson da Silva questions why some people have a tendency to accept paranormal phenomena.[19] He points out 'collective delusions have occurred throughout history' and that human perception is 'prone to being unreliable'. According to da Silva symptoms of mass hysteria include 'rumours and extraordinary public anxiety' as well as 'shared cultural beliefs or stereotypes'. He also cites 'amplification of these by the mass media, as well as reinforcing actions by the authorities such as the politicians, the police or the military'.

Let's have a quick look at such scientific notions in regard to the Westall event. The more people who perceive an event, the more inherent veracity we can assume it carries – and with more than 150 people claiming to have either seen the flying saucers or the landing rings, it is doubtful the reports could be put down to unreliable human perception. With the Easter holiday weekend approaching at the time, it could be projected the witnesses were not suffering undue anxiety; in fact, to the contrary, most were probably looking forward to a relaxing break. A potential contributing factor could have been that the Westall sightings were reported near the apex of the Cold War, and that recently the new medium of television had taken hold in most lounge rooms across Australia, supplying a near endless spectacle of science fiction programs including *Star Trek*, *Lost in Space* and *The Twilight Zone*. But although amplified by the media, the Westall incident was certainly not reinforced by authorities, which from the sound of things did their best to shut down all reference to alleged extraterrestrial activity.

'It's been a total cover-up from long ago,' insists Joy Clark. 'I think it was hushed up because it was a genuine sighting and they were scared to admit it.' To put this assertion to the test we contact the Department of Defence and enquire whether they acknowledge any army or air force involvement in the incident. We are informed that Department of Defence records dating back more than 30 years are transferred to the

National Archives; if any records pertaining to the Westall event exist, that is where they would be held. National Archives informs us there are no such files. We inform the Department of Defence about this and ask for their comment – but are soundly ignored. Next we make similar enquiries with the Department of Infrastructure, Transport, Regional Development and Local Government (incorporating what was in 1966 the Department of Civil Aviation). The response is the same. Finally, we are informed by Clayton Police Station there are no records of such an incident ever being reported.

We compare notes with veteran UFO researcher Bill Chalker, who in 1982, 16 years after the Westall event, was the first civilian researcher to be granted access to classified RAAF files at the Directorate of Air Force Intelligence offices in Canberra and also files from the Department of Aviation (as it was known in the 1980s) in Melbourne. He informs us that after an exhaustive search over a two-year period, during which he did find reference to other UFO sightings, he found no files pertaining to the Westall incident.

More recently ufologists Dianne Harrison and Keith Basterfield commenced the task of establishing the Australian UFO Disclosure Project, aimed at getting secret government files opened up. Citing the Freedom of Information Act, and not without some struggle – including initial claims from the RAAF that some of the files had been destroyed – they managed to secure thousands of pages of classified information.[20] But once again nothing on Westall.

Nevertheless the fact remains that more than 60 people, including students and teachers, insist three UFOs hovered above two schools in 1966. More than 100 claim to have seen proof of a landing site. After 45 years of government denial of the incident, not one witness has retracted their testimony. The fall-out still seems almost tangible; talk to some of the witnesses involved and you can feel how real is their angst, how painful their need to know what actually happened. Despite numerous entreaties to government bodies for an explanation or investigation, Westall's eyewitnesses still have no sense of closure.

For some witnesses it may never end. As Joy Clark puts it: 'I don't care what anyone says. You can't take it out of my brain. I had never seen anything like it in my whole life. And I've never seen anything like it since.'

In many ways, it could be said some witnesses are themselves 'lost in space', caught in a surreal state where although they are certain of what they experienced, they are equally certain that, to the extent of current scientific knowledge, what they saw was inexplicable. Some cling together like members of a support group, with a 40th anniversary reunion staged in 2006 and a web group founded by researcher Shane Ryan constantly gathering more members. Hopefully there is some solace for them in the knowledge the truth is out there and could someday prevail.

Meanwhile, the mystery lives on.

Chapter 18
The Valentich disappearance

Terrifying tales of the Bermuda Triangle, a stretch of water in the North Atlantic where dozens of aircraft and vessels supposedly vanished into thin air, remain amongst the most perplexing of modern paranormal folklore. Beginning with the mysterious loss of Flight 19, a squadron of five bombers in 1945, fascination with whatever dark forces were at play in this region flourished through ensuing decades. With government agencies never quite able to present convincing reasons for the baffling disappearances, many UFO researchers turned to laying blame on alien hands. But just as Bermuda Triangle fever was hitting its peak in the late 1970s, a disappearance was to occur on this side of the world, one easily as chilling as anything to occur in the Atlantic, and which would go on to earn one of Australia's iconic stretches of water its own sinister sobriquet: the Bass Strait Triangle.[1]

At 6.19 p.m. on October 21, 1978, 20-year-old Frederick Valentich, a pilot with 150 hours flight experience,[2] took off from Moorabbin Airport outside of Melbourne aboard a Cessna light aircraft. His destination: King Island, situated in the middle of Bass Strait. The conditions: light wind with good visibility.[3] But Valentich was never to arrive. Approximately 45 minutes into what should have been an 80 minute flight, and having just passed Cape Otway on the mainland to head out into the Strait, he reported sighting a large unidentified craft passing above him at high speeds. A little more than five minutes after his initial sighting, radio transmissions from his Cessna ceased abruptly and inexplicably. A sea and air search was launched the next morning, but tragically no traces of evidence were found.[4] It was as though both pilot and craft had vanished into thin air . . .

The case hit headlines not just in Australia but across the globe. Making the disappearance particularly haunting was the final exchange between Valentich and the Melbourne Flight Service Unit based at Essendon, Victoria. Indicating very strongly a UFO was involved in the disappearance, it commences with Valentich asking air traffic controller Steve Robey about other aircraft in his vicinity:

> Valentich: Melbourne, this is Delta Sierra Juliet. Is there any known traffic below five thousand [feet]?
>
> Robey: Delta Sierra Juliet . . . No known traffic.
>
> Valentich: Delta Sierra Juliet, I am . . . seems to be a large aircraft below five thousand.
>
> Robey: Delta Sierra Juliet, what type of aircraft is it?

> Valentich: Delta Sierra Juliet, I cannot affirm. It is four bright . . . and it seems to me like landing lights.

Pilot Valentich then reports the mystery craft dipping towards his Cessna:

> Valentich: Melbourne, it's approaching now from due east towards me . . . It seems to me that he's playing some sort of game. He's flying over me two, three times at speeds I could not identify.
>
> Robey: Delta Sierra Juliet. Roger. What is your actual level?
>
> Valentich: My level is four and a half thousand [feet] . . . Four, five, zero, zero.
>
> Robey: Delta Sierra Juliet . . . and you confirm you cannot identify the aircraft?
>
> Valentich: Affirmative.

Within moments the UFO looms closer, affording Valentich a clearer view:

> Valentich: Melbourne . . . Delta Sierra Juliet . . . It's not an aircraft! It is . . . [open microphone crackle]
>
> Robey: Delta Sierra Juliet . . . Can you describe the — errr — aircraft?
>
> Valentich: Delta Sierra Juliet . . . as it's flying past it's a long shape . . . [crackle] . . . cannot identify more than it has such speed . . . [crackle] . . . It's before me right now Melbourne!

> Robey: Delta Sierra Juliet. Roger. And how large would the — errr — object be?
>
> Valentich: Delta Sierra Juliet. Melbourne, it seems like it's stationary. What I'm doing right now is orbiting and the thing is just orbiting on top of me also! It's got a green light and sort of metallic-like, it's all shiny on the outside.

After providing his most detailed description of the UFO, Valentich then loses sight of it:

> Valentich: Delta Sierra Juliet . . . [crackle] . . . It's just vanished!
>
> Robey: Delta Sierra Juliet?
>
> Valentich: Melbourne, would you know what kind of aircraft I've got? Is it a military aircraft?
>
> Robey: Delta Sierra Juliet . . . Confirm the — errr — aircraft just vanished.

But as quickly as the UFO disappears, it reappears:

> Valentich: Delta Sierra Juliet . . . It's . . . [crackle] . . . now approaching from the southwest!
>
> Robey: Delta Sierra Juliet!
>
> Valentich: Delta Sierra Juliet . . . The engine is rough-idling . . .

As the Cessna exhibits the first signs of engine trouble, Robey enquires what action Valentich intends to take. The pilot seems unsure whether to continue for King Island or head back to Melbourne. It will be a decision he never gets to make:

Valentich: That strange aircraft is hovering on top of me again... [crackle]... It is hovering... and it's not an aircraft!

Robey: Delta Sierra Juliet!

Valentich: Delta Sierra Juliet! Melbourne... [open microphone crackle (17 seconds)... followed by an unexplained sound... and then silence]...

With the last words uttered by Frederick Valentich, Australia's greatest air mystery had begun. Initially with an Orion long-range reconnaissance plane, joined later by four more RAAF aircraft and assisted by several civilian sea vessels,[5] the region was scoured for almost a week. Search parties failed to recover any traces of plane or pilot.[6] An official Department of Transport investigation was launched. Its findings, delivered three years later, were inconclusive: 'The reason for the disappearance of the aircraft has not been determined' but was 'presumed fatal'[7] for Valentich.

So what did happen to Valentich and his Cessna? The transcript of his final exchange leaves no doubt he believed something was in the sky above him. Could a close call with an alien vessel have caused his engine to stall, sending him plunging into the ocean? A popular precept of UFO lore, as featured in the classic Steven Spielberg film *Close Encounters of the Third Kind*, is that proximity to a flying saucer can make a vehicle's engine stop. UFO researcher Keith Basterfield has compiled a detailed list of 79 cases of vehicular interference by alien craft in Australia,[8] and ex-NASA scientist and ufologist Dr Richard F. Haines has investigated 56 cases worldwide involving electromagnetic effects on aircraft caused by proximity to a UFO.[9] Haines's report shows these effects range from obstruction of automatic direction finders to total electrical system power loss. Could this have happened to Valentich's Cessna?

There is much debate amongst the UFO fraternity as to exactly how flying saucers might be powered, but one of the more popular theories is electromagnetic propulsion — some type of ion drive which would operate by charging atomic particles and directing them into a jet-like thrust. A natural progression of this theory would be that such a craft would in turn cause an electromagnetic field, possibly capable of interfering with the electrics of other engines in the vicinity.

Such a virtual scenario could fit the Valentich case. The pilot first reported engine trouble as the unidentified object flew over him. Radio silence less than a minute later suggests a critical event such as high speed impact with the water may have occurred. Of course, in such a case, one would expect to find debris on the ocean's surface — a major sticking point for many ufologists who have studied the case. To explain the lack of wreckage, some have gone so far as to suggest not only Valentich — but his craft as well — was subject to a mid-air alien abduction. This is not a new notion, having been used before by Bermuda Triangle researchers to explain both vanishing airplanes and vessels. Of course, it is a hypothesis reliant on a certain stretching of the imagination, incorporating as it does not only an alien craft, but a craft equipped with a 'tractor beam' (a hypothetical device referred to in many science fiction works with the ability to attract one solid object to another).

According to news reports at the time, Guido Valentich, the pilot's late father, expressed hope that Frederick had not crashed but actually been taken by a UFO: 'The fact that they have found no trace of him really verifies the fact that UFOs could have been there.'[10]

In an interview with *The Age* in 2008, now-retired air traffic controller Steve Robey expressed doubt Valentich was taken by aliens. When asked if he believed in the existence of UFOs he commented, 'I suppose I do. But not in the definition of spaceships and little green men. I mean, you've got to keep an open mind about these things.'[11] Robey still has no explanation for the incident.

But what about simple mechanical failure? After all, if we apply Occam's razor — a favoured principle of scientists worldwide, which suggests the simplest explanation of an event is usually the best — is it not likely that Valentich's Cessna merely suffered an engine malfunction and plunged into the ocean?

There were precisely 17 seconds between Valentich's last communication and the cessation of radio transmission. Depending on the drag coefficient, a small aircraft would be more than capable of reaching a terminal velocity leading to a drop of 4500 metres in such a timeframe.

But then we still have the radio communication between Valentich and Robey to deal with. Valentich seems adamant that something — 'not an aircraft!' — was interacting with his Cessna. According to respected Melbourne ufologist George Simpson, who has done extensive research into the incident, several other pilots were gathered at radio control as the drama unfolded. One reported to Simpson that as Valentich was describing the mystery craft whizzing past, the Doppler effect could be heard in the background. (The Doppler effect is the change in sound frequency when the source of a sound is moving relative to the observer. It is most commonly noticed when a vehicle with a siren approaches, passes and recedes into the distance. The pitch of the sound is higher on approach and lower upon passing.) This would reinforce Valentich's startled claim that a mysterious flying object was buzzing him.

Simpson also relates how the Department of Transport had intended to quash the contents of Valentich's radio exchange until one of the aforementioned pilots passed his story on to the media, whereupon a censored version of the transcript of the exchange was ultimately released. Unfortunately, no copy of the original taped exchange is available today. Its whereabouts is one of the mysteries of Australian UFO history. Valentich's father Guido was furnished a copy by the authorities, a duplicate of which was sent by a UFO group to Dr Richard F. Haines in the US for analysis.

Haines reported back an interesting anomaly; prior to the end of transmission, after Valentich's final words, a series of metallic scraping noises can be heard, described by the ufologist as '36 separate bursts with fairly constant start and stop pulses bounding each one', and with 'no discernible patterns in time or frequency'.[12] Although intriguing, the source of these noises and their significance has never been established. Authorities suggest it may have been the sound of the Cessna striking the water, but as author and researcher John Pinkney points out in his excellent dissection of the event in his book *A Paranormal File*, aircraft equipped with VHF radio technology – such as

Valentich's Cessna — could not communicate a signal below 3000 feet (900 metres). In Pinkney's words, 'They simply couldn't have heard him, via radio, hitting the water — and they damn well know it.'[13]

As in any case visual evidence is more compelling than audio evidence. And the sheer number of UFO reports from across the southern coast of Victoria on the night of Valentich's disappearance is astounding[14] — some sources claiming up to 50.[15] Of these sightings, which came from a cross-section of the local community,[16] more than a dozen refer to an 'erratically moving green light in the sky'[17] partially matching Valentich's description of the other craft.

Adding weight to these sightings is a series of photographs by amateur photographer Roy Manifold, who was taking sunset snaps with a tripod-mounted camera at Cape Otway 20 minutes before Valentich first encountered trouble over Bass Strait. When Manifold viewed his prints he discovered some revealed a mystery aerial object. Due to the efforts of Pinkney, along with Paul Norman from the Victorian Unidentified Flying Object Research Society, one photograph made it onto the front page of *The Australian*. The RAAF contended it was merely a shot of a dissipating cloud. Looking at the photo today, it's hard to tell. The blurry object on the righthand side of frame, silhouetted by the setting sun, certainly appears to be in motion. Our first impression is that it may be an out-of-focus seagull, but apparently an analysis by a US saucer group concluded it was in fact a UFO, possibly leaving a vapour trail.[18] Could Manifold's eerie photo have actually captured the alien craft heading towards its fateful interaction with Valentich's Cessna?

Not all theories included the involvement of a flying saucer. One suggested a disoriented Valentich was flying upside-down and mistook the reflection of his own craft in the water for another craft. This theory is unlikely due to the fact that a Cessna has very little aerodynamic propensity for upside-down flight.[19] Another posited that Valentich was actually flying towards the mainland, and the green lights he reported were navigational lights marking the Apollo Bay harbour. This scenario has Valentich crashing in scrubland beyond the bay, but no wreckage has ever been stumbled upon.[20]

A more sinister conspiracy theory had it that Valentich faked the event, flew to Tasmania and disappeared. This was based around the fact that Valentich filled the Cessna's tank with substantially more fuel than necessary for a return trip to King Island – during which he was intending to both pick up some crayfish[21] and make up some hours he needed in order to qualify for a commercial pilot's licence. Also considered curious was the fact he had not organised for landing lights to be turned on at King Island's airstrip.[22] Much like Elvis but on a smaller scale, a spate of Valentich sightings made the news, the most publicised being at a service station in Tasmania. But as a seemingly stable and content man with ambitions to take up flying professionally, it seems unlikely Valentich would have a motive to stage his own disappearance. As Guido Valentich told reporters at the time, his son 'was not the kind of person who would make up stories. Everything had to be very correct and positive for him.'[23]

Until his own death in 2000, Guido Valentich never let go of the memory of his son Frederick's tragic and mysterious disappearance. He joined various UFO groups, continued to gather information on the incident and pushed the government for answers. In 1998 the Valentich family erected a monument for Frederick at Cape Otway, overlooking the strait where he vanished. Air traffic controller Steve Robey, the last man to speak to Frederick, and who had become close to the Valentich family throughout their turmoil, unveiled the memorial.[24] Ironically, it too has now disappeared.

Chapter 19
The Min Min Lights

There's not much to see in the tiny western Queensland town of Boulia. A higgledy-piggledy collection of old farm machinery, dinosaur bones and cobwebs serve as a labour-of-love museum; there's only one pub; and there are a couple of camels that plod around a dusty racetrack once a year. But for the 300 residents of this remote settlement halfway between Mt Isa and Winton, 'nothing' is where the tourist dollar is at. In fact, Boulia has very successfully made something out of nothing.

What Boulia does have is a mystery – and a darn good one. It's the home of the infamous Min Min Lights – inexplicable glowing balls of light that, over the past 150 years or so, have 'terrorised and terrified' locals and passers-by. Like any good mystery, the intrigue is in the storytelling, and to capitalise on the widespread interest in this outback phenomenon, the good folk at Boulia have taken the yarns out of the pub and into its very own attraction – the Min Min Encounter.

Built at a cost of $1.8 million, this theatrical experience has attracted up to 200 visitors a day since it opened in April 2000,

The Min Min Lights

a considerable feat considering there's really no other reason to visit the town. Incorporating animatronics, fibre optics and high-tech wizardry, it's a 45-minute tribute to the art of outback bullshit, introducing visitors to the story of the Min Min Lights through waxwork characters who claim to have witnessed the mysterious glowing orbs themselves.

Visitors move through darkened passageways from scenario to scenario, where the figurines – themselves rather creepy and sure to scare the pants off little children – give their version of the spooky events. Each story is based on a 'true' encounter, and reflect characters from the town's history. The show concludes with a 'ride' through time, allowing the visitor to imagine their own Min Min sighting, and whetting the appetite to further explore the phenomenon.

Of course, like any good tale of the unexplained, the Min Min Lights do not appear on cue. As the Min Min Encounter concludes, 'You don't go looking for the Min Min – it comes looking for you.'

J.T. Wearne, of Bingara, New South Wales, first saw the light back in 1929 when he was droving cattle on an 1800-mile trip from Brunette Downs in the Northern Territory to Goondiwindi in Queensland. He and his cattlemen partners had set up camp outside of Boulia, and J.T. had drawn the midnight watch:

> The night was pleasantly cool, and George stayed out yarning whilst we did a few circles around the camping bullocks . . .
> At that moment we saw a car coming from the direction of Winton, and George said, 'There's a car coming, I'll stay out here until it gets past, in case it scares the bullocks.' He stayed

with me for at least another 10 minutes, during which time the light did not seem to get any closer . . . Only a few minutes after George had left me, I was amazed to see the same light again on the other side of the bullocks . . . There were no reflections from it, nor did it light up the ground directly beneath it. It appeared to be just the same as when George and I saw it first – a light from a car with a rundown battery. If I was forced on pain of death to make an explanation, I would say electricity, static or otherwise, but don't ask me to explain how the light could move so swiftly from one spot to another without any trace or sign of its passing.[1]

Nearly 70 years later, at the same campsite but in a very different era, John and Pamela Brown from Cargo, New South Wales, would also confuse the lights for oncoming headlights:

I saw what appeared to be the headlights of a car coming down the track towards us . . . I called out to Pammy, 'Here's a car coming down the track, better put the light out.' This she did and stood in the doorway to watch. To our surprise the two lights separated. One moved slowly to our right, the other moved very quickly to our left then rose in the air and moved slowly back. The other light remained motionless, increasing and decreasing in intensity, sometimes dazzling bright.[2]

In March 2007, Noel Anderson, a truck driver from Alice Springs, was driving towards Boulia after stopping for a cold one at the lonely Middleton Hotel:

On my right at about 30 degrees, I saw a light at about the height of two trees. It caught my attention because it was so much brighter than a star. The most observable fact was the pure white colour . . . It would appear for about two seconds then disappear for almost 10 minutes . . . The same white lights then appeared smaller and further away. This time at about 15 degrees to the right of my travelling direction and lower in the sky. It would appear for half a minute to one minute. This happened three of four times . . . I must say I was not scared when the light was coming towards me. However there was no way I was going to stop the truck.[3]

During the 25 years that Austrian immigrant Herda Szijarto has been delivering mail in the Boulia district, she has encountered the Min Min Lights on many occasions. The first was in 1978 — back then she had not heard of the phenomenon, so she kept quiet about the experience. Later she would tell ABC Radio, 'I saw a big round ball, a beautiful orange colour — trees standing there, and he came straight through, and of course not knowing what it was, I got sort of scared.'

As her sightings became more frequent, so Herda began to challenge the mysterious lights. 'This Min Min Light was coming fairly close, and I said right, I couldn't take photos of you, I'm gonna shoot ya — and I know I shot it because it was so big and I couldn't possibly miss it, and all it did was go away as if to say, "Well, you're a lousy shot".'[4]

So what exactly are the strange lights that provoked Herda to draw her weapon? Some claim they are supernatural in origin, ghosts of the past, tormented souls. Others swear they are extraterrestrial in nature, precursors to alien probes. Sceptics and scientists alike claim the phenomenon is a natural occurrence, anything from torch light bouncing off dingoes' eyes, to the reflection of distant headlights caused by atmospheric inversion, to emu or owl feathers tainted with a bioluminescent fungi.

What is certain is that the local Indigenous people knew of these lights before European settlement, believing they were *debil debil* – the souls of departed relatives or stillborn babies. Others believe the sightings 'after white man started killing the blackfella' – perhaps the result of a mass slaughter which took place in 1878 in retaliation for some killings of white settlers.

The phenomenon of lights associated with death is not unique to Indigenous Australian society – in other parts of the world, they are known as 'ghost lights', 'will-o'-the-wisp', 'jack-o'-lanterns' or 'ignis fatuus', meaning 'foolish fire' (as it is considered foolish to attempt to follow or capture such a phantom light).

In the British folktale about the jack-o'-lantern, Jack was a man so despicable that even the devil didn't want him, condemning him to wander the Earth for all eternity. When Jack complained about having no means to light his path, the devil tossed him an ember from hell, which Jack placed in a carved pumpkin – the genesis of the Halloween tradition.

On the vast plains of outback Queensland, imagination fuelled by alcohol and loneliness, it's little wonder such evocative tales from the mother country found a home, perhaps morphing with local Indigenous folklore to create the legend of the Min Min. It certainly wasn't too long after the establishment of the town of Boulia in the 1800s that the stories started flowing in, becoming as much a part of the local ethos as bulldust and flies.

While the lights have been experienced in a wide radius surrounding the town – and indeed in other parts of Australia, including Central Australia and the Grampians in Victoria – the epicentre of activity is the old Min Min Hotel, a ruin located 73 kilometres east of Boulia, just off the road to Winton. Surrounded by hectares of dusty, flyblown nothingness, all that remains of the former pub is a bottle dump and a couple of decrepit graves, an eerie and spine-tingling sight, particularly when a chill wind whips over the flat plain.

Legend has it that the old Min Min pub was once a roaring shanty, a den of iniquity so notorious for its murders and rapes that it was burnt to the ground in righteous retribution. It was not long after this act of vengeance in 1918 that the strange lights began to mysteriously appear, terrorising unsuspecting passers-by who chanced upon the ruins.

The most famous of these tales recounts the story an unfortunate stockman who, on passing one cloudy night, was set upon by a glowing ball the size of a small watermelon hovering over the graveyard. Terrified, the man galloped towards Boulia with the light in hot pursuit, arriving in a lather of sweat two hours later.

Considering the drive from the desolate site to Boulia in an airconditioned four-wheel drive takes a good hour, this story does seem a little far-fetched – but since that encounter, many people claim to have seen strange lights rise up from the graveyard and go bounding through the air across the stony expanse.

Not surprisingly, alcohol has played a role in many of these encounters; in fact, the town admits that many of the stories are fuelled – or at least exaggerated – by rum.

While some locals (drunk or otherwise) suggest the lights are the result of extraterrestrial exploration, the UFO theory has largely been dismissed by serious Min Min researchers. More common is the theory of 'earth lights', or 'unidentified aerial phenomenon (UPAs)', natural physical mysteries such as extreme forms of ball lightning or 'earthquake lights' – luminescent displays triggered by seismic activity.

In 2003, a neuroscientist from the University of Queensland, Professor Jack Pettigrew, claimed to have unlocked the secret of the Min Min, even purporting to have created his own spooky lights. He embarked on the research after personally encountering the lights, which he first thought was the planet Venus.

'But it didn't set,' he told ABC Science Online. 'It went down to the horizon and then sat on the horizon for some time.'

On another occasion, he was driving with two other colleagues when they saw what they thought was the eyes of a cat shining 50 metres in front of their vehicle. When they stopped and turned out their own headlights, the lights remained aglow, bouncing around with a life of their own.

'We had a big argument,' Pettigrew said. 'No-one could agree what it was and how far away it was.'

Science was to provide some clues. Using a car compass, Pettigrew and his companions drove off across the plains, calculating that the light they'd seen was 300 kilometres away over the horizon.

Pettigrew theorised the Min Min lights were caused by the same factors responsible for Fata Morgana, a phenomenon whereby landforms beyond the horizon appear to hover above it in an inverted form. These mirages are caused by temperature

The Min Min Lights

inversion, where cold air is trapped under a layer of warmer air, making light near the ground refract in a curved path.

To test his theory, Pettigrew decided to create his own Min Min. First he had to choose appropriate weather conditions — a cool evening following a hot day with little wind. He then set out in his car, driving 10 kilometres away over a slight rise and into a watercourse, below the normal line of sight of such a distant light.

According to Pettigrew, six witnesses observed the light of the car floating above the horizon. And to back up his claims, a spectacular Fata Morgana of a distant mountain appeared on the horizon the following morning, supporting his theory the Min Min had been due to specific atmospheric conditions at the time.[5]

While this explanation may be scientifically plausible, there are many who have been terrorised by the mysterious 'ghost lights' who insist the theory is too simplistic, failing to take into account the often sinister approach of the lights, or the fact the legend pre-dates the existence of cars.

What is certain is the Min Min Lights remain a compelling mystery, as well as an endearing part of Australian folklore. Personally, next time we visit Boulia we intend to stake out the site of the old Min Min Hotel at midnight, thermos of Bundy in hand and an infrared camera by our sides. If nothing else, we will have experienced a quintessential night under a starry outback sky, an extraordinary event at any time . . . in a place where anything is possible.

Chapter 20
UFO hotspots

It can be difficult to define exactly what constitutes a UFO hotspot. The number of sightings and reports in any given area tend to wax and wane over time – corresponding with, amongst other factors, the number of UFO enthusiasts in the local region and the relative interest shown by local news editors.

In the United States the UFOCAT database – maintained by the Centre for UFO Studies, which was founded by renowned scientist Dr J. Allen Hyneck who, initially hired by the military to debunk flying saucers, went on to become a believer – geographically pinpoints tens of thousands of UFO reports from around the world. A table gleaned from this database, ranking the top UFO hotspots in Australia, bases itself on complex criteria, including the numbers of various types of close encounters per head of population.[1] Oddly to some ufologists, it lists Tully in Queensland as Australia's top UFO stalking ground, whereas in our own investigations we found the skies above this tiny town in the Sunshine State to have been less busy than others since its infamous 'saucer nest' case in 1966.

Because it is our intention to untangle rather than further entangle this confusing puzzle, we took a more straightforward approach — defining Australia's UFO hotspots simply as those places which have generated the most buzz.

The Top End, Northern Territory

One such place is the Top End, where it seems UFO hunter Alan Ferguson's 'little black thingies' aren't the only mystery craft being spotted in the skies. In fact, if local headlines are to be believed, one could even fear Darwin is again under threat of invasion — this time by aliens. 'UFO "dive-bombs" couple' . . . 'Sceptic politician saw UFO' . . . 'Miners saw UFO' . . . 'Fishos catch sight of UFO' . . . From engineers to housewives to itinerant 'long-grassers', the sightings seem almost incessant.

According to Rebekah Cavanagh, reporter for the *Northern Territory News*, 'reports just come in randomly'. Witnesses tend to pop by or phone up the paper's offices any time, sometimes with photographic evidence. Amongst the more fascinating photographs are those taken near the centre of Darwin in January 2009 by retired Department of Conservation worker Mark Schmutter. The three shots, snapped during the day, show a strange airborne object against a partially cloudy sky. Quite startling is that while UFOs are usually described as chrome-coloured, silver or silver-grey, the one in Schmutter's snaps is a bright metallic blue — not dissimilar to the 1970s retro blue recently repopularised for muscle cars.

Meeting Schmutter at his home in a quiet northwestern suburb of Darwin, we find him to be a sincere, upfront and intelligent bloke with no apparent agenda, simply someone who saw something he couldn't explain and photographed it. His shots were captured from the balcony of a high-rise city apartment rented by a vacationing friend whom Schmutter was visiting.

'I was taking some shots of the city. And I spotted this thing go across the sky. So I followed it, and clicked off some shots before it disappeared,' he explains. 'I saw it both with my bare eyes and through the camera. My mate saw it too.'

Schmutter describes the astonishing object as moving away from him in an easterly direction: 'The sun was setting and reflected on it. It hovered for a while then shot straight up into the clouds. It moved really quickly. We kept looking, but it didn't come back.'

A self-possessed 79-year-old, Schmutter radiates the demeanour of a man who has seen a lot, and of whom it would take a lot to rattle. He was intrigued but not overly excited by his photographs until showing them to his daughter Robyn: 'I wasn't going to report it at all. But I told my daughter and she put them on the computer and enlarged them. She said, "Jesus Christ! I've got to ring the *Northern Territory News* about this." She got on to the *News* and the *News* got on to me.'

Schmutter, the reluctant UFO photographer, soon found himself a front page headline. Today, he remains bemused by the whole experience. 'I didn't really believe in UFOs before that,' he says. 'Now I don't know what to think.' Nor does Schmutter know what to think about the vivid hue of the object in his photo – then again, there's no reason to assume outer space is necessarily any more hoon-free than Earth.

A series of photographs very different in nature but similarly compelling were taken several months after Schmutter's by mother-of-three Kym over the suburb of Palmerston, southeast of the city and coincidentally where the studios of Buzz FM (from which Alan Ferguson broadcasts his UFO reports) are located. They were snapped from her patio with a recently acquired camera phone as a storm was approaching her house.

'I was playing around with it so I could send my family pictures of what happens most afternoons in the wet season,' explains Kym, who for 'occupational reasons' prefers not to reveal her full name. Until she downloaded the shots onto her computer she had no idea what she had caught on photograph.

'I noticed the lights in one of the pictures then I went back through the other photos and saw there were more unexplained lights in the photos,' she says.

In the clearest shot an elliptical circle of light can be seen hovering directly beneath a heavy build-up of dark, ominous cloud. A similar object can be discerned further in the distance. In other shots, more objects are apparent. A fleet of lit-up flying saucers invading suburbia? Or a bizarre electrical effect?

'There was some lightning at the time. But the shape of the lights is very different,' says Kym. 'If it was streaks you'd think it was lightning. But these are circles.'

If not flying saucers, what are they? Sheet lightning has been known to create a diffuse brightening on the underbelly of cloud formations. But it typically lights up larger areas and exhibits undefined edges. Also worth taking into consideration is that the photos reveal several objects of seemingly the same shape, and the fact that neither Kym nor her husband, who was with her at the time, saw anything strange in the sky.

Some ufologists put this phenomenon down to alien technology, with talk of advanced cloaking devices which can render craft invisible to certain spectra of light. They posit that although the naked eye may not glean the presence of such a concealed UFO, a camera potentially would. And as far-fetched as the idea of invisibility fields may sound, earthbound scientists have recently conducted experiments with artificially engineered 'metamaterials' to bend light around objects,[2] with the ultimate aim of developing devices that actually cloak objects from visual light.[3]

Meanwhile, Kym remains unsure about what she managed to inadvertently capture in her photographs: 'The concept of UFOs is rather scary. I don't like thinking about it. I'm not terribly keen on believing in them. So I'm still on the fence.'

Not unknown for their ability to fence-sit on any number of issues, politicians too are hopping down to claim close encounters of their own. In July 2008, poultry-farming parliamentarian Gerry Wood, MLA, was taking his usual early morning constitutional outside his home in Howard Springs, not far from Palmerston. Power-walking past a paddock at dawn, Wood was surprised to witness a soundless object whiz overhead.

'It was travelling at high speed like a jet fighter. But it made no noise whatsoever. It was low to the ground. Just above the treetops. It had no lights, although there was light reflecting off its nose,' declares the Member for Nelson. Unlike Alan Ferguson's hamburger-shaped UFO, the mysterious craft observed by Wood suggested another form of fast food: 'It was like a hotdog roll.'

Wood viewed the airborne object for approximately ten seconds before it disappeared into the distance. With his mobile phone he immediately contacted relevant departments to see if any aircraft were officially aloft in the area at that time. They were not.

'Now I'm a chook-farming UFO spotter!' jokes the politician. Although, describing himself a 'science man rather than an astrology man', he is cautious to admit what he saw was of alien nature, speculating, 'It may have been some secret military aircraft.'

Whether such advanced aircraft are linked to alien intelligence remains a big question mark. But unless the tropical heat is getting to the locals, something is in the air over Darwin.

The Grampians, Victoria

In stark contrast to the open landscape and searing climate of the Top End are the rugged but temperate Grampian Mountains in western rural Victoria, once referred to as Australia's 'Gateway to UFOs'.[4] As we pull into the tiny town of Halls Gap, nestled in the shadows of this spectacular ancient sandstone range, its otherworldly grandeur cannot help but invite thoughts of alien activity.

We are here because of stories of strange lights in the mountains. In 2002 a spate of sightings in a Grampians valley prompted a *Melbourne Herald Sun* reporter, along with a staff photographer, to investigate. Perched above the valley, equipped with both binoculars and a telephoto camera, they viewed and snapped shots of 'white lights . . . hover[ing] above the tree line' and 'a small red light [which] flew towards a companion and disappeared'. Reporter and photographer alike were left with 'no understanding whatsoever' of what they had seen.[5]

Representatives of a Melbourne-based UFO research group have also ventured into the Grampians, claiming to have captured similar images on video tape. The director of the group was quoted as proclaiming, 'There's a big one called "the commander" and it operates in concert with smaller ones.'[6] This sounded interesting, and we contacted the group with a view towards the possibility of examining their footage. Our enquiries went ignored.

But sightings have continued unabated, with reports coming in at the rate of roughly one per month. So what's going on in the skies around the Grampians?

We commence our investigation by wandering into the pub at Halls Gap and casually dropping the term 'UFO'. Within minutes, we unleash a deluge of stories. We hear from a local restaurant chef who, one night two years previous, was witness to an enormous green light flying overhead as he stood in his backyard — 'bright enough to light up the sky'. The next day, when he related his bizarre experience to other locals, some claimed to have experienced exactly the same phenomenon at exactly the same time. We also hear from a young lady who swears that while horseriding beneath the mountains with her sister on a clear and cloudless day, they both saw a shimmering silvery craft silently dive from the atmosphere at incredible speed, swoop over the field, arc back into the sky, then disappear.

The tales continue, but we find ourselves most intrigued by mention of a shadowy local figure referred to as an 'alien hunter', and described as tall, moustachioed, bearing an ET tattoo on his neck and gun-shy with the media. Informed that he, too, has collected video footage of the 'lights' — as many locals simply refer to the phenomenon — we make it our mission to track him down.

A lead from a local café sends us to the town of Stawell, home to the Stawell Gift, one of the world's richest annual foot races, and the Stawell Clock, underneath the face of which two bronze gold-diggers become re-animated on the hour at certain times of day. They are swinging into action to the sound of Winchester chimes as we arrive, and we wonder momentarily if we've actually taken a wrong turn into *The Twilight Zone*.

We have learnt the alien hunter works here at the local abattoir. Being a weekend, the facility is eerily deserted. With the stench of rotting carcass and congealed blood, and the plaintive bleating of a herd of lambs packed tightly in a parked trailer in the background, the slaughter yard might yet prove a suitably creepy backdrop for our first meeting with the man — who by now has grown in our minds into a larger than life figure. But he is nowhere to be seen.

Then a chance encounter with a coworker leads to us to a quaint and well-kept home in the back streets of Stawell. We are introduced to a charming retired couple who refer to each other as 'Mum' and 'Dad'. Dad, as it turns out, has accompanied the alien hunter on several nocturnal excursions in the Grampians — and he has in his possession a DVD copy of the UFO group's video! For a brief moment we think we've hit pay dirt. But as we view the footage over a freshly brewed cup of tea, we can't help feeling somewhat disappointed. The grainy footage, shot at night, randomly follows a group of white and red lights that seem to be cavorting on the valley floor. At no point do they appear to rise above the skyline. When the camera zooms in for a closer look, the low levels of illumination reveal nothing more than shapeless moving blurs. We can't figure out what they are — although they seem to a having a good time.

We are still keen on viewing the alien hunter's personal footage, in the hope it can shed more light on the 'lights'. Having failed to raise him on the phone for the last hour, Mum provides us with his address. Bidding the couple a fond farewell we head to the other side of town. Our desperate knocks elicit no response, so we insert a handwritten note in his flyscreen door, entreating him to contact us.

Our valued acquaintance George Simpson, an informed and approachable UFO researcher and a great ambassador for the field, has warned us of the dangers of getting too excited about the 'lights'. Since lights can potentially emanate from a variety of sources other than flying saucers, they too often lead to cases of misidentification. Simpson insists the principal aim of a UFO researcher should be the collection of either physical proof or a definitively clear photograph. Nevertheless, we decide to head back into the Grampians to conduct our own night-time vigil.

Driving up the steep winding pass cut into the wave-shaped cuesta escarpment of the Grampians, we arrive at Reed Lookout, fronting onto the impressively expansive Victoria Valley, just prior to sunset. From our perch we see vast stretches of woodland, broken only by tiny thread-like tracts of snaking dirt road. As night falls the temperature drops with it, and chilly winds slicing across the Victoria Range make our stake-out almost unbearable. Teeth chattering, we endeavour to hold our camera lenses steady as we scan the valley floor for any sign of lights. But apart from a giant inky void we see nothing. Frozen to the bone in less than an hour, we beat a hasty retreat to the warmth of our vehicle and descend the pass, heading back for Melbourne.

On the road out of Halls Gap we pass a phalanx of kangaroo shooters heading into the mountains, spotlights attached to the roll bars of their four-wheel drive pick-ups. As we stop at a service station to top up our tank, some of these 'spotlighters' pull in beside us. Striking up a conversation, we learn they are headed for one of their favourite hunting grounds – the Victoria Valley. Have we just discovered the secret of the Grampians lights? Could the glowing white objects be the 'roo shooters' spotlights, zigzagging the valley floor as they hunt their quarry? The glowing red objects their tail lights as they hit the brakes?

We toss the theory around until, on the outskirts of Melbourne, the mobile phone rings. It is the elusive alien hunter – finally!

For the next hour he regales us with tales of UFO sightings (as well as, oddly enough, tales of panther, puma and Tasmanian tiger sightings: he is a man who sees a lot). We listen intently and take notes diligently, the call ending with him agreeing to provide stills of his footage for further examination. Perhaps we will be proven wrong. Perhaps the mystery lights in the Victoria Valley really are of extraterrestrial origin . . .

But next morning he retracts his offer via an email sent from a public computer in a library. Did the men in black get to him? All we can do is shrug off our disappointment, mark it down to the alien hand of fate, and beam ourselves up the east coast to an appointment with our final UFO hotspot.

The Blue Mountains, New South Wales

Ever since renowned artist Norman Lindsay settled in the Blue Mountains of New South Wales in the early 1900s, the area has grown into somewhat of a haven for creative types — as many drawn by the preternatural hue of the landscape as the idyllic Bohemian lifestyle.

The mysterious majesty of the mountains also draws countless visitors, making the area a popular destination for daytrippers and weekenders out of Sydney. But if an ever-expanding stack of reports is to be believed, this renowned range, once considered so forebodingly impenetrable by early settlers, is also attracting visitors of another kind.

According to ufoinfo.com, a website representing a conglomerate of established UFO magazines and societies, the Blue Mountains has been Australia's number-one hotspot for UFO encounters since the 1950s, when a flying saucer flap in the region created such a stir it made the front page of the *Sydney Morning Herald* and prompted the RAAF to be put on standby – with a warning issued to not provoke aliens.[7]

As we step off the train at Katoomba station and make our way through a pedestrian underpass leading to the town centre, we pass a vividly coloured mural painted by local artist

Vernon Treweeke — a man known as 'the father of Australian psychedelic art', and featuring flying saucers hovering in the sky. We emerge from the unearthly tunnel into the light of day of Katoomba town centre, and continue our trek to the home of Ann Taylor, a witness to one of the more spectacular UFO sightings of the past decade.

Taylor has been an astronomy enthusiast from an early age. Armed with a Schmidt-Cassegrain C8 telescope, capable of magnifying an object almost 50 times original size, and having spent countless nights scanning the heavens with amateur astronomy clubs, she's a woman who knows what she's looking at in the sky.

In April 2000, after sketching some star constellations near Katoomba's Echo Point, overlooking the Jamison Valley and its renowned Three Sisters rock formation, she was returning to her daughter's home nearby when she noticed a bright glow begin to emanate from some distant clouds above.

'I stopped to have a look and — to my amazement — saw a spherical object descend through the cloud base,' she recalls. 'It just hovered there, as if suspended.' Fortunately, Taylor was carrying her camera. She snapped off the first of three photos while the orb-like glow, according to her estimate, was about a kilometre away.

'It then started to descend in a diagonal manner down towards me across the valley,' she continues. 'It stopped about 50 feet up in the air above the tress and sat there, hanging in mid-air, glowing. All the night sounds of birds and insects just stopped.'

At this point Taylor took her clearest and closest photograph of the object, in which a circle of bright white light can be seen, radiating incandescent beams illuminating the surrounding bushscape. 'It hovered for about five minutes,' she says. 'Then it moved out horizontally across the valley. As it reached the other side I took another photo just as it shot off skywards to disappear.'

Ironically, for someone who has had such an extraterrestrial experience, Taylor is a longstanding member of SETI (Search for Extraterrestrial Intelligence), the collective dedicated to making contact with whatever developed alien life forms are out there in the cosmos. In 1974, SETI beamed a message into space via FM radio waves from a radio telescope in Arecibo, Puerto Rico. Encoded as binary digits, the message included information as simple as the numbers one through ten, to such complex data as the formulae for sugars and bases in the nucleotides of DNA.

While waiting for a response, SETI has enlisted the help of more than 180,000 volunteers worldwide who, working from home to crunch data on their PCs, provide the collective with one of the most powerful computers on Earth. A dedicated member, Taylor has so far spent more than 30,000 hours processing information.

As we view Taylor's UFO snaps on her computer, they form a compelling triptych – showing the apparent approach, arrival and departure of a mysterious glowing airborne object. Backed by her sincerity and experience in stargazing, we are left with no doubt something strange is in the skies over Katoomba.

But with much data to crunch ourselves we feel our heads starting to spin. To give the left (or analytical) parts of our brains a rest, we decide to tackle the UFO conundrum using the right (or creative) parts. As we leave Katoomba we make a snap-decision to drop in on the home studio of the artist whose work so enthralled us upon our arrival in town – Vernon Treweeke.

Treweeke is one of the great characters of the Blue Mountains, where he has made his home for the past 30 years. Amongst the influential crop of young artists which came of age in the swinging 60s, and which included former boarding school mate Brett Whitely, Treweeke has works in the National Gallery of Australia. UFOs and alien landscapes have been a recurring motif in his work, often sharing the canvas with voluptuous female figures of otherworldly proportions.

The radical artist greets us warmly and considering the busy schedule that has him working until dawn most mornings – preparing for his first Sydney exhibit in 30 years – he is very generous with his time. He also seems more than eager to explain his theories about UFOs and how his belief in alien life forms informs his work.

'Here in the Blue Mountains research groups head out at night looking for UFOs,' he explains as he leads us down to his dark studio basement. 'They've had a lot of sightings. I've been out looking with them. But I've never seen any. So I've based most of my work on people's descriptions of what they've seen. Which has been helpful. I can get quite a good detailed description from people.'

One might wonder why an artist would choose to have a dark rather than brightly lit workspace. The question is answered at the bottom of the stairs, where we are accosted by a large fluorescent painting of a UFO destroying twin pyramids with a laser beam – a comment, the artist tells us, on US military imperialism. The colours are so vivid that under the black lights fixed to the ceiling of the studio they virtually jump off the canvas, and we are reminded Treweeke is the man who introduced Australia to psychedelic art.

But for the full 'head trip' his works are best viewed through what Treweeke calls 'prismatic Fresnel lenses'; he hands us each a pair and as we don them we feel as though we've been transported to an alien planet. The lenses create chromatic depth, separating the fluorescent colours of his enormous paintings, the reds coming forward and the blues sinking back into the canvas. The effect is particularly startling on a portrait of a pair of aliens.

'I'm convinced we're not alone in the universe,' says Treweeke. 'We tend to think we're the only intelligence. But that's absurd when you think of the scale of the universe . . . It's mind-boggling just to think how big our galaxy is. And there are millions of other galaxies even bigger than ours out there. There are more stars in the universe than there are grains of sand on the beach.'

Our minds are boggled by the effects of Treweeke's psychedelic art. As we view another piece featuring numerous flying saucers hovering around a female face in outer space, we ask the artist if he has a theory as to where saucers such as those witnessed so frequently in the surrounding mountains come from.

'I'm sure some are alien craft,' he replies. 'But to me some could be travellers from the future travelling into the past.

The UFOs are their viewing platforms. They wouldn't be able to interfere with history. So they avoid contact.'

As we take in the alien-looking psychedelic landscapes in the works adorning Treweeke's studio walls, some seemingly enormous enough to step into, we ruminate on this theory. Physics tells us nothing can move faster than light. But theoretically, if one were to break the light barrier, one would find oneself travelling back in time. According to current scientific technology, the concept of exceeding the speed of light is considered impossible. But as Arthur C. Clarke once stated, in the second of his three laws of prediction, 'The only way of discovering the limits of the possible is to venture a little way past them into the impossible.'[8]

Just as we get our minds around the technologically-advanced-future-time-travellers theory, Treweeke hits us with another: 'I also think it's possible some UFOs are created by enlightened people who have trained their minds to levitate. I've heard descriptions from military pilots about how they've come across luminous discs that have flown circles around them. Like a collective halo. Running rings around a symbol of death and destruction. They could be sending us a message of peace.'

On that heartening note we bid the artist farewell. Descending the Blue Mountains after our mind-expanding experience, it takes a while for us to adjust to the reality of a non-psychedelic world. And as we sight the familiar cityscape of Sydney looming in the distance, the idea of a UFO streaking past – whether from an alien planet, the future, or a conglomerate projection of enlightened minds – no longer seems totally beyond the realm of possibility.

Part 3
Cryptozoology

Chapter 21

Yowie – Australia's biggest cryptid mystery

It was a sight Matthew James was not expecting, least of all in suburban Canberra. But as he stood in his garage in October 2009, packing boxes in preparation for a house move, he was confronted with an incredible vision – a stocky, hairy monster standing in the corner, staring him in the eye.

'It was covered in hair, with long arms that nearly touched the ground, and it didn't have much of a neck. I'd say it was a juvenile – and it was inquisitive about what I was doing. It was definitely trying to communicate with me,' says James. 'At the time, I had no idea what I'd seen – it was only later that someone told me it was a yowie. From what I know now, that's definitely what it was.'

The yowie, of course, is the big daddy of all Australian mystery monsters, the Aussie cousin of North America's Bigfoot or Sasquatch, Himalaya's Yeti or Abominable Snowman, and the Hairy Moehau of New Zealand. Like his hairy counterparts around the world, he is as elusive as he is controversial, often seen but never photographed; and he is also the unwitting recipient of many a hoax, with attention-seeking jokers announcing they have indisputable evidence of his existence.

To the original inhabitants of this continent, however, the yowie is an important part of folklore, making numerous appearances in Dreamtime legends, particularly on the eastern seaboard. According to the *Australian National Dictionary*, the name is derived from *yuwi*, a term used by the Yuwaalaraay people of northern New South Wales to denote a dream spirit. In other regions, the 'hairy man' is known as *yahoo*, *yaroma*, *doolagal*, *mumuga* or *quinkin*; and invariably he was a hideous monster – about the same height as a man or taller, powerfully built, with long arms and large hands equipped with sharp talons. In some descriptions his feet are set backwards, giving the impression he is travelling in the opposite direction, and he is said to have a horrible stench. He generally lives in dense bushland in mountainous regions, and he is a solitary, nocturnal creature with a frightful growl.

In the Blue Mountains of New South Wales, the fearsome *yaroma* was a human-devouring goblin of sorts, a large, powerful creature with human characteristics and hair on his body. In his book *Aboriginal Legends of the Blue Mountains*, author Jim Smith describes it as a flawed monster: 'If a man be pursued by a *yaroma* his only means of escape is to jump into a waterhole and swim about, because these creatures cannot wet their feet. They have long teeth which they sharpen on rocks in the high ranges.'[1]

According to Australian Museum archaeologist Val Attenbrow, the Dharawal people of the Sydney region spoke in fear of the *mumuga*, who lived in caves and mountainous country and overpowered his victims with his gaseous emissions — unless they had a firestick with them.

'He possessed great strength, had very short arms and legs, with hair all over his body but none on his head,' Attenbrow writes in his book *Sydney's Aboriginal Past*. 'He couldn't run very fast, but because of his stink he didn't need to.'[2]

While many of the 'hairy man' monsters of Indigenous lore are depicted as human sized or even smaller, the bigfooted, giant version also makes an appearance. In the New South Wales government's Register of Historic Places, it states that the Dharawal people believed in two other kinds of hairy men — *kuritjah*, little hairy leprechaun-type creatures 'about the same size as a milk carton'; and *dooligah*, giant hairy men 'almost as big as trees'.

The legend recounted in the Register says that the *dooligahs*, because of their size, could not find enough food to fill their bellies, so one day, one crept down to where some children were hiding from their friends:

> The Dooligah grabbed the children, burying their faces in his long hair so their screams could not be heard, and ran to his cave where he promptly ate the fattest one, and imprisoned the other two so he could fatten them up for later . . . The little Kuritjahs went to the Dooligah cave and waited until the giant hairy men had fallen asleep. Then they crept into the cave, found the children and released them.[3]

With the first European settlers' nerves shot to pieces by the strange sights and noises permeating the alien Australian bush, so the legends of hairy monsters began to filter into the new colony. One of the first reports came from 1790, when a handbill printed in England reported how English sailors had captured a giant at Botany Bay and brought him back to England to be exhibited at Plymouth. The handbill was headed, 'A description of a wonderful large wild man or monstrous giant, brought from Botany Bay', and featured a crude sketch of the beast, who was described as '9 feet 7 inches high' with a 'long beard strong as black wire, body and limbs covered with strong black hair', and 'the nails of his fingers and toes were like talons'. Although clearly a hoax, it's interesting that this description so closely resembled the Indigenous people's 'yowie', and soon reports began to flood the media, reaching hysteria levels by the middle of the 19th century.

In the mid-1880s, the wife of Sir Henry Parkes's caretaker at Faulconbridge, NSW, was gathering sticks in her garden when a commotion amongst the fowls attracted her attention. 'On looking up, before her stood a Thing about seven feet high,' a report in the *Sydney Illustrated News* states. 'The black hair growing on its head trailed weirdly to the ground, and its eye-balls were surrounded by a yellow rim. It was – the hairy man!'[4]

In 1882, a naturalist, H.J. McCooey, sent the following letter to the *Australian Town and Country Journal*:

> When I first beheld the animal it was standing on its hind legs, partly upright, looking up at the birds above it in the bushes . . . I think that if it were standing perfectly upright it

would be nearly 5ft high. It was tailless and covered with very long black hair . . . the length of the forelegs of arms seemed to be strikingly out of proportion with the rest of the body.[5]

According to the Australian Yowie Research (AYR) website, there have been almost 10,000 reported sightings of an ape-like creature in the Australian bush during the past 200 years. Another cryptonaturalist, Tim the Yowie Man, says he receives at least two or three reports a month: 'There's still a steady flow of people claiming there's something unusual in the bush, a hairy ape-like creature.' Tim says that most of these sightings come from average 'Joe Blows' – people not in it for publicity, who have simply seen something they can't explain.

Publicity, however, inevitably follows, with Australian tabloids lapping up any whispers of inexplicable phenomenon. So too do the small yet enthusiastic brigade of yowie researchers, who jump on each report with territorial voracity, claiming the story as their own like colonial explorers of old.

In one of the most recent yowie reports, two women from Wingham, near Taree, were terrified by a creature on the side of the road on August 7, 2009. 'We were about 200 metres from the top of the hill . . . when I looked back up at the road and . . . ahead in the headlights [was] this big hairy animal thing on the side of the winding road. It was about eight foot high and four foot wide,' one woman told the *Manning River Times*. 'I was s**t-scared and thought I better not mess with this thing in case it lifts the trailer up and tips us over the bank edge.'[6]

Absolutely convinced that what they'd seen was a yowie, the two women were happy to share their story with a local reporter as well as several yowie researchers. However, when we asked one witness if she was willing to elaborate on her experience further, she said she'd been advised by one yowie researcher 'not to talk unless there was money involved'. She went on to say she had reached her threshold on the situation, feeling it had all gone 'over the top'.

With interest in the topic bordering on hysteria, it comes as little surprise that people who claim to have seen a yowie are driven to ground, ultimately refusing to talk about the experience. This was certainly the case with Australia's highest profile yowie witness, former Queensland Nationals senator Bill O'Chee, who cheerfully admitted to the *Gold Coast Bulletin* on November 17, 1977 that he and several chums had seen a yowie during a school camp, an experience he remembered vividly.

'About 20 of us saw it,' he told reporters. 'It was about 3 m tall, covered in hair, had a flat face and walked to the side in a crab-like style. It smashed small saplings and trees like matchsticks as it careered through the bush.'[7]

As one of Australia's most controversial politicians, famously retiring from parliament at the tender age of 33 after just eight years in the job, the interest in O'Chee's yowie story was unparalleled, to the point that he now refuses to discuss or elaborate on his story for fear of ridicule.

Other yowie witnesses, however, embrace the mystery, making it their lifetime quest to uncover the truth. Before he wore the 'Yowie Man' moniker, Tim Bull was an economics student at Australian National University in Canberra; however, an experience in dense bushland in the Brindabella Ranges in 1994 was to forever define his life.

'Out of the corner of my eye I saw this movement, and my first reaction was that it was a big 'roo,' the man now known as Tim the Yowie Man tells us. 'I looked at it and it was a big, hairy, blackhaired, bulky ape-like creature. It had really long arms and didn't seem to have much of a neck. My immediate reaction was to turn and run, but I knew if I did it might chase me. So I walked backwards step by step for what seemed like minutes, but in effect was probably 15 seconds. For all intents and purposes, to me, it was a gorilla. I only looked at it for 15 seconds or so – but that 15 seconds changed my life.'

Despite many years in the field searching for evidence of the yowie, Tim the Yowie Man claims he has never found any definitive proof that the creature exists. 'All I ever came across was anecdotal evidence of encounters,' he says. 'There was never any hard evidence – it was really frustrating. I'm almost resigned to the fact that I don't think I will get to the bottom of this mystery. Everyone who claims that they've seen something, including myself, is 100 per cent sure they've seen something – but there's not one scrap of physical evidence in the whole country that they are out there.'

With what he perceives as a lack of hard physical evidence, Tim the Yowie Man has reached a new conclusion regarding yowies: that they are actually paranormal or supernatural beings.

'When someone suggested that to me in 1995, I laughed at them. In fact, I once went to a Bigfoot conference in the United States; I was late and missed the first session of the conference. When I arrived there was a fight in the carpark where people who thought Bigfoot was flesh and blood were fighting people who thought it was supernatural. There was actual fisticuffs, they were really getting stuck into one another. That was my first introduction to the paranormal theory, and I thought it was quite outlandish.

'I don't know if I've mellowed with age or if I've just become disappointed — and it's not just me, others can't seem to find any evidence either. So that's the theory I have now.'

It is this theory that carries most resonance for Matthew James, the aforementioned witness of a yowie in his garage. As a 'sensitive' and medium, James believes the hairy figure he saw was a transcendental being, a messenger or harbinger from another realm. 'It spoke my name, psychologically,' James explains. 'There was an understanding between the two of us.'

James's case is unusual in that it happened in a confined space, well away from a wilderness area. The incident occurred in Bonython, about 15 kilometres from the Brindabella Ranges, where Tim the Yowie Man had his hairy man encounter; and while it is feasible the creature may have just ambled off course, its presence in suburbia only makes sense if yowies possess supernatural powers.

According to another well-known yowie researcher, Rex Gilroy, however, the yowie is definitely a flesh-and-blood creature grounded in reality. This 66-year-old dynamo cannot and will not rest until he finds definite proof of the hairy man — which he believes he already has in his possession. But in Gilroy's case, what he calls a yowie no longer fits the traditional description.

'The big hairy monkey creature many people call a yowie simply doesn't exist,' Gilroy states emphatically. 'We're not dealing with some ape-like beast. There are idiots out there who prefer the hairy monster theory — but if you're looking for any rare creatures, you need to go to your fossil records.'

According to Gilroy, the yowie is a remnant of *Homo erectus*, a tool-making, fire-making hominid species generally believed by the scientific community never to have inhabited Australia. Gilroy, however, is adamant that not only did these 'hairy people' pre-date the modern Aboriginal population, but that relict groups still wander remote regions of the eastern mountain ranges of Australia — evidenced by his staggering collection of fossilised skulls, stone tools and plaster footprint casts.

During our visit to Gilroy at his home in Katoomba, he proudly produces what he claims are fossilised *Homo erectus* skulls, as old as 2 million years. To our untrained eyes, they look dubiously like roundish, pock-marked rocks; but Gilroy insists his methodology of collecting and dating his findings are scientific and accurate.

According to a report in the *Bega District News* on January 13, 2006, Gilroy has in his possession what he believes to be the endocast of a primitive hominid skull dating back 7 million years, found in a volcanic plug that last erupted during the Pliocene era. Gilroy claims his 'Bega Man' not only challenges the orthodox 'Out of Africa' theory, but also sheds new light on his theories concerning the 'hairy man' of the Australian bush.

'I decided to do what any other scientist does when he discovers a new race or a new species,' Gilroy told the ABC's *Australian Story* in 2004. 'He names it. So I've just called them "Rex Beast". And I thought, well, I think I deserve something for all the work I've done.'

Something is Out There

Early ancestor of mankind, ape-like creature, supernatural being or perhaps just a feral human, overgrown and under-deodorised, whatever the yowie is it has certainly captured the imagination of Australians, who will continue to scour the continent for proof of its existence. And whatever the truth, one thing is clear: that the Australian bush still harbours many secrets — and one it may not be prepared to give up too easily.

Yowie hotspots

All it seems to take is one report — and suddenly, an area can become a cryptozoological hotspot, abuzz with researchers, reporters and hoaxers all out to make their mark on the world and perhaps be the first to provide irrefutable proof that yowies, or large hairy hominids, do indeed exist.

Hotspots, of course, come and go; and sightings tend to be cyclical. But some areas — usually densely forested, remote regions — tend to appear in the press time and time again, such as New South Wales's Blue Mountains, the Brindabella Ranges, the scrubby Pilbara of western NSW, Tully in North Queensland, and most recently and frequently the Springbrook region in southeast Queensland.

Several years ago, Springbrook proudly wore the mantle of the yowie capital of Australia. A 2.7-metre statue of an ugly hairy hominid stood proudly outside the Springbrook Homestead, a restaurant serving yowie burgers, listed on a yowie footprint-shaped menu. Inside, proprietor Andre Clayden proudly displayed his casting of a yowie footprint, and a scrapbook featured hundreds of reports from around the area.

A self-confessed 'promotions man', Clayden also ran tours of the region in conjunction with Tim the Yowie Man, tourists – particularly Asian visitors – lapping up the stories (and the burgers) with relish.

With the homestead under new management, Clayden, who now runs the nearby Springbrook Observatory, admits the yowie legend is starting to fade in the area. However, as recently as May 2009, Tim the Yowie Man made an emergency dash to the Gold Coast hinterland, hoping that a recent downpour would flush the elusive hairy man out of his lair.

'The soaked soil and muddy bogs created by the heavy rain are more conducive to animals, including yowies, leaving their footprint,' Tim told AAP hopefully.[8]

Hot on his heels, the article continues, followed Dean Harrison from the Australian Yowie Research website, returning with photographs of footprints he believes are of a female yowie and her young trailing along. On the same trip, Harrison claims to have been rugby tackled by a yowie near Gympie: 'This one knocked me flying backwards. I landed in a rockpool,' he said.[9] Not a bad effort for one research expedition.

Another recent report, this time from the Top End in April 2009, speculated that a yowie may have been responsible for ripping the head off a pet dog – a report that caused umbrage for Tim the Yowie Man.

'There have never been reports of a yowie attacking a pet or a human, except for in self-defence,' he tells us. 'To take the head off a dog – there's no other evidence, no footprints or hair samples. Seems like a strange leap of faith to think that a creature ripping the head off a dog would be a yowie.'

Something is Out There

> Tim thinks it's unlikely that yowies even live in Darwin, considering there have been very few reports coming from that region.
>
> 'I wouldn't want to be a yowie living in that hot, sticky humidity,' he says. 'You'd smell it a mile away!'

Chapter 22
The river monster

When it comes to the field of cryptozoology, it's impossible to ignore the contribution of one man, Rex Gilroy. This self-proclaimed eccentric has spent the last half century scouring the Australian bush in search of yowies, marsupial cats, river monsters and other legendary creatures, and in that time he has been called many things – 'the father of Australian cryptozoology', a genius, a fraud and a joke.

He himself is partial to the term 'guru' – 'I like the idea of followers coming and placing jewels at my feet' – and he even puts a bright spin on being considered crazy. 'There's a fine line between genius and mad,' he says. 'In ancient times, mad people were the divine of the gods.'

When we first meet with this legendary character in his home in Katoomba, just a stone's throw away from the alleged bushland haunts of many a mysterious creature, he appears a little agitated, suffering from heart palpitations and concerned that we'd been waylaid by his research assistant, who we inadvertently met earlier in the day.

After retreating to his 36-seater cinema, located in the back shed of his garden, Gilroy visibly relaxes amongst his beloved collection of movie memorabilia – including lobby cards of *Creature from the Black Lagoon*, *Forbidden Planet* and other old-school classics. As we chat, the suspicion he first directed our way – based on his assumption that we were fellow cryptozoologists set to undermine him – dissipates, and soon he is talking openly about his career, his setbacks and his enemies.

Being a small and closed community, the world of cryptozoology is, in Gilroy's opinion, a competitive one, with splinter groups, factions and professional jealousies. Gilroy's resentment of pretenders to his 'yowie man' throne is palpable – he sneers at the mere mention of any competitor, eliciting the venom of megalania itself as he describes them as the 'idiot faction'.

Yet Gilroy's bitterness is somewhat justified – as the man who brought the term yowie into the Australian lexicon, he feels his very persona has been hijacked. Add to that the wrath and ridicule of the scientific community, and a lifetime of misunderstanding stemming from a learning disability known as Asperger's syndrome, and one begins to understand his paranoia.

Adding even more stress is the worry about what will happen to his life's research when he can no longer spend every waking hour tending to it. Gilroy's home itself is a veritable museum – piled high with notes, books, filing cabinets and boxes of skulls and plaster castings. He has more than 50,000 insects and spiders, pinned out in glass cases or jars, plus countless photographs and hours of video footage, all waiting to be analysed.

'I have the largest natural science collection in Australia,' he laments. 'I've tried to get the local council to open a museum, but they don't want to know about it – every time I get someone interested, they pull out because I don't have university qualifications, so what I do isn't taken seriously.'

To the scientific community Gilroy certainly pushes the boundaries, challenging the textbooks and offering theories well outside the comfort zone of academia. Yet after 52 years in pursuit of his dream, nine self-published books, frequent appearances in the media and countless field trips, there's no doubting his dedication to his field or his determination to make his mark on the world.

'I'm the father of cryptozoology in this country,' he proclaimed during an interview on ABC's *Australian Story* in 2004. 'I'm the father of yowie research. Cryptozoology is the study of animals either unknown to science, or species long thought extinct that might still be with us. I don't talk the same language, I suppose, as most people, but I've spent a lifetime trying to educate myself.'

Gilroy's interest in mysterious creatures stems from 1957 when, as a teenager at Liverpool High School, he first came across a library book about the bunyip – 'which doesn't exist, by the way – it was a device invented by the Aborigines to stop children from going near waterholes'.

With an uncanny ability to recall specific dates and times in his life, Gilroy recalls his first encounter with a hairy hominid, or yowie: 'It was August 7, 1970, at 3.30 p.m. I was sitting on the first saddle of the Ruined Castle near Mt Solitary, not far from here, when I saw a hominid coming out of the scrub about 50 feet from where I was sitting. He came out of tall tree ferns; he was stark naked, had hair down to his shoulders and was digging around in the dirt, maybe with a digging stick. His skin didn't appear dark – it had a light tone, and he seemed at peace with nature.'

Since them, Gilroy claims to have witnessed yowies on four occasions – once coming across a whole family group of giant hominids in the Macleay Valley of northern New South Wales. Unfortunately, the pressure of the moment proved too much for his camera assistant, whose failure to press the correct button may have robbed Gilroy of conclusive, world-shattering evidence.

Astounded by Gilroy's ability to be at the right place at the right time, whether it be during yowie sightings, driving past thylacines crossing the road, or finding archaeological evidence poking out of the ground, we ask him how he does it – and how he succeeds where others fail.

Gilroy puts his successful collection of evidence down to an innate psychic ability – something he's had since he was a boy. 'Heather [his wife] will just be driving along, and I'll say, "Stop – there's something here." And whether it's an ancient hominid skull, a footprint or a funnelweb spider – whatever it is I'm looking for – usually, there it is. Yes, I definitely would say I'm psychic.'

But one creature continues to elude Gilroy, despite his absolute belief in its existence; a creature which could even be a contender for the title of world's most famous cryptid – currently held by the Loch Ness monster. Believing it lurks just outside of Sydney, it is the subject of his next proposed opus. He calls it the Hawkesbury River monster.

The river monster

The surface area of New South Wales's Hawkesbury River is roughly the same as that of Scotland's Loch Ness – approximately 50 square kilometres. But whereas Loch Ness has only slightly over 100 kilometres of foreshore fringe, the Hawkesbury has more than 1000! So if Scotland can boast its own giant water-dwelling creature, a suspected plesiosaur affectionately known as Nessie, why can't Australia? The answer is: we can. That is, if we are willing to accept the existence of a Mesozoic reptile which became extinct 65 million years ago . . .

Gilroy believes the existence of the Hawkesbury River monster has been known to man much longer than that of the Loch Ness monster. The first account of Nessie was in the sixth century, when Saint Columba allegedly encountered a troublesome 'water beast' and sent it scuttling away with the sign of the cross. But according to Gilroy, Indigenous rock art found in the Hawkesbury River area, depicting a plesiosaur-like creature, dates back some 3000 to 4000 years.[1]

He contends that, although eroded with time, reptilian-shaped furrows in sandstone cliffs near Wisemans Ferry, around 30 kilometres upriver from the mouth of the Hawkesbury, were carved by the local Indigenous Dharuk tribe to represent a creature known as *Mirreeular*, the 'giant water serpent'.[2] Earliest accounts of the beast from white settlers also came from this area, invariably describing it as large and greyish, with two sets of flippers, an eel-like tail, and a serpent-like head supported by a long neck.

But the first sighting to create a real splash occurred just after World War II, when Douglas Bradbury claimed that while fishing with mates at Broken Bay near the mouth of the river, an enormous sea monster rose from the water to tower 6 metres above their vessel. The panicked fishermen dropped their rods and rowed frantically to shore.[3]

Gilroy reports a slew of sightings throughout the 1970s and 80s: bushwalkers spotting the beast through binoculars while hiking on the banks of the Hawkesbury; fishermen startled, like Bradbury, by giant snake-like heads bursting from the water; and mysterious humps emerging from under the water to overturn terrified teenagers in tinnies. According to his research, the creature in more recent times has ventured as far upriver as St Albans, a tiny settlement nestled on a tributary of the Hawkesbury called the McDonald River, where one afternoon a local farmer supposedly witnessed the creature's hump emerging from local waters.[4] Most who have seen the beast estimate its length at around 15 metres (plesiosaur sizes varied significantly in their time, the largest growing up to 20 metres and the smallest a mere 2 metres).[5]

Gilroy has spent decades searching for physical evidence of the monster — journeying up and down the river as he scours the habitat for clues. Although he has managed to take photographs of a 'long, brownish shape'[6] creating a disturbance on the river's surface, which he claims is consistent with the shape of a submerged travelling plesiosaur, he is also quick to acknowledge the shots do not constitute incontrovertible evidence. Nevertheless, he speculates up to 60 specimens may be skulking beneath the Hawkesbury's surface, 'breeding somewhere offshore and laying their eggs inland'.[7] With Ahab-like determination, he remains bent on proving it.

The river monster

Of course, sea monsters, lake monsters and river monsters have been reported across the world for eons, their legends entrenched in many cultures.

Apart from Scotland's Nessie, Canada boasts both the Ogopogo of Lake Okanagan and the Manipogo of Lake Manitoba; the US has Lake Champlain's 'Champ' (which once had a $50,000 bounty placed on its reptilian head by legendary circus impresario P.T. Barnum); Sweden has the Storsjöodjuret of Lake Storsjon; Congo has the Mokele-mbembe; and Japan has Lake Ikeda's 'Issie' (so feted by locals a viewing platform was built in its honour in 1978 and inaugurated by the reigning Miss Hibiscus).[8]

But it takes a giant scientific leap to believe plesiosaur specimens survived beyond the K-T extinction event, which caused all land- and water-based dinosaurs to perish 65 million years ago. Gilroy is a researcher prepared to make that leap. With water as shelter, he believes the plesiosaur could have swum under the radar of the fossil record: 'The land surface had an ecological change. Oceans didn't. There is no reason they don't exist and are moving between here and New Zealand.'[9]

To support his theory that plesiosaurs prowl not only the Hawkesbury but Australia's entire eastern seaboard, Gilroy puts forward a sighting by experienced trawler men several kilometres off New South Wales's Central Coast. Their description matched reports of the creature seen in the Hawkesbury, the alleged encounter lasting more than 15 minutes as the sea beast trailed their vessel before plunging into the depths.[10]

There is no doubt the plesiosaur once cavorted in Australian waters. In the past 25 years, three plesiosaur fossils have been uncovered: two in Queensland and one in South Australia. The big question is: does a living, breathing specimen exist?

We consider the possibility unlikely, but tenacious investigators that we are, we head for the Hawkesbury River to see what's going on in its waters for ourselves.

Our investigation will be based around the river settlement of Wisemans Ferry, location of the site of the earliest sightings and now a popular spot for caravanners, houseboaters and waterskiers. It is situated where the Hawkesbury both branches northwest into the McDonald River and snakes southwest towards larger towns such as Windsor (where Gilroy also claims the Hawkesbury River monster has been reported).

We descend the winding Wisemans Ferry Road as a heatwave descends upon Sydney and surrounding areas. As uncomfortable as the high temperatures are, we figure they should be ideal for bringing out the reptiles – especially big ones like plesiosaurs. We pass some eccentric-looking local homes, some with driveway signs boasting 'chainsaw blade sharpening here'. We're not sure why this should be such a popular business, and it puts us a little on edge. We stop at a vantage point to take some scenic photographs of the river, impressively wide at this point. But no 'strange humps' or 'snake-like heads' are apparent.

Arriving in the rustic village of Wisemans Ferry, our concerns over chainsaw wielding maniacs are quickly assuaged. It is a charming little spot populated by friendly and chatty locals. We canvass the town thoroughly, from bartenders at the local pub to shop assistants to people on the street. Not only has no-one seen the monster, no-one has even heard of it.

The river monster

We are directed to a slender road meandering along the river bank and which leads to a succession of waterski ranches and wakeboarding schools. We talk to several proprietors and once again any mention of a monster merely elicits a glazed-over gaze. Probably just as well; the last thing a waterskier would want is the possibility of a giant snake-like head rearing in front of him as he tries to negotiate his speedboat's wake.

We decide to venture further upriver, reasoning the smaller the population, the greater the chances of the river monster legend being in circulation. We drive onto a cable ferry and, as we cross to the other side of the Hawkesbury, interrogate the operators; if anyone is likely to have spotted a plesiosaur, it would be someone who spends every day travelling back and forth across the river. We are told they have seen both dolphins and bull sharks this far upriver, but nothing remotely resembling a dinosaur. They also point out, however, that the murky river is still 60 metres deep even this far up.

Heading towards St Albans, we feel our chances diminishing as the river dries up further at every bend. In fact, just outside the tiny town the waterway becomes so silted over it has almost shrunk to a trickle. Even a platypus would have trouble scrambling from pond to pond, let alone a plesiosaur. Pulling into the Settler's Arms, we ask around. Once again nobody in this tight-knit community has heard about a river monster, nor are they familiar with any story about a local farmer seeing the creature's hump in the water.

Driving back to Wisemans Ferry on the opposite bank, we are perplexed by our lack of success in finding even a single thread of evidence to support this creature's supposed existence.

Is there really a river monster, we ruminate, or is Gilroy engaged in a quixotic quest? As we stop on the verge of a gentle bend to take a few final snaps of the river, a pair of cyclists pulls in for a rest. We strike up a conversation, which eventually turns to our monster search. We can't believe our ears when they inform us they met some campers earlier in the day who thought they had seen a dinosaur. Just as we were about to give in — a lead!

Following their directions we race off, eyes peeled. This is a particularly picturesque part of the region, with rich green flood plains stretching from road to river bank. We finally spot the bright colours of a small cluster of dome tents breaking the greenery through some shrubs, right where the cyclists told us we would find them.

The campers, who request anonymity, are happy to share their bizarre experience, which occurred two nights previous when they were camping further down river. 'We were all asleep in our tents. It was a bit windy. I heard this splashing sound from the river,' one of the three explains. 'I stuck my head out and heard it again. But it was dark. I couldn't see anything.'

The camper searched inside his tent for his torch, but couldn't find it. Grabbing his camera, he stuck his head outside his tent again and took a shot, the flash illuminating the immediate area.

'I thought I could see something tall amongst the trees. Either that or one of the trees was moving,' he continues. 'I was really freaked. I heard more splashing.'

By this point his mates had awakened, and he urgently told one of them to grab a torch. When the beam was splayed across the stand of trees on the river's edge, nothing was to be seen.

They wandered to the bank but saw nothing. After copping a ribbing, he decided to look at his snapshot. What they saw disturbed them so much they immediately pulled camp and moved upriver to the spot where we'd found them.

We ask to examine the photograph. The camper flicks through to the shot in question on the LCD screen on his camera. Framed between two trees in an inky darkness is a curved slender form. It is the same hue as the trees but not quite as high, and set further back. Rather than being crowned by leaves, it is capped with what could be perceived to be a reptilian head. Looking at the shot, it is hard to get a proper sense of perspective. Is it a branch floating downstream? Or is it the Hawkesbury River monster?

The campers have never heard of the beast they may well have encountered. And as we leave them discussing the wisdom of spending another isolated night on the banks of the Hawkesbury, we find ourselves as mystified as they seem shaken, our chance encounter reflecting two of the confounding impediments of cryptozoological research, no doubt faced many times by Gilroy: anecdotal sightings do not comprise evidence and photographic evidence is so often inconclusive.

Whereas the Hawkesbury River monster is being hunted by one man, the Loch Ness monster, which thousands of witnesses claim to have seen, has been subject to underwater photography, hydrophonic recording and sonar studies. It has been investigated by manned submersibles and had several funded large-scale expeditions launched in its pursuit. Yet it remains elusive, considered by mainstream science a mythical creature.

Something is Out There

We suspect the chances of a Hawkesbury River monster ever surfacing to be scant. Yet we find we can't shake from our minds the mysterious image in the camper's photograph. And as we climb the gentle incline leading us out of Wisemans Ferry, we catch a glimpse of a lone waterskier trailing his wake on an appropriately serpentine bend of the river, and can't help but wonder what lurks beneath.

Chapter 23
Mega shark

There are few creatures in nature which inspire more terror than *Carcharodon carcharias* — the great white shark. After all, it was the jagged gaping maw of the great white that spurred *Jaws* to become the most successful horror movie in history. The fictional shark in *Jaws* was 7.5 metres long, a surprisingly slight exaggeration for Hollywood considering the largest specimen ever caught was actually 6.5 metres. But imagine a monstrous eating machine more than 18 metres long! Such a creature existed millions of years ago. It was called *Carcharodon megalodon* — the megatooth shark. With jaws that opened wider than a man's height and teeth almost 20 centimetres long, it was the ultimate killing machine. Disturbingly, some say it still exists . . .

In October 2009 a monster shark panic hit the coast of Queensland when a drum-line, commonly used as an alternative to a shark net, hauled in a 3-metre great white off a North Stradbroke Island beach.[1] The hysteria was caused not so much by the captured shark but the state of its carcass, with huge chunks of flesh missing from both flanks. From measuring the bite radius, experts estimated the specimen which attacked the stricken shark to have been almost 6 metres in length. The perpetrator was most likely an oversized great white, but shocking photographs of the mega bites certainly brought the notion of a surviving megatooth to the forefront of the subsequent media frenzy.

In fact, considering the coasts of Australia are such a favoured feeding spot for big sharks like the great white, it is understandable many alleged sightings of megatooth have taken place in or near our waters. The most infamous of these came out of Broughton Island, 2 kilometres off Port Stephens on the New South Wales coast, in 1918 when lobster-men reported a giant shark patrolling their fishing grounds in deep water. Some described it as 30 metres long, although these estimates were no doubt prone to at least exaggeration. They claimed the enormous creature was apparently capable of swallowing whole metre-wide lobster pots — each holding up to three dozen lobsters. After menacing the island for several days the gargantuan sea beast was never seen again.[2]

Their reports were investigated by David Stead, an eminent naturalist of the time. Arriving too late to witness the creature himself, Stead nevertheless seemed convinced the men had encountered something not known to science:

> They were all familiar with whales, which they had often seen passing at sea, but [insisted] this was a vast shark . . . These were prosaic and rather stolid men, not given to 'fish stories' . . . The local Fisheries Inspector of the time . . . agreed

with me that it must have been something really gigantic to put these experienced men into such a state of fear and panic.[3]

A pair of sightings also garnering international notoriety occurred ten years later, in 1928. They were made by author Zane Grey, arguably the most successful writer of western novels of all time. Ironically, considering the bulk of his books were set in the deserts of the Wild West, the author's real passion was the sea. Grey was a fervent fisherman who made many expeditions to Australia. In fact, he is celebrated for helping to establish the sport of deep-sea fishing in Australia, particularly at Bermagui in New South Wales, which is now famous for marlin fishing. He was a patron of the Bermagui Sport Fishing Association and set a number of world records with fish caught off its coast.

He also made frequent trips to the South Pacific islands, which is where his possible megatooth encounters occurred. Off Rangiroa Atoll in Tahiti, while fishing aboard the SS *Manganui*, he claimed to have spotted an enormous yellowish shark with a 'square head, immense pectoral fins and a few white spots'.[4] Grey guessed its length to be considerably longer than that of his 10-metre vessel. Other fishermen aboard agreed with his estimate. Initially Grey thought it to be a whale shark, but soon realised he was mistaken. He observed that only the size of the creature was the same as a whale shark, otherwise it was in no way similar. 'I figured out that the fish . . . was not a harmless whale shark but one of the man-eating monsters of the South Pacific. Then I was more frightened than I remember for a long time.'[5]

Grey had heard tales of such a giant shark from local natives, and on returning to the atoll informed his son Loren of the sighting. Initially unconvinced, Loren Grey shed all doubt two days later when he joined his father on another fishing expedition to the same patch of water. In a 1994 newspaper interview he described his own sighting of the shark:

> We saw birds flying erratically over a yellow-coloured patch of water ... That patch was the giant shark swimming just beneath the surface ... It was not a whale shark ... Its tail stuck 10 feet out of the water ... I looked right down at him, and the head was as wide as [a] room. It had to be 50 feet long ... Everyone on the boat saw it. And then Pa, who had been up on the deck, comes running down and said, 'See, son, I told you; I'll make you eat crow!'[6]

In his book *Tales of Tahitian Waters*, Zane Grey elaborated even further on why both father and son were certain they had not confused the immense creature with a whale shark:

> When the great brown tail rose in the ship's wake ... I knew immediately that it was a monstrous shark. The huge round head appeared to be at least 10 to 12 feet across if not more ... It was my belief that this huge, yellowish, barnacled creature must have been at least 40 or 50 feet long. He was not a whale shark: the whale shark has a distinctive white purplish green appearance with large brown spots and much narrower head. So what was he — perhaps a true prehistoric monster of the deep?[7]

Did the Greys actually encounter what Polynesians traditionally refer to as *Magantu*, the Lord of the Deep — a mythological monster shark capable of devouring a *pahi* sailing canoe whole?

There are stories of human sacrifices being made to this giant shark, and of young islanders being sent to face him as a coming-of-age rite. Could *Magantu* in fact be the megatooth — or are both plain myth?

A more contemporary sighting of a giant shark occurred on the outer edge of the Great Barrier Reef in the 1960s. A 26-metre vessel experiencing engine trouble was forced to weigh anchor for repairs. While they waited, the captain and his crew spotted an immense pale shark swimming slowly past. They were awed by its size, which they estimated to be as long as their vessel. Experienced seamen all, they insisted the creature that skirted their vessel was not a whale.[8]

As the largest carnivorous fish ever known, the megatooth shark was firmly entrenched at the top of the marine food chain. According to Renaissance accounts, its large fossilised triangular teeth — first found embedded in rocky formations — were believed to be petrified dragon tongues. They were identified as shark teeth in 1667 by Danish naturalist Nicolaus Steno, whose paper 'Head of a Shark Dissected',[9] in which he compared the 'tongues' to shark teeth, was the first such scientific work to recognise they were the remains of a giant ancient shark which had died and subsequently become fossilised. The shark's genus — or unit of classification between species and family — was identified by Swiss naturalist Louis Agassiz as *Carcharodon megalodon* in 1835.

Megatooth stalked the world's oceans from 18 million years ago until (scientists of Agassiz's time theorised) it mysteriously became extinct 1.5 million years ago. This spanned part of the Miocene era, all of the Pliocene era and the first half of the

Pleistocene era. But their theory was thrown into doubt only decades later, by a discovery from the British oceanographic *Challenger* expedition. Under the direction of Professor Charles Wyville Thompson and naturalist Sir John Murray, the corvette *Challenger*, specially equipped for oceanographic research, sailed the Atlantic, Pacific and Antarctic oceans for four years between 1872 and 1876, collecting data and dredging specimens from the ocean floor. The expedition resulted in the discovery of 715 new genera and 4717 new species of ocean life.[10]

In the Pacific Ocean, Thompson and Murray also discovered two unfossilised specimens of megatooth teeth. One was dated at 24,000 years old and the other at only 11,000 years old, although some scientists maintain these estimates to be questionable due to manganese dioxide encrustation, caused by sea water over thousands of years and which, when scraped off, can result in a bone specimen looking younger than it actually is.[11] However, if these calculations were correct, it means megatooth was still patrolling the world's waters at the *end* of the Pleistocene era, when Palaeolithic man had already commenced farming land and was on the cusp of stepping out of the Stone Age and into the Bronze.

But could a relict population of this gargantuan shark still lurk at the bottom of our oceans today? Scientists cannot convincingly explain why an apex predator, after millions of years of dominance, would suddenly become extinct. They speculate it fed largely on whales, but realistically it would have had its choice of any course from the seafood buffet.

Fossil records indicate it was a warm water pelagic fish (found neither on the bottom of the ocean or near the shore), and would have flourished in oceans all over the world. But even if the megatooth was still around at the commencement of the geological epoch known as the Holocene Period, would it have endured the last great ice age? Between 15,000 BCE and 8000 BCE temperatures dropped dramatically. Earth lost almost one hundred genera of animals, renowned land-based casualties including the woolly mammoth and the sabre-toothed tiger. Perhaps the oceans just became too cold for the megatooth . . .

Or perhaps it survived. After all, in 1938 the coelacanth – a fish previously thought to have perished with the dinosaurs in the Cretaceous–Tertiary extinction event 65 million years ago – was discovered off the east coast of Africa. Since that first living specimen was identified, many more have been found throughout the waters surrounding the continent. A second species was even discovered in Sulawesi, Indonesia, in 1998.[12] This makes the coelecanth a classic example of *Lazarus taxa*, a term palaeontologists use to describe species which disappear from the fossil record only to rise Lazarus-like from the dead and reappear eons later. There have been many examples of *Lazarus taxa* – both on land and in the sea. Perhaps in time the megatooth will prove the most spectacular of all.

Previously unknown species also have emerged from the depths of the sea. In 1976 the scientific world was shocked by the discovery of a shark similarly named to the megatooth – the megamouth – off the coast of Hawaii. Nothing near the size of the monstrous megatooth, the megamouth is nevertheless a big fish – growing up to 5 metres in length. Yet despite its bulk, this deepwater shark's existence was previously unknown to science. Since then, 44 specimens have been caught and identified.

Something is Out There

The ocean is vast. It covers more than 70 per cent of Earth's surface, and at its deepest point, the Mariana Trench, plunges 11 kilometres. The notion that in this immense, largely uncharted matrix a very rare species of very large shark could continue to exist is by no means beyond the realm of possibility.

One problem encountered when assessing the viability of the existence of many cryptids is the sheer volume of alleged sightings by enthusiasts. As Arthur C. Clarke so aptly put it, 'I would take reports . . . more seriously if there were not so many of them.'[13] After all, if a supposed species puts in so many appearances, why is there not more hard evidence in the form of carcasses, bones, teeth or even photographs or video? The megatooth is not a cryptid to suffer from this syndrome. Sightings have been sparse but well documented, and from seemingly reliable sources.

In 1990 cryptozoologists the world over were excited to hear evidence of megatooth's continued existence might finally have surfaced. A research team commissioned by *National Geographic* had been exploring the depths of Japan's Suruga Bay, off the coast of Honshu, on the steep edges of the Nankai Trough, which plunges almost 5 kilometres below the ocean's surface. On September 13, 1989, aboard the French submersible *Nautile*, the crew was observing a series of baited cages placed on the bay floor to attract marine life. The late, legendary underwater cinematographer Ralph White, who would go on to work with top Hollywood director James Cameron on both his Academy Award-winning feature film *Titanic* and his 3D IMAX film *Ghosts of the Abyss*, was manning the camera.

Thirty minutes into the descent, at a depth of 1.3 kilometres, White was filming a shoal of deepwater sharks loitering near a cage. Suddenly a huge mass bumped the wall of the sub, which shook violently. In White's footage, the sharks can be seen scattering as an enormous dark figure skirts the periphery of the frame. The creature's head then enters frame, revealing itself as a gigantic shark, dwarfing the other specimens. It nuzzles the box then lumbers out of sight. White, along with the other occupants of the craft, was stunned: 'Parasites hung from the fluttering gills. All we could think was holy mackerel!'[14]

The research team estimated this goliath of the sea to be at least 7.5 metres long (the same size as Jaws!). It was ultimately identified as a disproportionately large specimen of the Pacific sleeper shark: a rare species, also recorded off the southern waters of Australia, but not previously known to grow more than 4.5 metres. The monster may not have been megatooth, but it certainly was an astonishing example of the colossal, unimagined denizens lurking deep in the Pacific.

But the most recent possible megatooth shark sighting came from the Indian Ocean – perhaps not surprisingly considering three of the finest examples of fossilised megalodon teeth were uncovered off Western Australia's Ningaloo Reef. The report, featured on the website of the cryptozoological television show *Animal X*, came from a petty officer with 15 years' service aboard a US navy ship sailing to Goa, India, in January 2000.

Stationed on the forecastle with two other crew members, the petty officer, who asked to remain anonymous for military security reasons, heard a loud, drawn out splashing 'like something thrashing around'. All three peered over the railing of the deck, only to see a pod of dolphins which had been following the vessel for days scattering wildly:

> We were amused at first thinking they were in a feeding frenzy when the largest dorsal fin I have ever seen broke the water and was chasing after the dolphins. At first I thought maybe it was a whale due to its huge bulk . . . The fin itself was over 10 feet tall.[15]

But the petty officer was shocked to realise the enormous creature he and his crew members were witnessing was not a whale:

> The whale theory went out the window when I saw the head of this thing. I grew up in the Florida Keys. I have seen tiger sharks, bull sharks . . . and so on. This was a shark plain and simple! The head of this shark resembled that of a tiger's. [It] came out of the water . . . and we watched this thing munching on a dolphin.[16]

The creature was officially reported as a whale. Sonar readings estimated the behemoth's length at more than 25 metres. The only whale known to attack dolphins is the killer whale. The longest specimen ever reported was 9 metres long. Could the crew of the naval vessel have actually encountered the Lord of the Deep himself – *Carcharodon megalodon*, the megatooth shark?

In January 2010, one of the most terrifying shark attacks of recent years occurred in shallow water off the coast of Cape Town, South Africa, when Zimbabwean tourist Lloyd Skinner was taken at popular swimming spot Fish Hoek beach. Twitter-user Greg Coppen, who witnessed the attack, tweeted,

'Holy shit. We just saw a gigantic shark eat what looked like a person in front of our house.' Shortly adding, 'That shark was huge. Like dinosaur huge.'[17]

Like the waters off Port Lincoln in South Australia, Cape Town is a renowned stalking ground for great whites, making the species the most likely culprit in the attack. Nevertheless, Coppen's description of the shark as 'dinosaur huge' cannot help but evoke thoughts of the prehistoric megatooth. In a later interview with the *Cape Times* he went on to describe the creature as being 'longer than a minibus'.[18]

Another witness described the shark as having Skinner's entire body in its mouth. An accurate assessment of the fish's size could not be made, since no remains were recovered for a bite radius to be determined. But if nothing more, this grim attack was tragic testimony to the fact that man-eating creatures as terrifying as Jaws are out there somewhere.

Chapter 24
Giant ripper lizard

Once upon a time, dragons stalked Australia. Enormous, slavering lizards called megalania. Measuring more than 5 metres long and weighing at least 500 kilograms, they were the ultimate predators of the late Pleistocene era, savage reptilian killing machines with razor-like claws and jaws armed with serrated blade-like teeth.

Called the 'ancient giant ripper lizard' by palaeontologists, megalania preyed upon the megafauna of its day — including the massive marsupial diprotodon. When it was on the hunt, nothing was safe. And terrifyingly, it was still stalking the continent as the first Indigenous Australians arrived. The skeleton of Mungo Man, the earliest human remains found in Australia, was dated from the same period as the most recent megalania fossils — around 40,000 years ago.

The largest lizard ever is definitely not the kind of creature one would care to stumble upon hiking through the Australian bush today. But one high profile cryptozoologist, who claims to have in his possession a plaster cast of a megalania claw print — taken from a field and not a fossil — believes such a scenario is not impossible.

Modern day sightings of the lizard king are exceedingly sparse, so before commencing our investigation into megalania, or *Varanus priscis*, we decide to conduct some face-to-face research with what scientists suggest is its closest living relative, the currently proven largest lizard in the world — the komodo dragon, or *Varanus komodoensis*.

And so we find ourselves aboard a Buginese schooner, three days journey from Benoa Harbour in Bali. Our destination is Komodo Island, a tiny island in the Lesser Sundas archipelago in Indonesia. After dropping anchor, we wake at dawn to gather on the teakwood decks to view an unforgettable crimson sunrise illuminating the Flores Sea. With no time for second thoughts, we are bundled into a Zodiac and hurtled towards Komodo Island, looming in front of us like a real life Jurassic Park: craggy, primeval, and menacing. We are about to enter the dragon's lair . . .

At the Komodo National Park headquarters, we are met by a park ranger who will act as our tour guide and safety officer. He is armed with a large forked branch, but claims his main protection against these carnivorous killers is his ability to read their behaviour. As we depart the headquarters we pass a warning sign: 'Dangerous area. Watch out. Komodo crossing. Be silent.'

We notice infant dragons clinging to high branches of surrounding trees. Until they are of moderate size, we are told, this is their only means of defence: cannibalistic komodo dragons are more than happy to eat their young. Along with horses, deer, goats and, of course, humans.

In Komodo National Park – an 1800-square kilometre World Heritage Site spanning several islands between Flores and Sumbawa – there are as many komodo dragons as human beings, around 3000 of each. Until recently, it has been a harmonious coexistence, with the villagers keeping a respectful distance from the beasts and venerating them in traditional stories.

One local legend tells of a man who once married a dragon princess, who gave birth to twins – one a human boy, the other a lizard girl. Separated at birth, the siblings grew up separately. One day, the boy met a fierce-looking beast in the forest; but just as he was about to spear it, his mother appeared, revealing to him that the two were brother and sister.

In order to appease the dragons – and to keep them at bay – villagers used to feed them animal carcasses as sacrificial offerings. But recently the practice was outlawed, with park officials claiming hand-feeding made the dragons fat, lazy and unable to fend for themselves.

According to the villagers, this has had an adverse effect, with the dragons now hungry – and ready to attack.

'They never used to attack us when we walked alone in the forest, or attack our children. We're all really worried about this,' village elder Hajj Amin told the Associated Press. With authorities not responding, the villagers made a makeshift barrier out of trees and broken branches, and requested for a 2-metre concrete wall to be constructed. This idea was rejected on environmental grounds.[1]

In early 2009, a 46-year-old park ranger named Main was doing paperwork at his desk in the national park when a 2-metre long intruder slithered up the stairs of his wooden hut and lunged at his dangling ankles. When the ranger tried to pry open the beast's jaws, it sank its serrated teeth into his hand, creating gashes that would require 55 stitches.

'I thought I wouldn't survive,' Main told a reporter, his hand still swollen three months later. 'Luckily my friends heard my screams and got me to hospital in time.'[2]

Several months earlier, a 31-year-old fisherman had been mauled to death by a dragon as he was wandered into a field to pick fruit from a tree. Two years ago, an eight-year-old boy was killed as he defecated in bushes behind his home. Others have been badly wounded after being charged unprovoked.

'We're so afraid now,' an 11-year-old schoolboy said, recalling how just a few weeks earlier students had spotted one of the giant lizards in a field behind their school. 'We thought it was going to get into our classroom. Eventually we were able to chase it up a hill by throwing rocks and yelling "hoohh hoohh".'[3]

It's not just in the wild that the dragons have been known to attack. One famously took a chunk out of Sharon Stone's ex-husband Phil Bronstein during a visit to the Los Angeles Zoo in 2001, crushing his toe and severing several tendons in his foot. His movie star wife dramatically shared the ordeal with *Time* magazine reporter Jess Cagal:

> It took a piece of the top of his foot off completely . . . all the flesh. It severed the main tendon to his big toe, the main tendon to the next toe, crushed the casing to the joints

that join the big toe to the foot. His toe was completely hanging off . . . And while I'm tourniquetting his foot and screaming for help . . . there were 10 kids, four adults, the whole cage was lined with little faces pressed against the glass. Very irresponsible.

The poor zookeeper . . . was now trying to keep this thing away. And now it had the taste of blood from Phil, it was continuing to try to attack him. It was slamming against Phil's back and clawing him . . . The zookeeper is trying to kick this thing off and it's going crazy . . . . It's shoving its claws and its paws through the iron grill of the cage door. The zookeeper gets out and locks it and this dragon continues to slam its body against the door to try to get out and continues to attack him.[4]

According to Stone, the celebrity pair had been told the dragon was mild-mannered and was used to kids petting it. Stone told *Time* she was shocked that visits into the dragon's enclosure continued even after Bronstein's attack — a move the zoo defended on financial grounds. 'If we get calls from prospective donors or celebrities, we'll try to accommodate them,' said LA Zoo's spokeswoman.[5]

The discovery of komodo dragons in 1912 was one of the most surprising scientific finds of the 20th century, a cryptozoological victory over sceptics who considered monster lizards to be the stuff of legend. The beasts first came to Western attention after a party of pearl fishermen returned from Komodo Island with tales of an enormous prehistoric predator roaming the forests.

The Blue Mountains of New South Wales, where in 1970 cryptozoologist Rex Gilroy experienced his first encounter with a hairy hominid. (Julie Miller)

Rex Gilroy, the 'father of Australian cryptozoology', in his home theatre in the Blue Mountains, New South Wales. (Julie Miller)

The Hawkesbury River, New South Wales. A popular weekend holiday spot where a plesiosaur-like creature has been reported. (Julie Miller)

Is this the reptilian head and neck of the Hawkesbury River monster glimpsed at night between trees? (Anonymous by request)

A 3-metre long white pointer caught on a drum line off Bribie Island, Queensland, has two enormous chunks torn from its torso by a mega-proportioned shark. (courtesy of Fisheries Queensland, a service of the Department of Employment, Economic Development and Innovation)

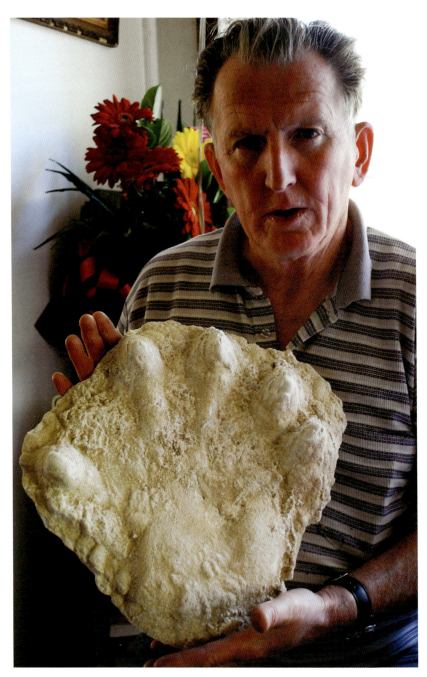

Rex Gilroy holding a plaster casting of what he claims is the footprint of a megalania. (Julie Miller)

A skull of a megalania, the most venomous predator ever to have walked this continent, and possibly still stalking remote locations. (Steven G. Johnson)

The Black Panther Café in Halls Gap, Victoria, where not panthers – but pumas – have been reported locally. (Julie Miller)

A stuffed puma spookily adorns the wall of the Wartook Teahouse in the Grampian Mountain Range, Victoria. (Julie Miller)

A plaster cast of a large paw print, believed to be that of a puma, compared to a domestic cat (left) and blue heeler dog print (right). (Julie Miller)

Some Blue Mountains 'panther' researchers believe the rogue canine to be not a black panther but in fact a melanistic jaguar. (Babirusa)

A kangaroo fends off attacking dogs, evidence of this beast's ability to slash and maim. (Julie Miller)

Reconstructed skeleton of the megafaunal predator *Thylacoleo carnifax* in Naracoorte Caves, South Australia. (Andrew McMillan)

An expedition followed from the Buitenzorg Zoological Museum in Java, but its report received little attention until 1926, when a group from the American Museum of Natural History, led by W. Douglas Burden, travelled to the island to investigate further. This expedition managed to bring home 12 dead and two live specimens.

These early expeditions claimed the largest male dragons weighed around 130 kilograms, though more typically they are around 70 kilos. Most of its hunting is based on smell – it can apparently sniff out carrion from several kilometres away when the wind is right. They are also very fast in short sprints, climbing a hill as quickly as a man can run on level ground.

As we follow our guide, traipsing a narrow trail skirted by trees and low-lying scrub, we can't help but feel we are being watched. As it turns out, we are actually being *stalked*, and we catch our first glimpse of a fully grown komodo dragon, silhouetted by the early morning sun, camouflaged by vegetation, lumbering beside us on top of a shoulder-high embankment. It is a chilling moment, but our guide reassures us we are in no danger – the giant reptile is only curious. Nevertheless, we all keep cautious eyes on the beast's progress as we wend our way to a currently disused 'viewing stadium'.

In 1988, for a visit to the island by then-president Suharto, a small wooden grandstand was built, overlooking a deep pit above which a hoist was installed. A clutch of komodo dragons was herded into the pit and – to demonstrate their awesome power to the president – a live goat was lowered on the hoist. The dragons tore into the goat with terrifying ferocity, like modern-day velociraptors, and Suharto was duly impressed.

A nearby helipad was even installed for return presidential visits, and the komodo 'goat sacrifice' was promoted as a tourist attraction. Understandably, this gruesome wild kingdom display proved unpalatable to tourists, and was thankfully discontinued.

At a nearby stream we encounter the largest concentration of dragons, basking on rocks in the heat of the sun. They truly are prehistoric-looking beasts, several of them more than 3 metres long and powerfully solid. It is hard to believe from their languid movements how swiftly they can move on the hunt. Fortunately, none appear hungry, and they evince no apparent interest in us.

It is on our return journey we really have the chance to get up close and personal with one of these lethal reptiles. A large specimen, identified by our guide as the lizard shadowing us earlier, appears on the track directly in front of us as we turn a bend. Its long, thin tongue darts out inquisitively, tasting the air, as dragons are known to do when assessing the suitability of prey.

The ranger tries to scare the four-legged predator off by waving his arms – but the beast is having none of it. It advances, prompting the ranger to thrust his forked stick against the animal's neck in an attempt to force it backwards. A tussle ensues, and we become quite concerned as we see him straining against the dragon's bulk.

Finally the dragon settles, and our guide instructs us to squeeze slowly and quietly past. We are less than a metre from the slavering reptile, able to catch a whiff of its fetid breath as we slink by. The ranger cautiously backs away as well, not taking his eyes off it, all the time speaking soothingly to the creature in a local Manggarei dialect.

He reassures us the reptile was not attacking, merely asserting its superiority; and indeed our last image of the massive dragon as we round the next bend is that of a monster claiming its turf — perched firmly on the track, head high, hissing loudly, and with drool seeping from its mighty jaws.

Until recently, the general belief was that the carnivore lizard killed via deadly bacteria in its saliva, the result of food rotting in its teeth. However, new studies debunk this theory, with researchers discovering in 2009 that the bite itself is venomous. The lizard uses its sharp teeth to open gaping wounds in its prey into which the venom is introduced, increasing the blood flow, reducing blood pressure and inducing shock in the victim.

'They are remarkably clean animals,' said Dr Bryan Fry from Melbourne University, head of a team reporting on the animal's arsenal in the US journal *Proceedings of the National Academy of Sciences*. 'Their teeth are shiny white and their gums pink.' And the reason why no-one had discovered this groundbreaking information earlier? 'Nobody looked,' Dr Fry said.[6]

According to Dr Fry, the lizards are extremely intelligent, with huge curved claws and teeth similar in shape to a tyrannosaurus rex. They can also distend their jaw, snakelike, to swallow large chunks of their victims. Although they usually snack on wild boar and deer, they have also been known to consume buffalo, snakes and even other dead dragons. And, of course, they are partial to human meat, having killed at least four people in the last 35 years.

While it was generally assumed that komodo dragons were native to the Indonesian islands they call home, the discovery of fossilised bones in Queensland recently turned that theory on its head. Dating around 300,000 years old, the fossils show the komodo dragon had its origins in Australia about four million years ago, possibly persisting on the continent until the arrival of humans around 40,000 years ago.[7]

Scientists now believe the dragons then dispersed northwestwards, eventually reaching the eastern Indonesian islands. But on the Australian continent, some unknown event – whether climate change or interaction with humans – caused the extinction of the lizard.

'It became extinct, we think, about 50,000 years ago, about the time that humans arrived in Australia, and of course it disappeared from every other island in Indonesia except Flores,' palaeontologist and former Australian of the Year, Tim Flannery of Macquarie University, told the ABC. Flannery added:

> The one interesting thing about Flores is that it is the home of the 'hobbit'. The hobbit was there for about two million years and maybe hobbit hunting was a bit like pre-school for the komodo dragon, they learnt how to deal with human-like hunters. Whereas in Australia and the rest of the island, the first thing that turned up was fully modern humans and they seem not to have been able to cope with that.[8]

While the thought of Indigenous tribes catching and feasting on komodo dragons seems plausible, it seems those early Australians may have had an ever larger carnivore to contend with – the dragon's 5-metre-long cousin, megalania. This was the king of all megafauna, a slavering beast that fed upon giant marsupials twice its own weight, as well as smaller mammals and birds. It had a lumbering body, stumpy limbs topped with giant talons, a huge skull and a massive jaw full of serrated teeth.

Dr Steven Wroe from the University of New South Wales, Dr Fry's colleague, compared the anatomies of both the komodo dragon and megalania, concluding that they shared skull and tooth adaptations that allowed them to kill large animals through rapid blood loss. Dr Wroe said:

> It all comes together as an armoury with a surprisingly sophisticated and complex tool kit. It doesn't have a powerful bite, but it is well adapted to bite and pull at the same time. And together with very sharp serrated teeth that is enough to open serious wounds in large prey. The affect of that is then amplified by the anticoagulant and hypertension toxins it is bathing the wounds in.[9]

According to Dr Wroe, it is not a stretch to suggest that megalania had the same killing arsenal as its living relative. 'Australia's megalania was probably the largest venomous animal that ever lived,' he said.

Depicted in rock paintings and engravings across the continent, there's little doubt megalania would have consumed *Homo sapiens*. According to historian Peter Hancock, a well-known Nyoongar story from Western Australia about a crocodile attack is in reality about a megalania.

'Something dramatic and memorable happened at the mouth of the Swan River all those centuries ago – so dramatic that the Aborigines named the river mouth after the "crocodile" and named seven hills in North Fremantle and Mosman Park after the dingoes that fought it,' he told *Perth Now* reporters. 'It is the Australian equivalent of Saint George and the dragon, but much more likely to be based on fact.'[10]

Megalania is believed to have died out in an extinction pulse around 40,000 years ago along with other megafauna such as giant kangaroos and the diprotodon. However, many Indigenous people as well as early European settlers claimed to have had encounters with oversized reptiles in the Australian bush, sparking speculation that the species did not, in fact, completely disappear.

One of the most famous incidents occurred during the 1890s when a huge reptile, reported to be a monstrous goanna 10 metres in length – terrorised the town of Euroa in Victoria. It tramped its way across properties, leaving behind gigantic footprints as evidence. A search party of 40 men, however, failed to find the elusive beast.

Nearly 100 years later, another giant reptile was spotted in the same region, gripping the border town of Mallacoota with 'lizard fever'. A female motorist claimed to have seen a 6-metre goanna on a road just outside of town, the claim attracting media including television program *A Current Affair*.

One man who firmly believes in the continued existence of megalania is Rex Gilroy, who possesses an impressive plaster cast of a footprint taken from a freshly ploughed field in Moruya on the New South Wales south coast in 1979.

With a passion for cryptozoology bordering on obsession, Rex Gilroy is an enigma often derided for his boundary-pushing beliefs and outrageous claims. Many of the so-called 'eyewitness' accounts of megalania peppered throughout the worldwide web have come via Gilroy – not all of them verifiable. However, with 50 years' experience in the field, it is little wonder people who have close encounters with mysterious creatures turn to Gilroy before more official (and perhaps more sceptical) bodies.

Gilroy is also the one and only source of the oft-recounted tale of Frank Gordon, a herpetologist who claimed to have seen a lizard more than 10 metres in length in the Watagan Mountains in New South Wales. Gilroy has stated that Gordon's experience in the field of lizards gave his story credibility and has used it to back up his own evidence.

If Gilroy's claims are to be believed, the area surrounding the Watagan Mountains on the New South Wales Central Coast has had more than its share of giant reptile sightings. In 1978, a farmer from Cessnock told Gilroy he had spotted a gigantic goanna ripping up a cow with its massive jaws and teeth, while another farmer said he'd seen a 10-metre monster moving in scrub near his barn.

On his mysteriouscreatures.com website, Gilroy also names Kuranda, in the hinterland of Cairns in northern Queensland, as another megalania hotspot:

> The creatures have left their large tracks across properties on the edge of jungle and taken the odd calf or two, even poultry. Some locals have even sighted these creatures but few talk about these things, no doubt fearing ridicule. Aborigines claim the reptiles wander a wide area of the Cape York and Gulf country forests.[11]

Another story Gilroy reports came from two sisters from North Queensland, Karen and Susan. One day the girls were walking with two boys along a jungle track in mountainous terrain near Townsville when they saw a huge reptile emerge from dense forest 100 metres ahead of them. One of the girls recalls:

> We took fright and hid behind some bushes watching the creature. It looked just like a goanna, only it was far far too big for that. It had a large, goanna-like head, long neck, a huge, almost elephant-like body, enormous legs and big claws, and a long, thick tail . . . It stood parallel with the swamp, and we estimated its length from head to tail to be a good 40 feet, and its height about six feet tall, standing on all fours . . . No one believes us to this day, but we know what we saw.[12]

Not to be outdone by others, Gilroy also claims to have seen megalania for himself, slinking through the bush. He recalls it was 'brownish', at least 8–10 metres long, and 'as tall as a cow'. 'It was the curse of the Aborigines,' he says. 'They hunted it to get rid of it and it fed the whole tribe.'

In his 2008 newsletter, Gilroy recounts a recent expedition into the Wollemi National Park west of Sydney with a camera crew from the History Channel, filming for a series called *Monster Quest*:

> There have been many reports over the years from over a wide area of the fringes of this wild forest and swampland region, and our friends from the History Channel hoped to capture whatever evidence we could find on film for a

one hour documentary . . . One place I showed the team was a campground on the edge of a pine forest, where one night a few years ago, a small party of campers spotted the long, dark shape of a large monitor lizard moving through the pines near the camp. Torches were flashed to reveal a mottle-coloured monster of up to 4m in length! . . . Had our History Channel team encountered an Australian giant monitor in the Wollemi we certainly would not have gone too close to it, preferring to film zoom shots of the creature at a safe distance.[13]

According to Gilroy, although the crew did not find a giant ripper lizard during this expedition, they did discover scuff marks of a large creature with five toes.

The closest relative to megalania confirmed to be living on the Australian continent today is the perentie or *Varanus giganteus* – but with an average length of just 2 metres long, it's unlikely eyewitnesses of purported megalania had confused the two species.

Is it possible, then, that giant ripper lizards could still exist in remote areas of Australian bushland? Remember that just 100 years ago, the komodo dragon was considered a creature of mythology – so anything is possible.

Interesting, palaeontologist Tim Flannery has suggested that the Australian ecosystem could benefit from the reintroduction of komodo dragons, as it could occupy the large carnivore niche left by the extinction of megalania. However, he argues for caution with such an experiment, since 'the problem of predation of large varanids upon humans should not be understated'.[14] Just ask those villagers living in fear on Komodo Island . . . or the hobbits of Flores.

Although officially found on just five islands – Gili Motang, Gili Dasami, Rinca, Flores and Komodo – there are often rumours of komodo dragons spotted on other nearby islands. This of course makes sense, as the dragons are known to be excellent swimmers.

However, just as recently as February 2008, there were reports of a komodo dragon sighted in Papua New Guinea, terrorising locals in the city of Lae. After a four-day 'komodo hunt' involving the army and Department of Environment and Conservation the search was called off, with authorities concluding the offending lizard was the similar-looking but smaller salvadori monitor, common to the Papuan region.[15]

A convenient result – or denial on the behalf of authorities too scared to continue the hunt? Could a prehistoric reptilian monster be lurking in the jungle of New Guinea, or even more terrifyingly, the bushland of Australia? Could megalania, or even a remnant population of the smaller komodo dragon, have survived against the odds? It seems in the intriguing world of cryptozoology, there is no such thing as 'case closed'.

Chapter 25
Beware the bunyip

Anyone who has heard the mating call of a male koala will surely agree it is the most incongruous sound in nature. Cute, cuddly and button-nosed, this benign ball of grey fluff perches silently in the fork of a gum tree, dozing and chewing, until, once a year, the urge to procreate shakes him from his slumber. He then announces his randy intentions with an unearthly, guttural bellow, before descending to the forest floor to stalk the object of his affections.

Similarly, the kitten-faced possum, all wiggly whiskers and bedroom eyes, becomes a snarling, hissing dragon during mating season rampages, its vocal ferocity belying its size and innocent, apple-nibbling demeanour.

Coming from a continent where much of the native wildlife merely whimpers, sniffs, snuffles or tweets, it's little wonder the first Europeans to arrive Down Under were horrified by the roars, cackles, guffaws and caterwauls emitted by the bizarre-looking creatures of the Australian bush.

Take, for instance, the crew of the French ship *Geographe*, nervously venturing inland along the Swan River back in 1801. Unfamiliar sights, smells and scenery already had them on tenterhooks, but when they heard a terrible roar, 'louder than a bull's bellow', emanating from the reeds of the waterway, they bolted back to their ship in fear, terrified of coming face to face with a man-eating monster.[1]

The Indigenous inhabitants of Australia were all too familiar with this mysterious, dangerous waterbeast. Generically known as the 'bunyip', it is described as a large, dark-coloured furred or feathery creature with glowing eyes and a fearsome roar that lurks around swamps, watercourses and billabongs, devouring anyone who ventures in its path. It appears in legends from all over the country (though mostly southeastern Australia), varying in its description but constant in its malevolence.

It is uncertain where the term 'bunyip' originated, or indeed which Indigenous language it stems from. Most likely it is a pidgin term adapted by white settlers, bastardised through cultural confusion like the word 'kangaroo'. On early maps of the area surrounding Melbourne, the Bunyip River was called the Buneep, named after a spirit said to live in its swamps, while in the Wemba-wemba language of western Victoria, the word 'banib' means an amphibious child-eating monster. In 1812, the term was recorded as 'bahnyip' in the *Sydney Gazette*. Whatever the derivation, the term was soon synonymous with the word 'monster' and became entrenched into the Australian vernacular.

According to Nicholas Holden, author of *Bunyips: Australia's folklore of fear*, the creature is also known as the *car-bunyah*, *gauarge*, *katenpai* and *too-roo-dun*, depending on the region. The Ngarrinderi people from the Murray River region knew it as *mulgewanki*, described by local Indigenous education worker Shane Karpany on ABC Radio:

> What I was taught what he looks like was half man and half fish, he's got a lot of ribbon weed on him, he's twice the size of the average man. He's still a bit hairy and furry with big red eyes, big teeth, real sharp claws but also web hands, feet like a duck and his colour is like the green-brown colour of the river.[2]

Stories of the bunyip played an important cultural role in teaching children to respect waterways. In many legends, women and children venturing out alone were the victims of this fearsome spirit, as told in this adaptation from Oodgeroo Noonuccal in the story of 'Biami and the Bunyip':

> Some of the younger women of the tribes foolishly disobeyed the elders, who told them they must have nothing to do with Bunyip. They went to find Bunyip to test his evil power. Bunyip lay in wait for the women, and when they were close enough to fall into his power he trapped them and made them his slaves. They lived with him as water spirits and were lost to the tribes forever.[3]

Confronted with bizarre creatures such as kangaroos, koalas and platypus, for the first European settlers the bunyip was no stretch of the imagination. Keen to find a source for strange noises heard around waterways, they latched on to the Indigenous legends, believing the bunyip to be just another yet unidentified creature of the Australian bush.

Something is Out There

As word spread amongst the European community about this strange and fearsome beast, so bunyip fever grew. In 1823, the *Sydney Gazette* published a letter from Edward Smith Hall, an early settler who claimed two years prior to have seen a bunyip in the shallows of Lake Bathurst, 40 kilometres south of present-day Goulburn: 'My attention was attracted by a creature casting up water and making a noise, in sound resembling a porpoise, but shorter and louder . . . It had the appearance of a bulldog's head, but perfectly black.'[4]

Giving authority to this story was the respected explorer Hamilton Hume who, in April 1818, claimed to have found several large bones from an unidentified amphibious creature near the same lake. Intrigued, the Philosophical Society of Australasia discussed the case during its meeting on December 19, 1821, offering to fund an expedition to retrieve a specimen; but Hume failed to produce any evidence, and his original findings remain a mystery.

William Buckley, an escaped convict who lived with the Wathaurong people near Geelong from 1803 to 1835, was as convinced of the bunyip's existence as his Aboriginal hosts. His experiences were published in a biography written by John Morgan in 1852 called *The Life and Adventures of William Buckley*:

> I could never see any part [of the bunyip] except the back, which appeared to be covered with feathers of a dusky-grey colour. It seemed to be about the size of a full-grown calf . . . When alone, I several times attempted to spear a Bun-yip; but had the natives seen me do so it would have caused great displeasure. And again, had I succeeded in killing,

or even wounding one, my own life would probably have paid the forfeit; they considering the animal . . . something supernatural.[5]

The golden age of bunyip tales was between 1840 and 1850, reaching near-hysteria levels. One person claimed a bunyip had killed his mother, while a report in the *Sydney Morning Herald* in 1847 stated a young stationhand had seen a bunyip while he was looking for cows during a flood:

> It was about as big as a six months old calf, of dark colour, a long neck and pointed head; it had large ears which pricked up when it perceived him [the herdsman]; had a thick mane of hair from the head down the neck, and two large tusks. He turned to run away, and this creature equally alarmed ran off too, and from the glance he took, he describes it as having an awkward shambling gallop; the forequarters of the animal were very large in proportion to the hindquarters, and it had a large tail.[6]

Several drawings of bunyips also appeared during this period. One, sketched by a western Victorian Indigenous artist called Kurruk, resembles an emu — two legs, feathery body, small bird-like head and three toes. The other, drawn by an Indigenous artist from Murray River in 1848, is more like a hippopotamus — rounded body, four legs and a horse-like head. Both artists claimed their subjects to be the real deal — but the drawings couldn't be more different.

Even the Governor of Port Phillip, Charles La Trobe, bought into the argument, concluding there were two distinct types of bunyip — a 'southern' or 'dog-faced' bunyip, and a 'northern' or long-necked species. It was said he personally possessed drawings of both types; unfortunately, these have since disappeared.

In 1847, La Trobe penned a letter to his friend Ronald Gunn, discussing the discovery of some interesting bones:

> You have heard probably the constant rumours of the existence of some unknown beast in the rivers and lakes of P. Phillip — under the native name 'bunyep' or 'bunyip'. That there is such a one whether round or square, fat or lean — and that of tolerable size — I have long been convinced. At last, Lonsdale writes me word that they have found the head of one in some stream near Murrumbidgee and that it has been brought down to Melbourne. According to description, it must be a long-snouted animal . . . its forehead rising abruptly, the eye placed very low, strong grinders, cavity for brain very large. The end of the snout is broken off but the blacks who have seen it say it ought to have two long tusks projecting downward at the termination.[7]

The weird and wonderful skull mentioned by La Trobe was soon to send the scientific world into a spin. Elongated, and with eye sockets sitting almost on the jawline, the strange bone, said by the local Indigenous people to belong to a *katenpai*, was put on display at the Australian Museum in 1847, attracting curious crowds and prompting a spate of bunyip stories.

On closer examination, however, Sydney's leading naturalist William Macleay concluded the skull belonged to a freak of nature — possibly a deformed horse or cow — and did not represent a new species. The *Australian Medical Journal* stated similar claims of bunyip skulls would in future be regarded 'an ostentatious display of our ignorance and credulity' – a warning that sent the boffins scuttling away in humiliation. The offending skull was quickly taken off display and stashed away in the dusty bowels of the museum where it conveniently disappeared, never to be seen again.

With science casting doubt on the existence of a new species, sceptics began to look for logical explanations for purported waterbeast sightings. A theory emerged that what (ignorant) natives and (drunk) white settlers were seeing was simply seals that had strayed inland, carried upstream by floodwaters and trapped in billabongs when water levels subsided.

In 1857, the naturalist Strocqueler sailed down the Goulburn River in New South Wales, sketching freshwater seals. Showing these to local Indigenous people, he was told the animal was 'bunyip's brother'. Around 1850, a seal was shot at Conargo in New South Wales, 900 kilometres from the sea, its stuffed remains holding pride of place on the walls of the local pub for many years to come. In the 1930s, a seal was identified in swamplands of the Murray River between Renmark and Loxton, stranded in a lagoon 500 kilometres from the sea.

One witness, E.J. Dunn, the director of the Geological Survey of Victoria, claimed in the early 20th century to have seen a whole herd of 'bunyips' swimming against the current in the Murrumbidgee River at Gundagai, New South Wales, 1200 kilometres from the sea. He later clarified his observations:

> My recollection of these animals is that they had round heads, with no visible ears, but eyes that could be seen, dark-coloured

fur, length of animals about five feet; while swimming the head and the top of the back were exposed above the water. Up to that time I had not seen seals, but since then many have come under observation, and I have to doubt the animals I saw in the Murrumbidgee were seals.[8]

Adding credence to the bunyip–seal theory is the raucous bark of the slick aquatic mammal, a sound guaranteed to frighten the socks off any unsuspecting passer-by. However, another popular theory attributes the bunyip's bellowing roar to an even more benign critter – the brown bittern, a nocturnal heron with a voice like a foghorn that inhabits reedy swamps.

However, the Reverend George Taplin, in his book *The Narrinyeri*, dismissed this possibility, believing the 'booming and explosive sounds' he regularly heard emanating from Lake Alexandrina 'cannot be the peculiar sound of the Murray bittern, as I have heard that too'.[9] And who can argue with a man of the cloth?

Similar booming noises coming from swamplands near the Victorian town of Greta sparked one of the country's most famous bunyip hunts. When the search parties failed to locate the source of the sound, the offending swamps were drained, the sound subsequently subsiding. Some locals believed the bunyip moved to another area; others thought it had died when its habitat was destroyed.

Of course, this would have been true if the creature was a stranded seal, a bittern or any other swamp inhabitant; and this may explain why bunyip encounters became less frequent in the 20th century, with many wetlands making way for dams, housing estates and industrial wastelands.

So the question remains — is the bunyip a case of mistaken identity, or could it indeed have been a real creature now extinct due to habitat loss? Considering the strange and wonderful creatures lost to science since European colonisation (up to 25 per cent of species are said to have died out in just over 200 years, giving Australia the world's worst track record for mammalian extinction), the latter is one of the more plausible theories thrown up by modern-day cryptozoologists.

The extinction theory brings us to another certainly worth considering — that the bunyip was inspired by the diprotodon, a creature extinct for almost 40,000 years that coexisted with early Indigenous people. This enormous marsupial, around the size of a hippopotamus at around 3 metres long and 2 metres high, had a large boofy head, a shaggy coat and lived around ancient lakes. Although a plant eater, its size alone would have been enough to inspire fear; doubtless it would have been the source of many embellished hunting stories, passed down through generations of Indigenous people.

Another contender for bunyip inspiration is *Palorchestes painei*, a lumbering, bull-sized relative of diprotodon described by Michael Archer, Suzanne Hand and Henk Godthelp in their book on Riversleigh as possessing 'huge koala-like claws, enormously powerful forelimbs, a long ribbon-like tongue and a large elephantine trunk'.[10] Depicted in rock art in Kakadu National Park, *Palorchestes* is considered by eminent scientist Tim Flannery as the animal most suited to have inspired the legend of the bunyip.[11]

Something is Out There

The last of these giant beasts died out around 26,000 years ago, along with other megafauna such as giant koalas, giant kangaroos and marsupial lions. Surely these historic creatures seem just as implausible, just as mythological, as the bunyip – yet they've been proven by science to have once roamed this very bizarre continent.

Chapter 26
The Binjour Bear

There is no doubt the yowie, with its impressive height, lengthy gait and colossal foot size, strides the landscape as the king of Australian cryptids. But allegedly, another hairy bipedal hominid is out there – less impressive in stature, we admit – but equally fascinating and utterly mysterious. At only 1 metre in height, it could be regarded as the 'Mini Me' of the yowie family. Amongst the townships surrounding Queensland's Binjour Plateau, where most sightings have been centred, it is called the Binjour Bear. But some local Indigenous people have been aware of its existence for eons. They know this elusive pocket-sized race as *jongari*.

The *jongari* – or *junjuddi*, *kuritjah* or *dinderi* (as it is variously known by different tribes) – is notoriously reclusive. In Indigenous folklore, it is described as tiny, hairy and with an elongated head. In the Dreamtime it supposedly lived peacefully alongside Indigenous people. According to local Indigenous folklorist Sam Hill, interviewed on the topic by the *Fraser Coast Chronicle*, 'They have always been here, always been in our culture as far back as we can remember.'[1]

Mr Hill believes one tribe used to live near the Glasshouse Mountains, north of Brisbane, and tells the story that many years ago his grandfather had to fight off some particularly aggressive *jongari* while ringbarking trees in the area.

White folk have also claimed encounters with the *jongari*. In 1979 a local resident, Mrs Locke, told the *South Burnett Times* how she and her husband saw a hairy, metre-tall creature standing by the side of the road as they drove towards the town of Kilkivan, southeast of the Binjour Plateau, just before dusk. 'It had broad shoulders and stood looking at us as we drove past,' she said.[2] That same year a youth reported being attacked by a small hairy man fitting the description of *jongari* at Charters Towers, north of the Binjour Plateau region.[3]

Local timber man Graham Griggs claimed to have been menaced by a group of territorial *jongari* while camping near Carnarvon Gorge, northwest of the plateau, in 1984. Apparently they leapt at him out of the shadows until, unable to cope with their campaign of terror any longer, he pulled up stakes and high-tailed it back into town.[4]

In 1994 the *Courier Mail* reported more *jongari* action from Carnarvon Gorge. Former National Parks and Wildlife Officer Grahame Walsh, who had been investigating encounters, described coming across fresh tracks near a river bank: 'They were like a five year old would make. I followed them up a hill but I lost them.'[5]

Most accounts describe the creature as 1 metre tall, with a torso like a man and limbs like an ape. It is also said to be very smelly — a trait apparently shared with the yowie. But how on earth could a tribe of hominids, no matter how tiny, remain so effectively concealed for so long?

There are certainly thick sections of scrub around the Binjour Plateau, but it's a far cry from the sort of impenetrable rainforests found in other parts of northern Queensland. And of course this is citrus country, with large sections developed as orchards — a difficult landscape for concealment.

As we drive into this picturesque part of Queensland in early spring, our senses assaulted by the aromas of orange, lemon and mandarin blossom, it immediately becomes evident it would take more than some cunning and determination for our metre-high men to stay hidden in these parts. We also can't help wondering what exactly the *jongari* are. Their descriptions seem to match nothing on the fossil record from any stage of our evolution . . . Or do they?

In 2003 the scientific world was turned on its head with the discovery of Flores Man (nicknamed 'the Hobbit'). While searching for evidence of the original migration trail of *Homo sapiens* from Asia to Australia in the Liang Bua Cave on the Indonesian Island of Flores, a group of anthropologists stumbled across a complete metre-tall skeleton of a previously unknown species of the genus *Homo*, which they named *Homo floriensis*. The remains were dated at 18,000 years old.

Ultimately the skeletal parts of six more specimens were uncovered in the cave, along with examples of the small tools these little people would have used. A scientific storm erupted. The discoverers asserted they had stumbled across a new species of the *Homini* tribe. Detractors argued the skeletons were merely those of microcephalic (small-skulled) humans. The debate was quashed when a cladistic analysis, a form of biological systematics based on evolutionary relationships, confirmed *Homo floriensis* was indeed a newly discovered and separate species from *Homo sapiens*.

Since the dawn of evolutionary theory, science had no idea Flores Man existed. But there he was, living contemporaneously with modern man on the island of Flores, just as some Queensland Indigenous people claim *jongari* used to live alongside them for thousands of years. Could these *jongari* be living breathing examples of *Homo floriensis*? After all, the first wave of Indigenous people only drifted into Australia from southeast Asia somewhere between 50,000 and 100,000 years ago. Is it such a stretch to imagine tiny Flores Man scurrying along behind them? We were beginning to think our theory might have legs – albeit small ones. Until we heard of a more recent sighting . . .

In early October 2000, citrus-farming siblings Alan Bucholz and Shirley Humphreys both witnessed a mysterious furry creature snooping around their respective properties outside the town of Gayndah, southeast of the Binjour Plateau. The sighting occurred shortly after they had been intrigued by a spate of inexplicable fruit raids on Humphrey's orchard, nestled on the verge of the Burnett River, where at the time she grew mandarins, oranges, lemons and grapefruit. Apparently the fruit thief was partial to the mandarins. 'There was a mandarin tree with lots of ripe fruit on it,' explains Humphreys. 'And something used to peel the fruit, eat it and drop the peel about a metre from the tree.'

The Binjour Bear

On one particular night, the food bandit stepped up its nocturnal incursions, ransacking a storage shed on the orchard. Humphreys recalls, 'We used to pack food in the shed to have morning tea in the orchard. And I've got a container I used to keep full of biscuits. It got hold of that and opened it, and ate all the biscuits. It was a difficult container to open, and it was covered in teeth marks. It even took a couple of cartons of eggs out of the shed and ate most of those. There was also a jar of Vegemite lying on the ground. But it couldn't get into that.'

Brother and sister alike were perplexed as to what was behind the raids. Until October 3, when Bucholz could barely believe his eyes as he spotted the potential suspect prowling his own orchard about a kilometre away. 'It was about a metre tall. It was walking on its hind legs. It was a dark colour – between a black and a brown . . . And it was similar to a bear!'

Before he could get a better look at the creature it wandered off into scrub. But the very next day it put in an appearance on his sister's property, on a stretch of sand beside the river, and this time lingering longer. Humphreys watched it for 20 minutes, and remembers her encounter vividly. 'I got a good look at it. It was only a metre tall. It looked like a bear. Sometimes it stood up and sort of ambled along. Other times it got down on all four legs. It was brownish-black.'

Eventually the creature sauntered off into the thick tangle of berry trees and vines comprising the scrub that stretches along the edge of the river. Humphreys and Bucholz felt they had finally found the phantom food forager. But what on earth was a bear doing roaming the Queensland citrus belt?

Broken by reporter Jill Flack, the story hit the local papers. National media pounced on the story, creating perhaps the biggest cryptozoological media circus in Australian history. Tim the Yowie Man arrived in town to investigate, trailed by a crew from Channel Nine's television program *A Current Affair*. He dubbed the creature the 'Gayndah bear' and offered a $10,000 reward for its capture or $1000 for photographic evidence. Sam Hill asserted Humphreys and Bucholz had actually seen a *jongari*.[6] But a longstanding local legend gave credence to their insistence it was an actual bear.

Local historian Brett Green tells of a Bullen's Circus trailer that upended in torrential rains while descending the Binjour Plateau in 1959. Some animals were killed in the accident. Others, including an injured elephant, had to be put down. Some escaped and were recaptured. Others were never seen again. Amongst those not accounted for were one male and two female bears — described as either Himalayan or Asian black bears.

Over the following years many bear sightings were reported, so much so that a 'Danger — Wild Bears Cross Here' road sign was erected at the base of the plateau.[7] A mango tree atop the plateau, under which bears were subsequently spotted, was dubbed the 'Bear's Mango Tree'. But could a breeding population have feasibly developed from three escaped bears?

Even Tim the Yowie Man admits the odds are against it. Then again, the Asian sun bear — smaller than the Himalayan and Asian black — does not hibernate, which means it can reproduce all year round. In fact a female sun bear can give birth to up to two cubs a year. Trainable, the sun bear was known to be included in circus acts in the past. Most interestingly, it only grows to a little over a metre in height. Either way, sightings eventually abated, becoming all but forgotten, until the orchard raid of 2000 again had the region gripped by bear fever.

Reporters from across the state flocked to Gayndah, and the story spread internationally. For a brief shining moment, the humble little Queensland town seemed like the most exciting place on the planet. Shirley Humphreys could barely keep up with interview requests: 'I got phone calls from all over. America. England. I couldn't get any work done!'

Unfortunately, after examining the orchard where the rogue bear had struck, as well as the river bank where it appeared and the bush where it slunk off, Tim the Yowie Man failed to come up with even so much as a claw print. Confusing the matter was a photograph taken by one of a couple of local men, supposedly showing the bear's rear end protruding from bushes, which one of the pair has since admitted to have been faked.

Just as unfortunately, *A Current Affair* in its report opted to mercilessly send up the town of Gayndah, raising the ire of many locals. 'They made a fool of everybody,' says Bucholz, still aggravated today at the town's treatment by national media. Because of this, most locals have since clammed up on the subject of the bear. Sightings still come in – including as recently as two years ago when some teenagers sighted the creature further upriver on the Burnett – but they are rarely reported to the press.

Meanwhile, Shirley Humphreys remains adamant about what she saw. In fact, she still keeps the scarred souvenir of her plastic Tupperware-like container, its deep scratch marks and tooth indents certainly giving it the look of a biscuit tin ravaged by ravenous ursine. But was it an actual bear, or an ancient *jongari*? In part due to the clumsy footprints left by tabloid television, the world of cryptozoology will probably never know.

Chapter 27
Panthers on the prowl

In 2008 then-premier of New South Wales, Nathan Rees, announced he was concerned about the threat posed by alleged wild panthers in the northwestern suburbs of Sydney. 'I don't think it's necessarily an urban myth,' Mr Rees told reporters in September of that year. 'There are too many people reporting sightings.'[1]

Had Rees shown similar concern for the more direct threat of trouble brewing within his party he may well have gone on to a longer and more illustrious political career. But at that point in time one of the issues foremost on his mind seemed to be whether or not pupils of the northwest could walk safely to school without being pounced on by a giant predatory feline. 'Of particular concern is if there are little kids out there, and there actually is one of these things,' he was quoted as saying.[2]

A study was duly commissioned by the Department of Primary Industries (DPI), resulting in a 38-page report in December 2008,[3] followed by a three-page abridged report in

March 2009.⁴ Upon public release, both were met with suspicion by members of Australia's tightly knit crypto-community, and with cynicism by the hard-nosed newshounds of the print media.

Although the reports did little to calm the shaky ground Rees's public persona was already standing on, they did at least serve to refocus the public spotlight on a question which has bothered some Australian communities for more than half a century: what the hell is that four-legged thing prowling the bushes in the darkness on the edge of town?

Of course, Sydney's northwest is not the only region to have been plagued by the panther phenomenon. Throughout the decades the creature has snatched headlines under such colourful sobriquets as the Kingston killer and Tyagarah lion, both of northern New South Wales, the Grampians puma of Victoria and the Cordering cougar of Western Australia. Veteran panther researchers Tony Healy and Paul Cropper have collected well over 1000 sightings from across the country,⁵ and considering they are only two of many such researchers and taking into account the tendency of many witnesses to not report sightings, this is most probably only the tip of the iceberg.

So what's the deal with these big cats?

Despite not one irrevocable shred of solid evidence having been unearthed, they incessantly continue to be reported from representatives of all walks of life, from lawyers and doctors to farmers. Rees's 'The Black Cat' report was based on more than 280 sightings submitted to the Department of Primary Industries over a five-year period, including statements from such reliable sources as DPI and Rural Lands Protection field staff.⁶

Perhaps appropriately, considering the legendary fickleness of feline nature, the matter of the big cats' existence is both complex and confusing. Evidence aside, the 'elephant in the room' at any rational discourse is the furtive creature's hue. Depending on locale, the colour of the animal's coat – as one would expect for a panther – is generally reported as being jet black. In fact, more than two-thirds of Australian eyewitnesses say the big cats they've sighted resemble nothing so much as the black panthers seen in zoos or on television documentaries.[7] But why a panther and not a far more common spotted leopard?

In fact a panther is a leopard: its spots overlaid by dark pigmented fur giving the animal the appearance of being black. This sporadic condition is known as melanism, and if one were to look closely at a panther in broad daylight it would be possible to spot the black-on-black spots. Which leads to a perplexing quandary: essentially, a panther is an uncommon leopard. In fact, reports from the African savanna suggest that for every 100 spotted leopards in existence, there is only one panther. So how could it be that not one of the manifold Australian eyewitnesses has reported a leopard? This conundrum has confounded cryptozoologists for decades.

The answer may lie northwest of our continent, in the steamy jungle landscape of the Malay Peninsula, where the panther truly proliferates. It was traditionally believed in this part of the world that one leopard in two is melanistic. But a 2007 study in the Taman Negara National Park, utilising big cat traps mounted with cameras, resulted in *all* photographed specimens proving to be black.[8] Scientists speculate the melanism may be an adaptive advantage for camouflage in the dark tropical rainforest habitat.

If similar panthers are stalking the Australian bush, how did they get here? It is doubtful they island-hopped their way to the Great Southern Land. But there was a time when Australia was a part of the Asian mainland. Could antecedent panther specimens have drifted south and established a relict population? Science says otherwise, but it is nonetheless of interest that the world's highest concentration of melanisitic leopard is relatively proximate to the Australian continent – with which it was once conjoined.

A more commonly accepted theory is the panthers escaped from captivity. Over the last three decades at least seven lions have managed to escape from private zoos and circuses in New South Wales.[9] Of those, five were destroyed and two recaptured. Although there were no reported panther escapes, a change of state legislature in 1986 enforcing both licensing and strict security measures for the private keeping of such cats could have led to specimens being intentionally released in the wild.[10] And whereas lions are fearless animals, unafraid of humans, panthers are secretive, stealthy and eminently capable of escaping detection.

But could panthers let loose in the Australian bush have been capable of establishing a breeding population? A standard wild leopard litter consists of two to four cubs, from which one in two will survive. Mature by the age of three, a young leopard will wander off on its own to hunt and breed.

With reports mounting for decades, the New South Wales cat controversy festered publicly in 2001, when it was revealed the state government had been maintaining a secret 'x-file' on the creature.

This file disclosed that government wildlife hierarchy was so concerned about threats posed by rogue felines in the Blue Mountains that in 1999 it had commissioned a study, conducted by Sydney University lecturer Dr Johannes Bauer, a scientist renowned for carrying out big cat surveys in both China and Nepal.

Bauer's conclusion in regard to the mysterious Australian creature was direct and to the point: 'The most likely explanation of the evidence . . . is the presence of a large feline predator . . . I consider the habitat the animal occurs in as optimal leopard habitat, with probably abundant prey of macropods, possums, cats and stray dogs.'[11] He also felt there was more chance of the creature being a panther than a jaguar, which is indigenous to Central and South America, and which also exhibits a melanistic strain.

So what were the conclusions of the 2008 Rees study? As could be expected with a government report not a lot were actually drawn. An arcane grading system was applied to panther sightings to quantify their validity. This vague methodology awarded, for example, 50 per cent for a sighting at more than 100 metres and 100 per cent for one at less than 50 metres. A daylight sighting was regarded as being completely feasible, whereas a night sighting of a panther had only 75 per cent credibility. This would mean in a scenario where a witness claimed to have spotted a panther (which is a nocturnal animal) during the day, his testimony would be regarded as reliable. But if one were to spot a panther at night, when the creature is known to be active, the sighting would only be given three-quarters as much clout.

The study also delves into the matter of faeces. After all, if panthers are as prevalent as witness numbers suggest, it stands to reason they must be dropping stool samples all over the place. The report refers to one such sample, purported to be from a panther and provided for analysis by the DPI, as being either dog or wallaby excrement. Leery of this result, Michael Williams, panther researcher and co-author of *Australian Big Cats: An Unnatural History*, independently collected droppings from a panther cage in a zoo and sent them off to two separate laboratories – one a preferred lab for state government testing. Both stool samples were returned with the same result: positive for dog!

Another potential source of panther DNA could be found in saliva swabs from the eviscerated remains of prey. Although it is difficult to ascertain exactly what predator attacked an animal, there have allegedly been numerous panther attacks on livestock such as sheep and cattle, as well as peacocks and wallabies. According to the report, DNA testing of saliva found on carcasses has proved as unrevealing as the stool sample tests. In one case a swab taken from a partially devoured wallaby tested positive for dog DNA from one university department and negative from another.[12]

But panthers also leave behind scratch marks and paw prints, which in some cases have proved more revealing. In one case, photographs of deep tree scratches, uncovered by an experienced wild-dog trapper after following 'panther-sized' footprints for several kilometres, are described in the report as 'not consistent with a native animal as they are too big and deep in the tree to be a koala, goanna or possum, nor are they from a domestic cat'.[13] Could they be from a big cat?

Similarly, a photograph of a paw print taken in the Blue Mountains was identified by Dr David Pepper-Edwards, formerly of Taronga Zoo in Sydney, as 'consistent with that of a medium sized cat – puma'. It is interesting Pepper-Edwards identified the footprint as a puma, since the term is rarely used by eyewitnesses to describe the Blue Mountains big cat. But such are the confounding variables of cryptozoology.

A puma is another type of cat altogether, sandy coloured like a lion but slightly darker, and with no melanisitic variations having ever been reliably reported. Also known as a mountain lion or cougar, it has one of the largest ranges of any wild mammal – from the Yukon in Canada to the Andes of South America. Although described scientifically as a *small* cat, it can reach a head-to-tail length of more than 2 metres and can weigh more than 100 kilograms. In comparison, the leopard, which along with the lion and tiger is described as a *big* cat, usually has a shorter head-to-tail length and with its slighter build weighs a good 10 kilograms less. There is no doubt the puma is a powerful and ferocious cat; with its heavily muscled shoulders and forelimbs, perhaps even more so than the leopard.

The Australian epicentre of puma sightings is the Grampians Range of northeastern Victoria. Rockier and more sparsely vegetated than the Blue Mountains in New South Wales, it certainly looks like cougar country. We arrive in the odd little town of Halls Gap, under the shadow of the mountains, and pull up in front of the Black Panther Café. We wonder why it's not called the Sandy Puma, but nevertheless it foreshadows that we're in the right spot to commence our search. The walls of the café are adorned with news clippings of local sightings, but the staff inform us that for real puma evidence we'll need to head up through the mountains to an even tinier place called Wartook.

We wend our way up the steep, snaking sandstone pass, eyes peeled for puma. It is a sunny autumn day, perfect weather for a wild cat to be out sunning itself on a rocky ledge. But none seem to be around today. Eventually, we pull into another café, the quaint but sizeable Wartook Teahouse. As we enter its cavernous darkness we are shocked to see a mountain lion crouching on a ledge, high on the wall, apparently about to pounce. We are relieved to realise it is only a stuffed animal, but are still curious as to how it got here.

The proprietors, a charming couple called Tony and Jenny Wilson who took over the teahouse two years ago, inform us the stuffed animal was not shot locally. The Wilsons inherited it from the previous owner, who in turn bought it from a taxidermist. Along with the stuffed puma, they also assumed the mantle as keepers of local puma lore. They present a scrapbook containing a mind-boggling collection of newspaper articles on Grampians big cat reports. There are hundreds of them, scattered across the decades, from both local and national publications.

As we flick through the cuttings a local wanders in and, upon hearing about our cat quest, regales us with the story of his encounter. He was out shooting, he says, when he turned to see a puma, just like the one on the wall, less than 30 metres away, hissing as it stared straight at him. Following his first instinct, he turned and ran.

This is typical of the stories we hear: local country people, who know their wildlife, are adamant what they saw was a big sandy cat, much too large to be a feral cat. But eyewitness reports do not constitute evidence and, as far as we could gather, no photograph has ever been taken of the reputed Grampians puma.

As we ruminate on this, the Wilsons pull out a carefully packed exhibit from beneath the bar. They unwrap it to reveal a plaster cast moulding of a supposed mountain lion print – one of only two such pieces of evidence collected in the area. The story goes that a local woman had sighted a puma on a dirt road on her property; the animal sprang off, leaving behind a print in the dirt. She contacted a local man with an interest in the big cats, who made the cast we currently hold in our hands. It seems huge for a cat – approximately 12 centimetres across, with markings on its pads certainly matching those of a puma. Initially suspicious the mould was made from our stuffed friend on the wall, we compare it for size: the cast is considerably larger and definitely from another cat.

Tales of pumas in these parts go back as far as the goldrush days. Some locals say American goldminers brought the cats over to guard their claims. Others have it that US airmen brought them over in World War II as squadron mascots. In a report commenced in the 1970s called 'Pumas in the Grampian Mountains: A Compelling Case' – the largest official big cat study made outside of the New South Wales state government's more recent efforts — the latter theory was considered the more credible.

Put together by Dr John Henry, head of the Puma Study Group at Melbourne's Deakin University, the report cites testimony from two Australian guards stationed at an airstrip in Nhill, northwest of the Grampians, who witnessed a US bomber arriving from the Philippines with a puma cub aboard. The cub was allegedly released at the foothills of the mountain range.[14] Of course, to establish a breeding population the cub must have both survived and come into contact with other pumas. Nevertheless, the group concluded the possibility that 'a big cat population is established in the Grampians . . . beyond reasonable doubt'.[15]

The Deakin report also refers to sheep carcasses found on rock ledges hundreds of metres above the valley floor and cattle bones found in cave-like shelters,[16] evidence reflecting the behavioural patterns of mountain lions. But for us, as we drive back to Halls Gap along the winding road dividing sparse fields of livestock, the legendary predatory cat of the Grampians remains elusive.

In contrast, the New South Wales panther seems far less coy. In March 2004 it was reported not only as extending its territory from the Blue Mountains into the heavily populated Hills District northwest of Sydney, but also perpetrating its first known attack on a person.

According to the *Hills Shire Times*, Kenthurst teenager Luke Walker was in the yard of his family home when he heard the sound of a cat growling behind him. 'I turned around and saw it about three to four metres away,' related Walker. 'It leapt and

I put my arm up and its front claws then dug into my arm and its hind legs ripped into my gut.'[17]

Describing the rogue feline as 'the size of a labrador', Walker claims he deterred the animal by striking its head as it pounced. 'It jumped off and ran into the night,' he said. 'When I got back inside there was blood all over my T-shirt.' Lacerations on his skin required medical attention and he allegedly suffered cat-scratch fever for the following two weeks.

More sightings were made over ensuing months, including from local woman Judy Pope, who claimed the beast took one of her kittens. 'I got the fright of my life when I heard this awful noise coming from the garage,' she explained. 'I went to investigate and there were kittens scattered everywhere and this massive cat with a face three times the size of our cat. It grabbed one of the kittens in its mouth and ran off.'[18]

The largest feral cat ever caught in Australia weighed in at 16 kilograms.[19] A standard male labrador weighs more than twice that. The mystery as to whether Walker's mauling and Pope's kitten snatch were the work of a monstrous moggie or smallish panther was never solved.

In semi-rural Grose Vale, northwest of Kenthurst, in the foothills of the Blue Mountains, Chris Coffey is the creator and keeper of a database dedicated to bringing such mysteries to an end. Since encountering a big cat herself she has been both fascinated by the creatures and fearful of the threat they pose. She maintains a hotline on which anyone who has made a sighting can report it and have the details logged.

Coffey was also the 'whistleblower' on the state government's x-file in 2001, and although she agrees with some of the conclusions drawn by Dr Johannes Bauer in the report that was eventually released she does diverge on one important point. Coffey believes the creature is not a panther but a melanistic jaguar. This is a somewhat disturbing thought, considering what a terrifying animal the jaguar can be.

Not as long as the panther or puma, the jaguar is more muscular and much heavier – weighing up to 160 kilograms. It is the national symbol of Brazil and, as a figure of power and strength, became the focus of a cult in pre-Columbian Central and South America. Like leopards, jaguars are covered in black spots known as rosettes, although arranged in chunkier patterns; like panthers, melanistic jaguars – estimated to comprise 15 per cent of the population – have black fur between rosettes creating the look of an all-black cat. Australia shares similar latitudes with parts of South America but the obvious question can't help but rear its head again. How did they get here?

'Smuggled into the country from Mexico,' suggests Coffey. 'I have it on good authority even 12 years ago you could buy a black jaguar cub on the black market for as little as $5000. People bought them as pets or for private zoos. It's all very well to buy something when it's the size of a miniature poodle. But it will grow bigger than a rottweiler. That's when they get let go.'

And it heads for the mountains, obviously. But why is Coffey so sure the creature is a jaguar and not a panther? Apparently it has to do with bite radius.

'When you look at the remains of an animal attacked by a big cat, you can see the puncture marks made by their long sharp canine teeth. Panther canine punctures are 4.5 centimetres apart. Jaguar canine punctures are 6 centimetres apart. The bulk of carcasses we've studied have 6-centimetre punctures. That would indicate jaguar attack.'

Although Coffey, after a personal conversation with Nathan Rees, was crucial in getting the state government's panther report up and running, she is not impressed with the results — pointing out inconsistencies between the initial 2008 report and the more widely circulated three-page edition released in 2009. The 2008 report concluded that, 'It seems more likely than not on available evidence that such animals do exist in New South Wales.'[20] Somewhat contradictorily, the abbreviated 2009 report states, 'There is *still* nothing to conclusively say that a large black cat exists.'[21]

In previous years Coffey has a received a steady flow of reports. Since the media vilification of panther sightings following the more recent report, she believes witnesses have become backward in coming forward due to risk of ridicule. Undaunted, and with her database approaching 500 sightings from throughout the state, she remains committed to cracking the big cat puzzle. 'All we've asked the government to do,' she insists, 'is issue some kind of public warning for people living on the edge of the bush.'

Emerging mysteriously from the bush, the Australian mystery cat has certainly clawed its way into popular culture. Penrith, at the base of the Blue Mountains, calls its rugby league team the Panthers; the Australian music scene's most renowned groupie, the 'Lithgow Leaper', was affectionately nicknamed by a rock group (which prefers to remain anonymous) in honour of her hometown's other wild icon of the 1970s, the Lithgow panther; and in award-winning author Tim Winton's chilling

Something is Out There

1988 novella *In the Winter Dark*, an elusive predatory beast prowls the valley scrub where his protagonists make their home.

Next time you hear a rustle in the bushes followed by a deep growl, beware. Something more sinister than you think could be out there.

Chapter 28
Phantom kangaroos

The big cats that allegedly stalk the Australian bush are classified as cryptozoological creatures due to the fact they are anomalously spotted outside their native habitat. But one of our native animals is also prone to putting in the odd overseas appearance in the wild – the kangaroo!

Sightings of 'phantom kangaroos', as they are known in the crypto-world, have emanated for some time from the United States, the United Kingdom and various parts of Europe – although the bulk of these expatriated macropods appear to have no phantom-like qualities whatsoever.

In 2003 it was reported a colony of approximately 50 kangaroos was living wild in the Rambouillet forest west of Paris, France. Apparently a breeding population broke free during a bungled burglary on a wildlife park in the 1970s, not only surviving but thriving on a diet of buds and leaves. Road signs signalling their presence have since been erected outside nearby villages, with locals seemingly unperturbed. 'Kangaroos have been part of our daily life for 20 years,' the mayor of the town of Emance was quoted as saying.[1]

Similarly, Derbyshire in the east midlands of England was subject to an invasion of wallabies; not of the rugby union–playing kind but the red-necked species. The wallabies were believed to have been descended from a small group that escaped a private zoo in Staffordshire in the 1930s. Although local temperatures might at first seem a little chilly for a marsupial macropod, it should be remembered red-necked wallabies have been known to survive high in the mountains of Tasmania and Australia's east.[2]

In the 1970s Derbyshire wallaby numbers also rose as high as 50, but very few have been sighted since the turn of the millennium. Locals are unsure whether the colony died out or drifted to more remote areas.[3]

More curious are kangaroo reports from America – including one from Chicago in 1974 where police officers, called to investigate a kangaroo on a suburban porch, were able to corner it in an alleyway but unable to take the feisty marsupial in. Several more sightings were reported after the incident.[4]

But the most bizarre tale emerged from Tennessee, decades earlier in 1934, where a kangaroo – possibly taking the 'boxing kangaroo' concept one step too far – is alleged to have killed and partially devoured several dogs. A reverend who sighted the creature described it as 'fast as lightning, and looking like a giant kangaroo as it ran and leapt across a field'.[5] A search party followed the animal's prints until the trail ended at a cave.[6]

Obviously the concept of a carnivorous kangaroo takes things one leap too far. However, kangaroos in the wild in Australia are well-known for killing dogs, disembowelling them with their claws or drowning them in rivers by dunking them underwater.

America's fascination with the costar of our Commonwealth Coat of Arms was evident even as far back as 1909 in a renowned cryptozoological hoax. It involved the Jersey devil, a gargoylish creature reportedly sighted in New Jersey since the early 1800s and so ingrained in local pop culture the state's National Hockey League team, the Jersey Devils, is named after it. The greatest Jersey devil flap occurred in 1909, when in the space of a single week thousands of Jerseyites claimed to have seen or been attacked by the hideous beast. The Philadelphia Zoo offered a $10,000 reward for its capture. The most infamous fake put forward was a green-painted kangaroo with artificial wings.[7]

But is the Jersey devil an urban myth, the subject of hoaxes or a cryptozoological wonder? Described as a flying biped with a horse-like head, kangaroo-like torso, bat wings and hooves, it is speculated by crytozoologists to lurk in coastal pine lands in the south of the state.[8] As with the phantom kangaroo, sightings of the bizarre beast continue to this day.

Chapter 29
The Queensland tiger

With its picture perfect beaches and three hundred cloudless days per year, Queensland's aptly named Sunshine Coast, a short drive north of Brisbane, is one of Australia's most appealing holiday destinations. Drawn by its relaxing atmosphere, visitors flock to this upmarket resort hub virtually all year round. But few are aware that lurking in its lush hinterland – a mere stone's throw from its welcoming sand – may well be one of the most fearsome beasts to ever stalk our continent. It is known as the Queensland tiger, and according to local researcher Steve Rushton, who has spent more than a decade in its pursuit, 'It is a "top order" predator. An animal of great speed. Of great stealth. And with the ability to kill a man in seconds.'

For eons the east coast of Queensland has been deluged with reports of striped, dog-sized cats with large teeth and vicious temperaments. Local Indigenous tribes have traditionally accepted the existence of the elusive creature; calling it *yarri*, their tales of the carnivorous tree-climber were first noted in the late 1800s by Norwegian ethnographer Carl Lumholz, a scientist renowned for meticulous research:

> It was described . . . as being very savage. If pursued it climbed up the trees, where the natives did not dare follow it, and by gestures they explained how at such times it would growl and bite their hands.[1]

But what exactly is this animal? However much credibility one gives tales of mysterious panthers and pumas in other states, they at least resemble known species. If descriptions of the Queensland tiger are accurate, however, it is unlike any other cat currently existing on the planet.

According to cryptozoologists Tony Healy and Paul Cropper in their meticulously researched book *Out of the Shadows*, the first officially reported sighting of this furtive feline by a settler occurred in 1871, when a letter published in *Proceedings of the Zoological Society of London* detailed a police magistrate's report of his son's encounter with the creature northwest of Townsville:

> Its face was round like that of a cat, it had a long tail, and its body was striped from the ribs under the belly with yellow and black. My dog flew at him. I fired my pistol at its head; the blood came. The animal then ran up a leaning tree. It then got savage and rushed down the tree at the dog and then at me.[2]

Across the turn of the century reports continued to mount. Australian ornithologist George Sharp, while collecting bird specimens in far north Queensland, described seeing the carcass of a dead animal similar to a thylacine, or Tasmanian tiger, but larger and darker, and with different stripes.[3] Celebrated and prolific author Ion Llewellyn Idriess, credited for bringing bush tales to the city, claimed to have seen a Queensland tiger disembowel a kangaroo on the York Peninsula.[4] In the same region he also observed the carcass of a Queensland tiger, describing it as being the dimensions of a dog, striped black and grey, with a tiger-shaped head and 'lance-like claws of great tearing strength'.[5]

In 1930 a Queensland tiger was encountered northwest of Gympie, a sighting that would prove significant, as it was one of the first to be reported on the fringe of the Sunshine Coast. A pair of local men described the beast as 'nearly the size of a mastiff, of a dirty fawn colour, with a whitish belly, and broad blackish stripes', its head was round with 'lynx-like' ears.[6]

Of all Australian cryptids, the Queensland tiger has come closest to earning official recognition. In fact, sightings were so well-documented in the first half of the 20th-century naturalists of the day assumed it to be a legitimate species. In their seminal text on indigenous fauna *The Wild Animals of Australasia*, Albert Sherbourne le Souef (of the prominent le Souef zoological family) and Henry Burrell described it as the 'Striped marsupial cat'.[7] It also warranted mention in *Furred Mammals of Australia*[8] by Ellis Troughton, long-time curator of mammals at the Australian Museum.

The Queensland tiger was deemed to be out there somewhere. But what was it meant to be?

It was the Belgian–French scientist Bernard Heuvelmans, the 'father of crpytozoology' who, in his groundbreaking publication *On the Track of Unknown Animals*,[9] first speculated the Queensland tiger might in fact be a prime example of *Lazarus taxa*, defined as a species erroneously thought extinct according to previous fossil records. The controversial cryptozoologist's most likely choice of suspect? *Thylacoleo carnifax* – the marsupial lion.

There are few animals to ever stalk the Australian landscape more fearsome than *Thylacoleo carnifax*, an aggressive carnivore growing to the size of a mountain lion and estimated to weigh up to 120 kilograms. Its pre-molars were razor-sharp guillotines, perfectly designed for shearing flesh from prey – with a bite force twice that of a present-day lion. Each paw on its muscular forelimbs was armed with a huge retractable killing claw. Scientists also believe it to have been a tree-dweller, one which would wait patiently for prey to pass beneath before dropping on it from above. In short, thylacoleo was not the kind of creature one would want to stumble across on a bush walk.

Thylacoleo was a genus of Australian megafauna which existed from approximately 16 million to 50 thousand years ago. As far as the food chain was concerned, the marsupial lion was top cat, predating on pretty much whatever it wanted, up to and including the 3-metre long, 3-tonne diprotodon – more than 20 times its body weight. But could thylacoleo really be the Queensland tiger?

All species of megafauna are considered extinct by science, but the actual cause of their disappearance is somewhat baffling and for some cryptozoologists contentious. Recent results from radiometric dating of fossils suggest extinction occurred directly after human arrival, the use of firestick farming in hunting by Indigenous Australians generally considered to having been a major contributor. Another theory suggests increased aridity during peak glaciation may have been an added factor, although oxygen and carbon isotopes from fossilised teeth indicate such megafauna as the marsupial lion were well adapted to arid climates. And of course it should be noted some megafaunal species previously endured two million years of climate change.

Could the marsupial lion have survived extinction? Eyewitness reports all seem to point towards an animal with similar features: large cat-like head, dog-sized torso, long claws, long tail, striped back, aggressive behaviour, and arboreal tendencies. Much of which could fit *Thylacoleo carnifax*, or at least some form of descendent species, down to the bone.

Most encounters with the creature up until the mid-20th century came from Queensland's far north. But across the next few decades sightings began to drift south, and since the 1970s especially seem to have centred on the town of Buderim, located 10 kilometres inland from the Sunshine Coast. In fact, reports have flowed so copiously from this tiny town the striped mystery cat has earned itself a local sobriquet: the 'Beast of Buderim'.

The beast was perhaps most famously spotted by local dentist Dr Lance Mesh in 1995, when driving with his daughter at night on the edge of rainforest just outside of Buderim. 'It was striped and like a combination of a goldy, brindly cat and dog,' explained Mesh in a *Sunday Mail* interview. 'My headlights froze on him. He arched his back and crouched before running off the road into the rainforest. I couldn't believe it. For a moment I thought someone had painted a strange-looking dog with stripes.'[10]

It was this sighting which drew the attention of Steve Rushton – a man with a longstanding interest in cryptozoology. Setting up traps near Mesh's property in a failed attempt to capture the beast, he nevertheless became fascinated by its possible existence, and has been both researching and searching for it ever since.

After running with the Mesh sighting, *Sunday Mail* journalist Toni McCrae was deluged with similar accounts from her readers.[11] One of the more vivid came from retired marine engineer Roy Swaby. Shocked by a panicked kangaroo bounding past his vehicle's headlights one night, he was stunned to see the creature from which it was fleeing:

> This incredible sandy-coloured striped animal leapt a full 15 feet out from the side of the road . . . It stopped on the road, turned to look at me, and fell back on to its huge hindquarters, its large green-yellow eyes glowing to the light, and then it opened its jaws and snarled at me. I have never seen anything like it. The white teeth were large and the jaws like a crocodile, like a mantrap. It took two steps and then suddenly crouched and sprang again . . . I drove home shaking.[12]

The accounts received and published by McCrae came from a cross-section of credible local witnesses: a biologist who saw the beast pounce out of his kitchen window after disembowelling his cat;[13] a naturalist who passed the striped cat on a highway north of Brisbane;[14] even a woman who claimed to have hit the creature as it reared in front of her car one night, and was doubly startled to see it bound away with seemingly no injury.[15]

Well-known local businessman Ron West, proprietor of the Majestic Theatre in Pomona, north of Buderim, spotted the striped beast near his home one night:

This animal was probing some sort of dead animal on the white centre line of the road ... It almost sauntered, loped off the road and into the scrub. It was ... not at all like a dog. There wasn't much hair ... The stripes were the arresting thing.[16]

Buderim woman Doris Crerar made headlines when it was speculated she had captured photographic evidence of the creature. But Crerar herself was not quite so sure. Even today she feels the infamous snap she took was more probably that of a stricken member of another cunning family. 'My son said, "Come and take a look at this creature." It was under the avocado tree eating avocadoes. I came out and took a photo of it. It was a strange-looking creature. But I got very close. It was most probably a malnourished fox. I think it had the mange, and therefore had a very stripy appearance. It slunk off quite slowly.'

Crerar's photo of the less than agile animal was sent to the late Dr Eric Guiler, known throughout Tasmania as the 'Thylacine Man', and who unfortunately was unable to identify it. The media flurry abated but Steve Rushton has continued his quest undiscouraged; throughout the past decade and a half he has personally collected more than 50 eyewitness reports from around the local area. Added to these are mounds of information collected from other veteran Queensland crypto-researchers, including the legendary, late local historian Stan Tutt, whose brother Nigel, interviewed on ABC Gold and Tweed Coasts in 2009, provided one of the more colourful descriptions of an encounter with the tiger:

> In my early 20s my brother Charlie and I went up into the scrub. There's a thing I'll never forget. There's an old pine stump. And there's this huge cat sitting on it. Now don't anybody tell me I don't know what a cat looks like. I've seen plenty of cats. But this fellow, he was about the height of a very large cattle dog. And his arms were three times as thick![17]

Tutt's description of the creature he and his brother happened upon on the slopes of nearby Mt Stanley could certainly fit with the muscular feline physique of *Thylacoleo carnifax*. But why weren't the siblings attacked? Rushton speculates that 'Fortunately, the animal is not a manhunter. It basically hunts wallabies and kangaroos.'

Rushton is also keen to clear up confusion between the Queensland tiger and other species. He points out, 'There is no evidence thylacoleo had striping on it. But then again, the Queensland tiger may be the wakaleo – a megafaunal species that could be described as a cross between a kangaroo and a cat.' Some scientific renderings of thylacoleo show it with stripes. Others without. Many renderings of wakaleo have it sporting spots.

It is a confusing area, obfuscated more by the existence of the northern quoll. Ranging from 25 to 75 centimetres long and with tails 20 to 35 centimetres long, quolls are carnivorous marsupials native to Australia and Papua New Guinea. An infamous photograph from 1953 titled the 'Tiger Cat Kenilworth', and portraying the carcass of a long spotted carnivore with a huge head, has been misconstrued by many a novice cryptozoologist as evidence of thylacoleo, thylacine, wakaleo or some hybrid species. Rushton is quick to point out it is in fact a giant northern quoll, a species which grows to more than a metre in length, much larger than its southern counterparts. 'It is known as a "northern wonder", or more commonly a "tiger cat",' states Rushton, vexed at the misnomer. 'It should be called a "leopard cat" because it's spotted and not striped. It is not the Queensland tiger. The Queensland tiger is striped!'

Apart from his ever-growing mounds of research papers, Rushton is yet to collect indisputable physical evidence of the creature's existence. But he knows it's out there. The most substantial footage he has seen came from a German couple holidaying in Charleville, and taken on June 25, 1995 at the height of Queensland tiger mania. In the video, the animal – which appears only fleetingly on the edge of a railway track – appears to have a muscular torso and a very large head. It is impossible to discern whether it is canine or feline, but it certainly looks both wild and unusual, and unlike anything we have ever seen.

Somewhat disenchanted by his lack of success in trapping a specimen, Rushton has in the past few years embarked on less field trips. But he has recently found fresh enthusiasm in the form of a state-of-the-art trap he designed himself. It has a fibreglass frame and ducting, as Rushton believes anything metallic to be anathema to these wary creatures. The spring-loaded trap, Rushton reassures us, 'is not meant to harm the animal in any way – it does not snatch it by the leg'. Instead, the creation will potentially 'ensnare and entangle' the beast.

Rushton has constructed a prototype with which he has conducted preliminary experiments on his pet Staffordshire bull terrier. 'It works perfectly!' he enthuses. 'I was able to untangle him in seconds.' Of course, one can't help but wonder how much longer it would take to untangle an angry snarling thylacoleo. Planning to reduce the size of his new lightweight trap so it can be easily stuffed into a backpack, Rushton intends to resume his tiger quest with renewed vigour. We wish him all the best, hoping he does not suffer too many scratch marks from 'lance-like' claws or bites from 'guillotine-like' pre-molars in the process.

Chapter 30
The Tasmanian tiger

It's impossible to comprehensively cover the subject of extinct Australian species intent on reappearing without mentioning *Thylacinus cynocephalus*, or the Tasmanian tiger. The demise of the thylacine less than a century ago was one of the great catastrophes of Australia's marsupial world.

The last captive specimen of a Tasmanian tiger passed away in its cage at Hobart Zoo on September 7, 1936. In the same year it was added to the protected wildlife list – not officially being declared extinct by international standards until 1986.

For the previous four million years it had prowled not only the Apple Isle but the Australian mainland, feeding on pretty much whatever it wanted: kangaroos, wallabies, wombats, possums and birds. Its disappearance from the mainland 4000 years ago is considered to have been caused by the introduction of the dingo, possibly brought here aboard vessels by Indonesian seafarers.[1] The dingo hunted the same prey as the thylacine, but had the advantage of an omnivorous diet.[2] More pressure was placed on its food sources by Indigenous use of dingos as hunting companions.³ Ultimately, this inimitable creature seems to have been starved out of mainland existence.

It fared better out of the dingo's reach in Tasmania – at least until the arrival of European settlers. As sheep farming became established on the island the thylacine made the mistake of adding mutton to its diet, leading to the establishment of a bounty scheme to cull numbers. Until 1909, the Tasmanian government was paying 1 pound per head for a fully grown thylacine and 10 shillings per pup. The last known kill occurred in the northeast of the state in 1930. Tragically, six years later, the species was gone for good.

Or was it? Since its demise, sightings of the unique marsupial have continually cropped up on the mainland as well as down in Tassie, with figures varying radically depending on the source. The Australian Rare Fauna Research Association claims nearly 4000 reports on mainland Australia alone.[4] Independent thylacine researchers Buck and Joan Emberg estimate the number of overall reports collected nationally at more than 600.[5] In comparison, the Department of Conservation and Land Management in Western Australia has reported more than 60 sightings.[6] Whatever the true figures, thylacine reports are regular enough for official bodies to take note. As Tasmania's Department of Primary Industries, Parks, Water and Environment asserts, 'The incidence of such sightings makes even authorities reluctant to make emphatic statements on the status of the species.'[7]

Where once bounties were placed on the thylacine's scalp, rewards have since been posted for its live capture. In 1983 American media mogul Ted Turner put up an offer of $100,000, since retracted.[8] In 2005 news magazine *The Bulletin* offered $1.25 million,[9] the offer expiring before the magazine itself met its demise. Currently a Tasmanian tour operator is offering $1.75 million.[10] Nevertheless, no hard proof of the creature's continued existence has surfaced.

The most frequent thylacine sightings tend to come from the southern part of Victoria.[11] Indeed, the most recent spate of reports have emanated from Gippsland, southeast of Melbourne. In 2009, Melbourne school teacher and thylacine researcher Murray McAlister, who claimed to have seen the creature, revealed to the *Herald Sun* he was embarking on a quest into the Gippsland region to find conclusive evidence of its existence.

'Through the binoculars you can see everything that says it's a Tasmanian tiger. You can see his stripes, the dark colours on his rump and the way he moves,' McAlister said at the time. 'The problem is that we haven't had enough technology to capture the image close up.'[12]

McAlister intended to remedy this problem utilising a high-powered camera lens, worth $100,000 and capable of taking clear close-up images 1 kilometre away. So far, the thyla-seeker has had no success in procuring such a shot.[13]

Rather than being rediscovered, can the Tassie tiger be raised from the dead? In 1999 then-director of the Australian Museum Professor Mike Archer hatched a controversial plan to clone the creature with reconstructed DNA from a thylacine pup preserved in ethanol in the late 1800s. Archer theorised that once reconstructed, the gene could be cloned in a Tasmanian devil egg.[14] The scheme, which earned the palaeontologist a nomination in the Australian Sceptics' annual Bent Spoon

Awards for the 'perpetrator of the most preposterous piece of paranormal or pseudo-scientific piffle',[15] nevertheless attracted financial backing from the private sector. Abandoned when Archer left the museum in 2004, the plan was itself resurrected shortly thereafter when the palaeontologist took a position as Dean of Science at the University of New South Wales and procured backing from several other universities.[16] In 2008, detractors were partially silenced when scientific researchers successfully revived the thylacine gene in a mouse embryo,[17] although it should be noted one of the scientists working on the project, Professor Marilyn Renfree, was quoted as saying it was 'highly unlikely' an entire animal could be brought back to life via this process.[18]

Many conservationists believe such money would be better spent on preserving existing endangered species. For example, think of the plight of the poor Tasmanian devil, whose numbers, due to a rare form of communicable face cancer, have diminished more than 90 per cent since the mid-90s[19] – leaving this unique creature precariously balanced on the tipping point of extinction. Inversely, it could be argued technology from such research might potentially lead to a way to save it.

In the meantime, the Tasmanian devil's carnivorous marsupial relative the Tasmanian tiger – so proudly displayed on the state's coat of arms – continues to be sighted. And just like the devil, it does not seem likely to stray too far from headlines anytime in the near future.

Epilogue

The world is a strange place. And as science moves forward, with innovations such as digital still and motion picture capture technology becoming both ubiquitous and virtually instantaneous, we are learning it may be far stranger than we ever thought. Camera and video phones are all around us, and subsequently the number of reports of paranormal phenomena substantiated by visual evidence seems to increase with every turn of the news cycle.

Shortly before this book went to print, Sydneysider Fiona Hartigan snapped a picture of three circular silvery black objects streaking through the sky above a major thoroughfare in the city's western suburbs with her iPhone. The startling photograph made the news nationally both on television and in print.

Meanwhile, ghost tour participant Renee English took an eerie shot of two spectral children romping through the grounds of St Mark's Cemetery in Picton, New South Wales. The controversial photograph, which supposedly links back to a commonly reported ghost of a little girl who died tried tragically in the 1800s and is interred in the cemetery, spent weeks splashed across the papers and created a controversy between believers and naysayers.

These are only two recent instances chosen at random. Countless more could be cited, making all the more curious the dearth of visually documented evidence of crypto creatures. Regularly sighted as they are, they are rarely caught on camera.

Talking to cryptozoologists — as committed a bunch as anyone is likely to encounter — we could not help but sense undertones of fatigue and exasperation engendered by failure to accumulate definitive photographic proof of their quarry. Yet perversely, of all types of Forteana, it is the potential existence of certain cryptids such as the Queensland tiger and the Tasmanian tiger which are awarded most credence by some members of the scientific community.

In this regard — in fact in regard to the pursuit of any paranormal phenomena — it is worth citing the experience of the late Sir Edmund Hillary, the first man to scale Mount Everest and who in 1960 was contracted by *World Book Encyclopedia* to investigate legends of the yeti in the Himalayas. Accompanied by respected author and journalist the late Desmond Doig, Hillary spent nine months in and around the Nepalese village of Khumjung, an epicentre of sightings, equipped with trip-wire, time-lapse and infra-red cameras.

In that time they collected not one single photograph of a yeti. Hillary (who incidentally claimed to have encountered the ghost of fellow explorer Sir Ernest Shackleton in Mawson's

Hut in the Antarctic) became disenchanted, and the expedition ground to a halt.

Doig, however, remained convinced of the legendary Abominable Snowman's existence. 'We may not have seen a yeti,' he explained two decades later. 'But we didn't see a snow leopard either. And we *know* they exist.'[1] Cryptids are, by definition, rare. And rare creatures are of course furtive in nature and sparse in number.

Indeed, if there is one quality necessary for a paranormal researcher to stay true to their quest it's faith – without it, they are just chasing their evolutionarily defunct tails. Throughout the course of collating information for this book we have had not only our minds opened to the possibility of the impossible, but also our scepticism challenged as evidence, both visual and anecdotal, has revealed itself in myriad ways.

Not only have we been presented with stories from credible, intelligent and sincere sources, but we have also seen things with our own eyes that cannot be readily explained. We have been chased down dark highways by strange lights, watched doors open of their own accord, and felt the physical presence of invisible forces. Try as we might to justify these occurrences scientifically, acceptable answers have not been forthcoming, leaving us with no option but to believe. Or at least believe that anything is possible.

By no means do we wish to contend all the phenomena in this book exist. No doubt in time some will be disproved – cases of hoax, of misidentification, or of traditional myth being promulgated and distorted by urban legend. Some may even go on to be proven. And some will remain mysteries forever.

Epilogue

Despite our own exhaustive investigations, we are still far from being in any position to predict which phenomena might ultimately fall into what category.

But we are very certain of one matter: something is out there.

Glossary

Anomaly An unusual occurrence that does not fit a standard rule or law and cannot be explained by accepted scientific theories.

Apparition The visible appearance of a spirit, with imprints of distinct physical features it possessed in life. Can be either partially or fully formed, and is the rarest type of manifestation as well as the most classic.

Banshee An ancient Irish or Scottish tradition of a female spirit foretelling a tragedy or death. They are said to emit a sound like a mournful crying.

Clairvoyant A person possessing the innate ability to see physic phenomenon, including visual mental images of alleged spirits. Someone who hears voices of discarnate beings is called clairaudient.

Cold spot An energy area associated with a temperature change. The theory is that the presence of a spirit zaps the air of its warmth, transferring the energy to itself.

Something is Out There

Ectoplasm From the Greek words *ektos* and *plasma*, which mean 'exteriorised substance'. A semi-fluid material that is a product of psychic energy, usually forming as a fog-like mist or a solid white mass. It is said to be the second stage of manifestation after an orb. Movie ectoplasm is often green and slimy.

Ghost The image of a person, experienced after their death by the living, reflecting their appearance during life. An earthbound spirit, it is speculated that a ghost does not realise it is dead, has unfinished business or does not want to move on so remains in an area of emotional attachment. Also called phantom, spook or spectre.

Ghost lights Strange lights that appear where there is no natural source, indicating the presence of a ghost or entity. They often appear outdoors and have been attributed to natural as well as spiritual sources. They are also known as phantom lights, jack-o'-lanterns or *ignis fatuus* (meaning 'foolish fire'). In Australia they are known as Min Min Lights.

Grounded spirits A spirit trapped in the earthly or material realm.

Harbinger An entity which brings warnings of impending events.

Haunting A repeated manifestation of supernatural phenomena occurring over a period of time in a specific location.

Intelligent haunting When spirits seem to inhabit a specific location—not necessarily at the place they die, sometime a place of attachment such as a home or hotel. The spirit appears to act with free will, shows intelligence, attempts to make its presence known, and interacts with witnesses at a location.

Ley lines The Earth's natural energy lines, which often correspond with significant landmarks or ancient sites. It is suggested that where two ley lines cross, there is a possible portal to another dimension.

Manifestation The appearance of an entity taking form, either partially or fully. It can also mean the outbreak of paranormal activity.

Medium A person who has the innate ability to communicate with the deceased, conveying messages from them to the living.

Men in black A term used to describe government agents who reportedly visit UFO witnesses in an attempt to stop them telling others what they have seen.

Orb An anomalous ball of energy, either white or coloured, that is generally considered an incomplete manifestation of a spirit at an allegedly haunted location. Orbs usually show up when a camera flash is used, and many skeptics dismiss them as unreliable indicators caused by natural elements such as dust, pollen, insects or moisture. Orbs can appear stationary or travelling at high speed, in which case they appear with a 'tail'.

Paranormal Above or outside the range of the natural order of things or beyond scientific explanation.

Poltergeist The literal translation from German means 'noisy and troublesome ghost'. Often manifests in a violent or aggressive manner, or sometimes just playful.

Portal A doorway or gateway to the 'other side', a path between the physical and spiritual realms or between dimensions.

Residual energy Energy left over after a person has died, sometimes in a home or even on a piece of furniture associated with the deceased.

Residual haunting The psychic imprint of a scene from the past repeated at intervals. Perhaps the spirit is trapped in a specific moment in life, or it may be just a flash from the past reliving a traumatic moment. The ghostly participants often seem unaware of their living observers.

Sensitive A person who is particularly sensitive to the psychic emanations of his or her surroundings and other people.

Visitations A term used to describe the occasional and inconsistent presence of a ghostly entity.

Vortex Believed to be a portal through which spirits travel between the earthly and spiritual realms. These often appear in photography as spiraling white mist or tornado-like slashes, indicating a moving spiritual presence.

Ghost-hunting devices

EMF A hand-held device (sometimes called a trifield meter) used to measure fluctuations within an electromagnetic field. These fields surround and permeate all physical reality and include X-rays, radio waves and ultraviolet rays. Anything that conducts energy, from televisions to power boxes—even human beings and animals—will emit a reading, and these must be taken into consideration when ghosthunting. The theory is that ghosts disrupt the EM field when present, their energy overriding other forms of electromagnetic energy. The devices measure in milligauss, with a reading above 7mG accepted as the level indicating a supernatural presence. EMF meters vary in quality and price; there is even a new iPhone app that claims to detect spiritual presence.

EVP Disembodied sounds or voices recorded on magnetic tape which are only heard upon playback. Discovered by Swedish researcher Friedrich Juergenson in 1959. Usually recorded in a range from 30–250 Hz (Human speech is generally within 500–2000 Hz, and has never been recorded below 280 Hz). Purists believe EVP recordings are more successful on old-style analogue tape recorders.

Digital cameras and camcorders The world of ghost hunting has opened up to the populace since the invention of digital photography. A camera is a necessary tool when ghost hunting—and for some reason the cheaper point-and-shoot versions tend to capture better images than more sophisticated DSLR (Digital Single Lens Reflex) cameras that require manual settings. Budding ghost photographers should take as many images as possible when a ghostly presence is suspected, with flash both on and off. Some video cameras come with night vision, or infrared settings, which is used when there is insufficient light to see an object with the unaided eye.

Since paranormal experts believe a spirit is composed of energy not always visible to the naked eye, this is a particularly useful tool for ghost hunters.

Divining rods Also called dousing rods, these forked sticks were traditionally used for finding water. In paranormal circles, they are usually L-shaped brass rods, used in pairs, which move when in contact with spiritual energy. Often used in conjunction with questions, prompting the entity to make the sticks cross or move apart.

Infrared thermometers Temperature tends to drop suddenly in the presence of a ghost, the theory being that the ghost absorbs the energy from the surrounding air. A thermometer is a useful tool to verify the existence of a cold spot. Infrared non-contact thermometers use an infrared laser beam accurate up to 30 metres for recording temperatures.

Bibliography

Ansell, K. and Farrell, P. (eds) *The Clayton Calendar*, Term One Edition, Westall High School, 1966

Archer, Michael, Hand, Suzanne and Godthelp, Henk, *Riversleigh, the Story of Animals in Ancient Rainforests of Inland Australia*, New Holland, Sydney, 1991

Arnold, Kenneth and Palmer, Ray, *The Coming of the Saucers*, property of the author, 1952

Attenbrow, Val, *Sydney's Aboriginal Past: Investigating the Archeological and Historical Records*, University of New South Wales Press, Sydney, 2002

Bartholomew, Robert E. and Howard, George S., *UFOs and Alien Contact: Two Centuries of Mystery*, Prometheus Books, Amherst, NY, 1998

Basterfield, Keith, *A Catalogue of Australian UFO Vehicle Interference Cases*, Project 1947, online at <project1947.com/kbcat/kbvehint0505.htm>

Blake, L.J., *Letters of Charles Joseph La Trobe*, Victorian Government Printer, Melbourne, 1975

Cartmell, B.C., *Let's Go Fossil Shark Tooth Hunting*, Natural Science Research, Venice, FL, 1978

Something is Out There

Chalker, Bill, *The OZ Files: The Australian UFO Story*, Duffy & Snellgrove, Sydney, 1996

Clark, Jerome, *The UFO Book: Encyclopedia of the Extraterrestrial*, Visible Ink Press, Canton, MI, 1997

——*Unexplained! 347 Strange Sightings, Incredible Occurrences, and Puzzling Physical Phenomena*, Visible Ink Press, Detroit, MI, 1993

Clarke, Arthur C., 'Hazards of Prophecy: The Failure of Imagination', *Profiles of the Future: An Inquiry into the Limits of the Possible*, Bantam, NY, 1962

Cusack, Frank, *Australian Ghost Stories*, William Heinemann Limited, Melbourne-London, 1967

Dapin, Mark, *Strange Country*, Pan Macmillan, Sydney, 2008

Favenc, Ernest, *The History of Australian Exploration from 1788 to 1888*, Turner and Henderson, Sydney, 1888

Flannery, Tim, *The Future Eaters: An Ecological History of the Australian Lands and People*, Grove Press, New York, 2002

——*Prehistoric Animals of Australia*, Australian Museum, Sydney, 1983

Friends of the Theatre Royal, *Hobart's Theatre Royal: A Brief History* (brochure), Mercury Press, Hobart, 1948

Fort, Charles, *The Book of the Damned*, Horace Liverlight Inc., New York, 1919

Green, William, *Warplanes of the Third Reich*, Doubleday, New York, 1970

Grey, Zane, *Tales of Tahitian Waters*, Harper and Brothers, New York, NY, 1928

Haines, Richard F., *Melbourne Episode; Case Study of a Missing Pilot*, L.D.A. Press, Los Altos, CA, 1987

Healy, Tony and Cropper, Paul, *Out of the Shadows: Mystery Animals of Australia*, Ironbark/Pan Macmillan, Chippendale, NSW, 1994

Heuvelmans, Bernard, *On the Track of Unknown Animals*, Bernard Rupert Hart-Davis, London, 1958

Hitch, G. and M., *Ghosts of Norfolk Island*, self-published, 1988

Holden, Nicholas, *Bunyips: Australia's folklore of fear*, National Library of Australia, Canberra, 2001

Jones, Granny, *Ghost Stories of Richmond*, Regal Publications, Launceston, Tasmania, 1992

Killey, Kevin and Lester, Gary, *The Devil's Meridian*, Lester-Townsend, Sydney, 1980

Lasby, Clarence G., *Project Paperclip: German Scientists and the Cold War*, Atheneum, New York, 1971

le Souef, Albert, Sherbourne and Burrell, Henry, *The Wild Animals of Australasia*, George G. Harrap, London, 1926

Liston, Dr Carol, 'Frederick Fisher and his Ghost', *Campbelltown: the Bicentennial History*, Campbelltown City Council, NSW, 1988

Llewellyn Idriess, Ion, *One Wet Season*, Angus & Robertson, Sydney, 1949

Lumholz, Carl, *Among Cannibals: An Account of Four Years' Travels in Australia and of Camp Life with the Aboriginals of Australia*, Rasmus B. Anderson (trans.), Charles Scribner's Sons, New York, 1889

Martin, Robert Montgomery, *History of the British Colonies, Australian Almanac & Directory*, O'Shaunessy, London, 1835

Maxwell-Stewart, Hamish, *Closing Hell's Gates: The death of a convict station*, Allen & Unwin, Sydney, 2008

McCloy, James F. and Miller, Ray, *The Jersey Devil*, Middle Atlantic Press, Moorestown, NJ, 1976

Morgan, J., *The Life and Adventures of William Buckley*, Hobart, 1852, reprinted by Australian National University Press, Canberra, 1980

Noonuccal, Oodgeroo, *Stradbroke Dreamtime*, Angus & Robertson, Sydney, 1993

Pace, Steve, *B-2 Spirit: The Most Capable War Machine on the Planet*, McGraw-Hill, New York, 1999

Pinkney, John, *A Paranormal File: An Australian Investigator's Casebook*, The Five Mile Press, Noble Park, Victoria, 2000

——*Haunted: The Book of Australia's Ghosts*, The Five Mile Press, Noble Park, Victoria, 2005

Poultney, Trevor, *Hangmen, Hunger and Hard Labour, Old Melbourne Gaol*, National Trust of Australia, Victoria, 2003

Pouyaud, L., Wirjoatmodjo, S., Rachmatika, I., Tjakrawidjaja, A., Hadiaty, R. and Hadie, W., 'Une nouvelle espèce de coelacanthe: preuves génétiques et morphologiques' [A new species of coelacanth: genetic and morphological evidence], *Comptes Rendus de l'Académie des sciences* [Proceedings of the Academy of Sciences], Paris, 1999

Rieusset, Brian, *Penitentiary Chapel, a Brief History of the Penitentiary Chapel and Criminal Courts*, Brian Rieusset, Hobart, 2007

Schnabel, Jim, *Round in Circles*, Hamish Hamilton, London, 1993

Smith, Jim, *Aboriginal Legends of the Blue Mountains*, property of the author, Wentworth Falls, NSW, 1992

Smith, Malcolm, *Bunyips and Bigfoots: In Search of Australia's Mystery Animals*, Millennium Books, Alexandria, NSW, 1996

Stead, D.G., *Sharks and Rays of Australian Seas*, Angus & Robertson, London, 1963

Steno, Nicolaus, *The Head of a Shark Dissected*, Royal Society, London, 1667

Taplin, George, *The Narrinyeri*, E.S. Wigg & Son, Adelaide, 1878

Tim the Yowie Man, *Haunted and Mysterious Australia*, New Holland, French's Forest, NSW, 2006

Troughton, Ellis, *Furred Mammals of Australia*, Charles Scribner's Sons, New York, 1947

Ullathorne, William, *The Devil is a Jackass*, Gracewing Books, London, 1995

Vincent, Liz, *Ghosts of Picton Past*, self-published, 2004

Welfare, Simon and Fairley, John, *Arthur C. Clarke's Mysterious World*, William Collins Sons & Company and George Rainbird Limited, Fakenham, UK, 1981

Whyte, Rob, *The Ghost Tour, Jenolan Caves*, self-published (brochure), 2006

Williams, Michael and Lang, Rebecca, *Australian Big Cats: An Unnatural History of Panthers*, self-published, 2010

Wilson, Colin, *Mysteries*, Putnam, New York, 1978

Winton, Time, *In the Winter Dark*, McPhee Gribble, Melbourne, 1988

Notes

Introduction
1. Jacqueline Maley, 'We believe in miracles, and UFOs', *Sydney Morning Herald*, December 19, 2009
2. Colin Wilson, *Mysteries*, Putnam Publishing, New York, 1978
3. Charles Fort, *The Book of the Damned*, Horace Liverlight Inc., New York, 1919

Chapter 1 Haunted houses
1. *Daily Telegraph*, May 23, 2009
2. *Ibid.*

Chapter 2 Terror towns
1. Liz Vincent, *Ghosts of Picton Past*, self-published, Picton, NSW, 2004, pp. 64–5

Chapter 3 Creepy convict colonies
1. Hamish Maxwell-Stewart, *Closing Hell's Gates*, Allen & Unwin, Sydney, 2008, p. 2
2. *Ibid.* p. 16
3. *Ibid.* p. 1

4   *Ibid.* p. 16
5   *Ibid.* pp. 16, 73
6   *Ibid.* p. 67
7   *Ibid.* p. 70
8   William Bernard Ullathorne, *The Devil is a Jackass,* Gracewing Books, London, 1995

Chapter 4 Paranormal prisons
1   *Sunday Herald Sun,* August 16, 2009
2   'Mansion may reach back', online at <www.starnewsgroup.com.au/story/43382>
3   Trevor Poultney, *Hangmen, Hunger and Hard Labour, Old Melbourne Gaol,* National Trust of Australia, Victoria, 2003, p. 17
4   Brian Rieusset, *Penitentiary Chapel, a Brief History of the Penitentiary Chapel and Criminal Courts,* Brian Rieusset, Hobart, 2007
5   *Ibid.*

Chapter 5 Wards of woe
1   Submitted experiences, Quarantine Station, online at <www.paranormalaustralia.com>
2   *Ibid.*
3   Investigation of Aradale Asylum, 2008, online at <ghost-researchinternational.com>

Chapter 6 Theatres of fear
1   Frank Cusack, 'A Round of Wraiths: Federici – and the Devil in the Evening Dress', *Australian Ghost Stories,* William Heinemann Limited, Melbourne-London, 1967
2   Mr Federici's Funeral: A Painful Incident at the Grave', *The Argus,* March 6, 1888
3   'Death on the Stage of F. Federici', *Illustrated Australian News,* March 31, 1888
4   Frank, Cusack, 'A Round of Wraiths'

5 *Ibid.*
6 *Ibid.*
7 *Ibid.*
8 *Ibid.*
9 John Pinkney, 'Uncanny "Extra" Invades a Movie Set', *A Paranormal File: An Australian Investigator's Casebook*, The Five Mile Press, Noble Park, Victoria, 2000, p. 18
10 *Ibid.*
11 Justin Murphy, 'The Theatre Ghost', *Rewind*, ABC Television, August 29, 2004
12 John Pinkney, 'Bert Newton's Extraordinary Encounter', *A Paranormal File*, pp. 15–16
13 *Ibid.*
14 *Ibid.*
15 Justin Murphy, 'The Theatre Ghost'
16 *Ibid.*
17 Boise State University, 'The D'Oyly Carte Opera Company', Frederick Federici (1879–87), online at <math.boisestate.edu/gas/whowaswho/F/FedericiFrederick.htm>
18 *Australian Dictionary of Biography*, online at <www.adboline.anu.edu.au>
19 Friends of the Theatre Royal, *Hobart's Theatre Royal: A Brief History*, (brochure)
20 'The Theatre Royal', *Dimensions*, episode 7, online at <www.abc.net.au/dimensions>, October 25, 2002

Chapter 7 Ghostly grottos
1 Rob Whyte, *The Ghost Tour, Jenolan Caves*, self-published, 2006
2 *Ibid.*

Chapter 9 Possessed pubs
1 John Pinkney, *A Paranormal File: An Australian Investigator's Casebook*, The Five Mile Press, Noble Park, Victoria, 2000

2 'Investigation of the Coach & Horses Inn', June 2007, online at <www.ghostresearchinternational.com>
3 Ibid.
4 ACT Paranormal Investigators website, online at <www.actparanormal.com>
5 Kate Grenville, 'Once Upon a Time in 1806', *The Guardian*, February 18, 2006
6 Michael Fitzgerald, 'Watery Grave of Secrets', *The Times*, September 2007
7 Brad Perry, 'Who is Haunting the Region', *Riverland Weekly*, August 13, 2009

Chapter 10 The banshee in black
1 Flora King, 'Ghosting through the Blue Mountains with Paranormal Pete', *Australian Traveller*, July 31, 2009
2 *The Australian*, February 19, 1839
3 *Sydney Gazette*, May 3, 1842
4 Ibid.
5 Ibid.

Chapter 11 Spooky cellars
1 'The Drives Investigation', June 14, 2008, online at <www.ghostresearchinternational.com>

Chapter 12 Australia's most infamous ghost
1 Frank Cusack, 'A Rattle of Leg Irons: Fisher's Ghost', *Australian Ghost Stories*, William Heinemann Limited, Melbourne-London, 1967
2 Dr Carol Liston, 'Frederick Fisher and his Ghost', *Campbelltown: The Bicentennial History*, Campbelltown City Council, NSW, 1988
3 Robert Montgomery Martin, *History of the British Colonies, Australian Almanac & Directory*, O'Shaunessy, London, 1835

4   Dr Carol Liston, 'Frederick Fisher and his Ghost'
5   Frank Cusack, 'A Rattle of Leg Irons: Fisher's Ghost'
6   Jeff McGill, 'How We Became a Ghost Town', *Campbelltown Since Federation*, Campbelltown City Council, online at <www.campbelltown.nsw.gov.au>
7   Jeff McGill, 'Have you seen Fisher's Ghost?: 180 years of the Fisher's Ghost Legend', *Campbelltown-Macarthur Advertiser*, June 21, 2006
8   Ibid.
9   Ibid.

Chapter 13 Wycliffe Well – Australia's UFO capital
1   Tash Henning, 'UFOs frighten Marlinja family', *Tennant & District Times*, June 27, 2008
2   A quote from the NPWS noticeboard at the Devils Marbles Conservation Reserve

Chapter 15 The great UFO flap of 1909
1   Kenneth Arnold and Ray Palmer, *The Coming of the Saucers*, property of the author, 1952
2   *Sydney Morning Herald*, August 10, 1909
3   *Clutha Leader of Balclutha*, July 27, 1909
4   Ibid.
5   *Otago Daily Times*, July 25, 1909
6   *Thames Star*, July 31, 1909
7   *Otago Daily Times*, July 29, 1909
8   *Southland Daily News*, August 4, 1909
9   *Sydney Morning Herald*, August 11, 1909
10 *Hobart Mercury*, August 19, 1909
11 Ibid., August 24, 1909
12 Ibid., August 23, 1909
13 *Sydney Morning Herald*, December 5, 1910
14 Ibid.

15 Robert E. Bartholomew and George S. Howard, *UFOs and Alien Contact: Two Centuries of Mystery*, Prometheus Books, Amherst, NY, 1998
16 Mowamjum Artists, Spirit of the Wandjina Aboriginal Corporation, online at <www.mowanjumarts.com>
17 Coo-ee Aboriginal Art Gallery, online at <www.cooeeart.com.au/wanjina/indec.html>
18 Mowamjum Artists, Spirit of the Wandjina Aboriginal Corporation

Chapter 16 Tully saucer nest

1 'Crop Circles: Mysteries in the Field', television documentary produced by Termite Art Productions & distributed by Discovery Communications, 2002
2 Bill Chalker, 'The 1966 Tully Saucer "Nest", A Classic UFO Physical Trace Case', *The OZ Files: The Australian UFO Story*, Duffy & Snellgrove, Sydney, NSW, 1996
3 *Ibid.*
4 *Ibid.*
5 *Ibid.*
6 *Ibid.*
7 *Ibid.*
8 *Ibid.*
9 *Ibid.*
10 *Ibid.*
11 *Ibid.*
12 *Ibid.*
13 *Adelaide News*, May 5, 1972
14 Jim Schnabel, *Round in Circles*, Hamish Hamilton, London, 1993
15 Cameron Outridge, '"Unfakeable" crop circles discovered at Conondale', *The Range News*, April 2, 2004
16 Bill Chalker, 'The 1966 Tully Saucer "Nest"'
17 *Ibid.*
18 *Ibid.*

Chapter 17 The Westall UFO conspiracy

1. John Pinkney, 'The saucer that shocked a school', *A Paranormal File: An Australian Investigator's Casebook*, The Five Mile Press, Noble Park, Victoria, 2000
2. Karen Ansell and Peter Farrell (eds), *The Clayton Calendar*, Term One Edition, Westall High School, 1966
3. Yahoo! Groups, Westall High School 1966 UFO incident, online at <tech.groups.yahoo.com/group/Westallhighschoolufo>
4. John Pinkney, 'The saucer that shocked a school', *A Paranormal File: An Australian Investigator's Casebook*, The Five Mile Press, Noble Park, VIC, 2000
5. 'Beam of Light like a Disc', *Dandenong Journal*, Thursday April 21, 1966
6. Ibid.
7. Karen Ansell and Peter Farrell (eds), *The Clayton Calendar*
8. Steven Cauchi, 'Academic throws light on 40-year-old UFO mystery', *The Sunday Age*, October 2, 2005
9. Ibid.
10. Yahoo! Groups, Westall High School 1966 UFO incident
11. Ibid.
12. Ibid.
13. 'Flying Saucer Mystery: School Silent', *Dandenong Journal*, April 14, 1966
14. Ibid.
15. Bill Chalker, 'The Westall School Sensation', *The OZ Files: The Australian UFO Story*, Duffy & Snellgrove, Sydney, 1996
16. William Green, *Warplanes of the Third Reich*, Doubleday, New York, 1970
17. Clarence G. Lasby, *Project Paperclip: German Scientists and the Cold War*, Atheneum, New York, 1971
18. Steve Pace, *B-2 Spirit: The Most Capable War Machine on the Planet*, McGraw-Hill, New York, 1999
19. da Silva, Wilson, 'Mass Hysteria', *Cosmos*, August–September, 2009, pp. 40–1

20. AUFORN, 'Disclosure Australia', The Australian UFO Research Network UFO Disclosure Project, online at <www.auforn.com>

Chapter 18 The Valentich disappearance

1. Kevin Killey and Gary Lester, *The Devil's Meridian*, Lester-Townsend, Sydney, 1980
2. Aircraft Accident Investigation Summary Report Ref. No. V116/783/1047
3. *Ibid.*
4. *Ibid.*
5. Graham Bicknell, 'The Mysterious Disappearance of Frederick Valentich', *Geelong Advertiser*, September 27, 2007
6. Aircraft Accident Investigation Summary Report Ref. No. V116/783/1047
7. *Ibid.*
8. Keith Basterfield, *A Catalogue of Australian UFO Vehicle Interference Cases*, Project 1947, online at <project1947.com/kbcat/kbvehint0505.htm>
9. Richard F. Haines, PhD, 'Fifty-Six Aircraft Pilot Sightings Involving Electromagnetic Effects', M.U.F.O.N. UFO Symposium, Albuquerque, NM, 1992
10. 'Pilot Missing after UFO Report', Associated Press, *Waterloo Courier*, October 24, 1978, p. 1
11. Mark Russell, 'Victoria's own X-File unsolved 30 years on', *The Age*, October 14, 2008
12. Richard F. Haines, *Melbourne Episode; Case Study of a Missing Pilot*, L.D.A. Press, Los Altos, CA, 1987
13. John Pinkney, 'The Bass Strait Vanishings', *A Paranormal File: An Australian Investigator's Casebook*, The Five Mile Press, Noble Park, Victoria, 2000
14. Richard F. Haines, *Melbourne Episode; Case Study of a Missing Pilot*; Paul Norman, 'The Frederick Valentich Disappearance', Victorian Unidentified Flying Object Research Society, Moorabbin, Victoria, 1998, online at <members.ozemail.com.

au/~vufors/valensum.htm>; Jerome Clark, *The UFO Book: Encyclopedia of the Extraterrestrial*, Visible Ink Press, Canton, MI, 1997
15 Paul Norman, 'The Frederick Valentich Disappearance'
16 John Pinkney, 'The Bass Strait Vanishings'
17 Richard F. Haines and Paul Norman, 'Valentich Disappearance: New Evidence and a New Conclusion', *Journal of Scientific Exploration*, vol. 14, no. 1, 2000, pp. 19–33
18 Pinkney, John, 'The Bass Strait Vanishings'
19 Graham Bicknell, 'The Mysterious Disappearance of Frederick Valentich', *Geelong Advertiser*, September 27, 2007
20 *Ibid.*
21 Mark Russell, 'Victoria's own X-File unsolved 30 years on', *The Age*, October 14, 2008
22 Graham Bicknell, 'The Mysterious Disappearance of Frederick Valentich'
23 'Pilot Missing after UFO Report', *Waterloo Courier*, October 24, 1978, p. 1
24 Chris Wisbey, interviewing historian Reg A. Watson, ABC Hobart, 'Frederick Valentich vanishes', October 6, 2008

Chapter 19 The Min Min Lights
1 Provided by The Min Min Encounter, Boulia, John and Pamela Brown, August 5, 1996
2 *Ibid.*
3 Provided by The Min Min Encounter, Boulia, John and Noel Anderson, March 22, 2007
4 ABC Radio, July 14, 2005, online at <www.abc.net.au/northwest/stories/s1414278.htm>
5 ABC, *News in Science*, March 28, 2003, online at <www.abc.net.au>

Chapter 20 UFO hotspots
1 'Top UFO "Hot Spots" for Asia and Australia', online at <www.ufoinfo.com/onthisday/hotspots/asia-australia.html>

2. Gary Sledge, 'Going Where No One Has Gone Before', *Discovery Channel Magazine*, Issue 3, August 2008
3. 'Next Generation Cloaking Device Demonstrated', <online at www.sciencedaily.com> January 16, 2009
4. 'Grampians gateway To UFOs', *The Warrnambool Standard*, June 14, 2003
5. Mark Dunn, 'Mystery lights have Victorians asking . . . What Is Out There?', *Melbourne Herald Sun*, June 27, 2002
6. *The Warrnambool Standard*, 2003, online at <www.cosmicparadigm.com>
7. Erik Jensen, 'The Visitors: Aliens and UFOs in Contemporary Art', *Sydney Morning Herald*, December 11, 2007
8. Arthur C. Clarke, 'Hazards of Prophecy: The Failure of Imagination', *Profiles of the Future: An Inquiry into the Limits of the Possible*, Bantam, New York, 1962

Chapter 21 Yowie – Australia's biggest cryptid mystery
1. Jim Smith, *Aboriginal Legends of the Blue Mountains*, property of the author, Wentworth Falls, NSW, 1992
2. *Sydney Morning Herald*, September 13, 2002
3. Register of Historic Places & Objects, online at <www.phasnsw.org.au>
4. *The Illustrated Sydney News*, October 2, 1889, online at <www.bmcc.nsw.gov.au>
5. *Australian Town and Country Journal*, December 9, 1882
6. *Manning River Times*, August 7, 2009
7. *Gold Coast Times*, November 7, 1977
8. *The Australian*, May 26, 2009
9. *Ibid.*

Chapter 22 The river monster
1. Ruby Lang, 'The Hawkesbury River Monster: What Lies, or Lurks Beneath?', *Australasian Post*, 2001

Notes

2. Rex Gilroy, 'Research of Australian Reptilian Water Monsters', online at <www.mysteriousaustralia.com>
3. *Windsor and Richmond Gazette*, August 8, 1979
4. Rex Gilroy, 'Our Own Nessie', *Australasian Post*, May 2, 1985
5. Rex Gilroy, 'Research of Australian Reptilian Water Monsters', online at <www.mysteriousaustralia.com>, 2006
6. Rex Gilroy, 'Our Own Nessie'
7. Ruby Lang, 'The Hawkesbury River Monster'
8. Simon Welfare and John Fairley, 'Creatures of Lakes and Locks', *Arthur C. Clarke's Mysterious World*, William Collins Sons & Company and George Rainbird Limited, Fakenham, UK, 1981
9. Jane Boler, 'Panther Old News, Hawkesbury now has a Dinosaur Problem', *Hawkesbury Gazette*, August 13, 2009
10. Rex Gilroy, 'Research of Australian Reptilian Water Monsters'

Chapter 23 Mega shark

1. Sarah Vogler, 'Monster shark spreads fear off Queensland coast', *Courier Mail*, October 24, 2009
2. Ben S. Roesch, 'A Critical Evaluation of the Supposed Contemporary Existence of *Carcharodon megalodon*', *The Cryptozoology Review*, no. 3, 1998
3. D.G. Stead, *Sharks and Rays of Australian Seas*, Angus & Robertson, London, 1963
4. Zane Grey, *Tales of Tahitian Waters*, Harper and Brothers, New York, NY, 1928
5. *Ibid.*
6. Pete Thomas, 'The Old Men and the Sea', *Los Angeles Times*, September 28, 1994
7. Zane Grey, *Tales of Tahitian Waters*
8. B.C. Cartmell, *Let's Go Fossil Shark Tooth Hunting*, Natural Science Research, Venice, FL, 1978; Ben S. Roesch, 'A Critical Evaluation of the Supposed Contemporary Existence of *Carcharodon megalodon*'

Something is Out There

9 Nicolaus Steno, *The Head of a Shark Dissected*, Royal Society, London, 1667
10 Tony Rice, 'The HMS Challenger expedition, 1872–1876', Natural History Museum, United Kingdon, online at <www.nhm.ac.uk/nature-online/science-of-natural-history/expeditions-collecting/hms-challenger-expedition/index.html>
11 Ben S. Roesch, 'A Critical Evaluation of the Supposed Contemporary Existence of *Carcharodon megalodon*'
12 L. Pouyaud, S. Wirjoatmodjo, I. Rachmatika, A. Tjakrawidjaja, R. Hadiaty, and W. Hadie, 'Une nouvelle espèce de coelacanthe: preuves génétiques et morphologiques' [A new species of coelacanth: genetic and morphological evidence], *Comptes Rendus de l'Académie des sciences* [Proceedings of the Academy of Sciences], Paris, 1999
13 Simon Welfare and John Fairley, *Arthur C. Clarke's Mysterious World*, William Collins Sons & Company and George Rainbird Limited, Fakenham, UK, 1981
14 David Doubilet, 'Suruga Bay: In the Shadow of Mount Fuji', *National Geographic*, vol. 178, no. 4, October 1990
15 Animal X, online at <www.animalx.net/welcome.html>
16 *Ibid.*
17 'Killer shark attack in South Africa witnessed on Twitter', *The Herald Sun*, January 15, 2010
18 *Ibid.*

Chapter 24 Giant ripper lizard

1 I. Firdaus, 'Komodo dragon attacks terrorize villages', online at <www.msnbc.com/id/30913500/>, May 24, 2009
2 *Ibid.*
3 *Ibid.*
4 *Time*, online at <www.time.com>, June 23, 2001
5 *Chronicle*, June 11, 2001
6 *The Australian*, May 19, 2009

7   *The World Today*, ABC online at <www.abc.net.au>, September 30, 2009
8   *Ibid.*
9   ABC Science Online, online at <www.abc.net.au>, May 19, 2009
10 *Perth Now*, January 22, 2007
11 'Giant Reptilian Monsters in the Australian Bush', online at <www.mysteriousaustralia.com>
12 *Ibid.*
13 Rex Gilroy newsletter, 2008 online at <www.mysteriousaustralia.com>
14 Tim Flannery, *The Future Eaters: An Ecological History of the Australian Lands and People*, Grove Press, New York, 2002
15 *Papua New Guinea Post Courier*, February 12, 2008

Chapter 25 Beware the bunyip
1   Ernest Favenc, *The History of Australian Exploration from 1788 to 1888*, Turner and Henderson, Sydney, 1888
2   ABC Radio, *Local Stories*, June 22, 2007
3   Oodgeroo Noonuccal, *Stradbroke Dreamtime*, Angus & Robertson, Sydney, 1993
4   *Sydney Gazette*, March 27, 1823
5   J. Morgan, *The Life and Adventures of William Buckley*, Hobart, 1852, reprinted by Australian National University Press, Canberra, 1980
6   *Sydney Morning Herald*, June 16, 184
7   L.J. Blake, *Letters of Charles Joseph La Trobe*, Victorian Government Printer, Melbourne, 1975
8   E.J. Dunn, 'The Bunyip', *Victorian Naturalist*, 1923
9   Reverend George Taplin, *The Narrinyeri*, E.S. Wigg & Son, Adelaide, 1878
10 Michael Archer, Suzanne Hand and Henk Godthelp, *Riversleigh, the Story of Animals in Ancient Rainforests of Inland Australia*, New Holland, Sydney, 1991

11 Tim Flannery, *Prehistoric Animals of Australia*, Australian Museum, Sydney, 1983

Chapter 26 The Binjour bear
1 Jim Martin, 'Bear Known to Gayndah Aborigines', *Fraser Coast Chronicle*, February 5, 2000
2 *South Burnett Times*, 1979
3 *Courier Mail*, January 29, 1994
4 Ibid.
5 Ibid.
6 *Fraser Coast Chronicle*, February 10, 2000
7 Brett J. Green, 'The Gayndah Bear Story', *Rainbow Spirit Warriors – Ka'ki Aboriginal cultural histories of S.E. Queensland, Australia*, online at <www.warriors.egympie.com.au/gayndahbear.html>

Chapter 27 Panthers on the prowl
1 Nick Ralston and Evyn Testoni, 'NSW Premier Nathan Rees believes panther roaming Sydney suburbs', *Herald Sun*, September 19, 2008
2 Ibid.
3 NSW Department of Primary Industries, 'The Black Cat: A Report on Information Available on the Reported Large Black cat in the Blue Mountains', Sydney, December 2008
4 NSW Department of Primary Industries, 'Reports of large black cats in NSW: Update Report: existence of large black cat in the wild', Sydney, March 29, 2009
5 Tony Healy and Paul Cropper, *Out of the Shadows: Mystery Animals of Australia*, Ironbark/Pan Macmillan, Chippendale, NSW, 1994
6 NSW Department of Primary Industries, 'The Black Cat'
7 Tony Healy and Paul Cropper, *Out of the Shadows*
8 Fiona Sunquist, 'Malaysian Mystery Leopards', *National Wildlife Magazine*, Dec/Jan, 2007
9 NSW Department of Primary Industries, 'The Black Cat'

10 *Ibid.*
11 *Ibid.*
12 Bernard Lagan, 'The Beast who walks', *The Bulletin*, February 3, 2004, pp. 37–8
13 NSW Department of Primary Industries, 'The Black Cat'
14 NSW Department of Primary Industries, 'The Black Cat'
15 Dr John Henry, 'Pumas in the Grampian Mountains: A Compelling Case', Puma Study Group, Deakin University, Melbourne, 1976
16 Bernard Lagan, 'The Beast who walks'
17 Gerald Rillstone, 'Monster cat stalks Hills', *Hills Shire Times*, March 25, 2003
18 Gerald Rilstone, 'Big Cat Mystery Deepens', *Hills Shire Times*, April 1, 2003
19 NSW Department of Primary Industries, 'The Black Cat'
20 *Ibid.*
21 NSW Department of Primary Industries, 'Reports of large black cats in NSW'

Chapter 28 Phantom kangaroos

1 'Kangaroos run wild in France', *Sydney Morning Herald*, November 12, 2003
2 'Derbyshire Wallabies', The Guide to Life, The Universe and Everything, *h2g2*, online at <www.bbc.co.uk>
3 *Ibid.*
4 Jerome Clark, *Unexplained! 347 Strange Sightings, Incredible Occurrences, and Puzzling Physical Phenomena*, Visible Ink Press, Detroit, MI, 1993
5 Horace A. Minnis, *Chattanooga Times*, January 1934; Loren Coleman, '1934's Murderous Monster Marsupial', online at <www.cryptomundo.com>, July 15, 2006
6 Loren Coleman, '1934's Murderous Monster Marsupial'
7 'The Jersey Devil Legend', online at <www.thefixsite.com>

8 James F. McCloy and Ray Miller, *The Jersey Devil*, Middle Atlantic Press, Moorestown, NJ, 1976

Chapter 29 The Queensland Tiger

1. Carl Lumholz, *Among Cannibals: An Account of Four Years' Travels in Australia and of Camp Life with the Aboriginals of Australia*, translated by Rasmus B. Anderson, Charles Scribner's Sons, New York, 1889; Tony Healy and Paul Cropper, *Out of the Shadows: Mystery Animals of Australia*, Ironbark/Pan Macmillan, Chippendale, NSW, 1994
2. B.G. Sheridan, Letter to the Secretary, *Proceedings of the Zoological Society of London*, November 1871, pp. 629–30; Tony Healy and Paul Cropper, *Out of the Shadows*
3. Tony Healy and Paul Cropper, *Out of the Shadows*
4. Ion Llewellyn Idriess, *One Wet Season*, Angus & Robertson, Sydney, 1949; Tony Healy and Paul Cropper, *Out of the Shadows*
5. Ion Llewellyn Idriess, *One Wet Season*; Tony Healy and Paul Cropper, *Out of the Shadows*
6. *Ibid.*
7. Albert Sherbourne le Souef, and Henry Burrell, *The Wild Animals of Australasia*, George G. Harrap, London, 1926
8. Ellis Troughton, *Furred Mammals of Australia*, Charles Scribner's Sons, New York, 1947
9. Bernard Heuvelmans, *On the Track of Unknown Animals*, Bernard Rupert Hart-Davis, London, 1958
10. Toni McCrae, 'Beast of Buderim', *Sunday Mail*, June 18, 1995, p. 10
11. Toni McCrae, 'Beast of Buderim on the Prowl', *Sunday Mail*, July 2, 1995
12. Toni McCrae, 'Buderim Beast Made Man Shake', *Sunday Mail*, August 27, 1995
13. Toni McCrae, 'Doris Captures Buderim Beast', *Sunday Mail*, July 9, 1995
14. Toni McCrae, 'Beast of Buderim on the Prowl'

15 Ibid.
16 Toni McCrae, 'Odd Beast Seen Again', *Sunday Mail*, June 25, 1995
17 Donna Meiklejohn, 'Big Cats – Big History', interview with Nigel Tutt, *ABC Gold & Tweed Coasts*, January 14, 2009

Chapter 30 The Tasmanian tiger
1 Richard Macey, 'Tiger's demise: dingo did do it', *Sydney Morning Herald*, September 6, 2007
2 Ibid.
3 C.N. Johnson and S. Wroe, 'Causes of extinction of vertebrates during the Holocene of mainland Australia: arrival of the dingo, or human impact?', *The Holocene*, no. 13, 2003
4 Australian Rare Fauna Research Association, 'The Tasmanian Tiger: *Thylacinuus cynocephalus*', online at <www.arfra.org>
5 Buck Emberg and Joan Emberg, 'Thylacine Sightings Map', online at <www.tasmanian-tiger.com>
6 Greg Herbele, 'Reports of alleged thylacine sightings in Western Australia', *Conservation Science Western Australia*, 2004
7 Department of Primary Industries, Parks, Water and Environment, Government of Tasmania, *Tasmanian Tigers*, 2009, online at www.dpiw.tas.gov.au/intertext.nsf/WebPages/BHAN-53777B?open>
8 Jason Steger, 'Extinct or not, the story won't die', *The Age*, March 26, 2005
9 Daniel Dasey, 'Researchers revive plan to clone Tassie tiger', *The Sun-Herald*, May 15, 2005
10 Ibid.
11 'Thyla seen near CBD?', *The Sydney Morning Herald*, August 18, 2003
12 Peter Rolfe, 'Tiger tales put to test', *Herald Sun*, March 29, 2009
13 Ibid.
14 Daniel Dasey, 'Researchers revive plan to clone Tassie tiger'

15 Wayne Miller, 'Tasmanian tiger clone a fantasy: scientist', *The Age*, August 22, 2002
16 Daniel Dasey, 'Researchers revive plan to clone Tassie tiger'
17 Andrew Pask, Richard Behringer, Marilyn Renfree, 'Resurrection of DNA Function In Vivo from an Extinct Genome', Department of Molecular Genetics, University of Texas, M.D. Anderson Cancer Center, Houston, TX and Department of Zoology, University of Melbourne, Melbourne, Victoria, May 21, 2008
18 Stephen Pincock, 'Extinct thylacine genome brought to life', *ABC Science*, May 20, 2008
19 Department of Primary Industries, Parks, Water and Environment, Native Plants & Animals, 'Tasmanian Tigers'

Epilogue
1 Simon Welfare & John Fairley, 'The Missing Ape Man', *Arthur C. Clarke's Mysterious* World, William Collins Sons & Company and George Rainbird Limited, Fakenham, UK, 1981, p. 27

Conversion table

Imperial to metric distances

1 inch	2.54 centimetres
1 foot/12 inches (15 feet)	30.38 centimetres (4.55 metres)
1 yard/3 feet (50 yards)	0.9144 metres (45.72 metres)
1 mile/760 yards (500 miles)	1.6093 kilometres (804.65 kilometres)